Hell, I'm Still Here!

Fifty Years a Gunwriter

Hell, I'm Still Here!
Fifty Years a Gunwriter

by

Jon R. Sundra

SAFARI PRESS

Frontis: *One of the first animals to fall to my original 7mm JRS was this 39-inch Dall sheep from the Wrangells of Alaska.*

The trademark Safari Press ® is registered with the U.S. Patent and Trademark Office and with government trademark and patent offices in other countries.

Sundra, Jon

First edition

Safari Press

2018, Long Beach, California

ISBN 978-1-57157-527-2

Library of Congress Catalog Card Number: 2017963813

10 9 8 7 6 5 4 3 2 1

Printed in China

Readers wishing to see Safari Press's many fine books on big-game hunting, wingshooting, and sporting firearms should visit our website at www.safaripress.com.

This book is dedicated to Judith, my late wife, who for the three years we dated and the forty-two years we were married, never uttered a discouraging word. She supported me in every way possible, and was always there for me, as well as for our two fine sons, Ian and Sean. I miss her terribly.

Table of Contents

Foreword

Jon Sundra was once the biggest mistake of my entire magazine editing career. Then he became one of the biggest achievements of that same career. The name Jon Sundra became a cornerstone in my daily efforts to bring reading satisfaction to the audience I served. These folks were dedicated to guns and hunting and were eager to plunk down their hard-earned dollars to read fresh, engaging prose about guns, loads, and game worth pursuing.

My "mistake," as I call it, happened in the 1970s when great fortune, a miracle really, favored me with my becoming editor of *Sports Afield* for six years, then *Outdoor Life* for two. As veteran readers will recall, the seventies were a time of ground-shaking change in the outdoor magazine field. In the short-sighted view of some of us who occupied the uneasy chairs atop the editorial pyramid, the outdoor field was dominated by the so-called "Big Three": *Field & Stream*, *Outdoor Life*, and *Sports Afield*, each with monthly circulations of one-and-a-half to two-million copies.

Like my colleagues, I failed to notice the barbarians at the gates, much less sound the alarm over their trespasses. Magazines like *Guns & Ammo* were thriving, with healthy growing circulations. The reason should have been obvious to those of us holding the reins at "The Big Three." Our magazines had to cover all phases of hunting and fishing, with camping and boating thrown into the mix. We simply did not have the space needed to satisfy readers thirsting for all the coverage they could get on guns and hunting. Fresh, new magazines sprang to life, bristling with the works of writers and photographers whose names seldom, if ever, cracked into the "Big Three."

Not that *Field & Stream*, *Sports Afield*, and *Outdoor Life* lacked firepower. Warren Page at *Field & Stream*, Pete Brown at *Sports Afield*, and Jack O'Connor at *Outdoor Life* were big guns. Jack O'Connor with his plethora of book club offerings at *Outdoor Life* no doubt sold more books than any writer of his time. When he jumped ship from *Outdoor Life* to join Petersen's new venture, *Hunting*, Jack was probably the best-known and most popular writer in the field.

So great was his following that he developed a severe case of what my Southern coaches of long ago called "The Big Head." Always irascible and self-centered, this former school teacher actually wrote an editorial in *Hunting* in which he described all writers in the field as: ". . . not knowing what they're talking about and not knowing how to write if they did."

It was also in the seventies that I chose Grits Gresham to succeed Pete Brown at *Sports Afield*. Grits was a strong contributor as well as an outdoor personality, but I should have been calling up more reinforcements to help us in the guns and hunting areas. By that point, it should have been obvious that we were losing readers to a new breed of writer, one not only with talent but loaded with knowledge and experience with guns, loads, and their practical application in the field for game.

Such a writer was Jon Sundra. In the early 1980s, I became fully aware of his work, and I reached out to him like a drowning man grabbing a rope. The "Big Three" were behind me at that time, but publisher Stanley Harris had offered me a new opportunity to develop a group of gun and hunting magazines. Jon Sundra's published works hit my tired old editorial eyes with a wake-up call. Full of freshness, vigor, documentation, and research, his printed pages were not only great reading but also illuminating journeys. As a bonus, his photography was sharp, detailed, and covered every key element in his articles.

From the moment I first opened an envelope containing a new Jon Sundra article and photographs, and for the next twenty years, Jon's work comprised the best stuff I've ever shepherded into print. We published hundreds of articles together, and I honestly cannot recall being disappointed in a single one. In fact, I firmly believe that Jon Sundra is the best writer published in the 1980s, 1990s, and well into 2000. No, I won't give him that title for the 1970s because Jack O'Connor and Warren Page weren't exactly chopped liver, but Jon was coming on strong at that time. By the 1980s there were other fine writers with dedicated readers, but Jon was "The Man," in my view. I will tell you why.

For openers, his prose has the sweep and feel of a fresh wind and his descriptions were never tired or clichéd or read like an instruction pamphlet in a computer box. Jon could take any subject on guns and hunting and wring it out so that gems of information and bursts of action would keep the readers' eyes glued to the page. As a professional editor who tried to get the commas in the right places, I would read Jon's articles with great joy, for they were written with precise punctuation requiring little or no editor's pencil.

When Jon takes on a subject like an improved rifle load, he tells you exactly how the load has been performing, why the new version is thought to be an improvement, and he then shows you how it performs on the range—in the field, too, if he has had time to test it. When Jon is describing a hunting scene, like the footfalls of a jaguar or black bear, or the challenge of a five-hundred-yard rifle shot, you are *there*—with him in the field.

To find the real Jon Sundra behind all this prose, you'll have to look far beyond the line-up of famed gunwriters—the Elmer Keiths, Jack O'Connors, and Warren Pages. The Jon Sundra I know is a man of character and depth unlike any of his fellow scribes, either past greats or struggling newcomers eager for publication. I'm sure they all have character and depth . . . but they are not Jon Sundra.

As a hunter, Jon has shaken more dust off his boots than others have walked over. His experiences are vast, for he has spent many years in many lands. As a writer, he is an educated bloke, schooled in the basics and beyond, and loaded with talent that he does not let lie fallow. His personal interests, outside of hunting, are so vast I'm constantly amazed at him fitting them into a single lifetime.

He is a gourmet cook, with French and Italian dishes his favorites. His wine cellar ebbs and flows as he makes new discoveries, but on any given afternoon, Jon Sundra will be popping the cork on a red or white of extraordinary vintage. So well does Jon know wine that he can go to any restaurant in the world and make sense of the wine list without calling the sommelier.

Jon's love of fast and beautiful cars dates back to his late teens when he followed his older brother on the Circuit of the Americas–Sports Car Club of America to race Porsches. He doesn't race today, but he drives a Lamborghini, a nod to those early memories still alive inside him.

This hunter, gourmet cook, wine expert, and car enthusiast is also a golfer who knocks the ball to kingdom come and posts scores in the seventies and eighties. This year alone, he has already shot his age three times. He's a very strong seventy-six as I write these words.

It took me awhile to realize that Jon is a true athlete. I had known him for years and had enjoyed good times with him at his homes in Pennsylvania and North Carolina and at numerous gun trade shows before I realized that his appearance had been creating the wrong impression for me. He appeared to be a bookish fellow, not a man of action. It was those glasses. Big lenses with dark frames hid the fact that Jon Sundra is a natural sportsman with the stamina, agility, and strength to master any sport he desires.

This man of action and adventure has always been unwilling to accept life in the slow lane. As a young man he once had a job as a machine operator, sharpening tools. He saw this as nothing more than a dead-end job, so he did something about it—he pursued his dream and found success.

There is only one Jon Sundra, and only he could have written this book. Jon has seen the monkey and heard the owl. He has hefted a few with legends of the gun world and has interesting stories about them. He has hunted with passion and love of the game he seeks, and he has written about his experiences with descriptive prose that puts you into the scene with him.

I feel privileged to write the foreword for his book, and I am urging you right here to turn the page and get into the fast lane with Jon Sundra.

Lamar Underwood
Pennington, New Jersey
December 20, 2017

The Seeds, an Introduction

I t is said you're a lucky man if you can look back on your life and say that you've achieved all your childhood dreams. I think I'm even luckier because I can recall the precise moment of that realization. It came one evening when I was on Lake Kariba on the Zambezi River in 1977, in what was then Rhodesia, in a dilapidated excuse for a boat called . . . if you can believe it, the *African Queen II*. An about-to-set sun hung just above the horizon like a gigantic orange golf ball sitting on a vaporous tee. I half expected to hear a hissing sound as the orb slowly sank into the water.

I can't recall how much time had passed since we had left Kariba, but we were closing in on our destination, Namembere Island, the largest body of land still above water after the mighty Zambezi had been dammed at Kariba Gorge to form Lake Kariba back in the late 1950s. It was on this short boat ride that it dawned on me that I was fulfilling a dream I had had as a young man: to be making a living—though just barely so—as a full-time gunwriter, and being in Africa on safari. To be on a boat called the *African Queen*, and knowing that the next morning I'd be hunting Cape buffalo on the very first day of my very first safari was . . . well, intoxicating. The only way it could have been more magical would have been for me to see the specter of Bogie as a weeping and horribly hung-over Charlie Allnut, watching helplessly as Kate Hepburn's Rosie, his prissy nemesis, empties his precious case of Gordon's gin one bottle at a time into the Ulanga.

To be there just once, as Lou Gehrig said, I considered myself to be the luckiest guy on the face of the earth. Little did I know at the time that I would be lucky enough to make nineteen more safaris to the Dark Continent, and some one hundred other hunting trips to three other continents. As to how many hunts I've made to the fifty States, I can only hazard a guess.

On the *Queen* with me were two friends, George Daniels, a hunt booking agent out of Chicago who had arranged the trip, and Howard Wells, a friend from Pittsburgh who was also on his first African safari, and our two professional hunters, John Tolmay and Clem Coutzee. Clem was the chief warden of the Matusadona Game Reserve who had arranged for a special permit that allowed Howard and me to hunt on the island. I have long since lost touch with all of them, but the memories come flooding back every so often, ever so vividly.

We slept on the *Queen* that night. I can still hear the rhythmic swishing as the Zambezi licked her wooden hull. I tried to sleep, but my mind would have none of it. I kept trying to imagine what the morning would bring. What would it be like to finally hunt an animal that could kill me? What if I wounded it? Would I have the courage to face a charge should it come to that? Was my decision to hunt with a single-shot rifle a stupid one, as John had already not-so-diplomatically suggested.

Then, oddly enough, my thoughts turned nostalgic. I was transported back to my first job out of college as I remembered a coworker of mine named Carl Hanley. In my mind's eye, I was sitting at my desk during lunchtime and there was Carl telling me to give up my dreams of hunting in Africa. . . . Smiling inwardly at the memory of dour, deadbeat Carl as I sat on the *African Queen II*, I couldn't resist the sweet revenge of this "I-told-you-so" moment.

The Formative Years

I wasn't really a problem child in the general sense of the term, but then I didn't exactly make it easy for my parents, either, especially my mom. Mom didn't work in those days, so she was always home, whereas my dad was working one of three shifts and, therefore, was either away or sleeping for two-thirds of the time I was awake. Consequently, I saw a lot more of my mom than I did of my dad, and to her fell the responsibility of manning the complaint department.

I used to dread seeing a neighbor even approach our house, let alone turn up the front walk, because I figured they weren't coming to visit. Nope, it was to grouse about me. (A guilty conscience is a heavy burden for a young boy!) For a while my name could have been "that boy of yours" because that's how the neighbors referred to me. As I said, I hated to see Mom talking to a neighbor because there was always a good chance there'd be hell to pay when my dad, who was a Cleveland cop, got home. But hey, they were only doing what my dad asked them to do. Cops were more respected in those days, and my dad was kind of the neighborhood authority figure.

"If you see my boy doing something wrong, something he shouldn't be doing, you be sure to come tell us," he'd tell the neighbors. He never really had to specify *which* boy. I had a four-year-older brother, Richard. To all the neighbors, then, I was "that boy of yours," but he was "Richard," the Sundra boy; the boy who never got into trouble and was an A student. By the time my brother graduated eighth grade, he had skipped two grades getting there, and after graduating high school with honors, he entered Case Institute of Technology—now Case Western Reserve University—with a scholarship at the age of seventeen. "Why can't you be like your brother" was an all-too-familiar refrain from my earliest recollections to the time I, myself, reluctantly entered college.

For some reason I can't remember anything about kindergarten other than I know I attended, and that I entered the first grade at the normal age of six. My debut as a first grader was a rather auspicious one. My dad, resplendent in his police uniform, delivered me personally to Sister Steven, the nun in whose charge I would be for the next nine months. Besides me, my dad presented Sister Steven with a paddle he had fashioned from a pine board with the instruction that it was to be used on me whenever she saw fit. It was artfully shaped to look exactly like what it was, sanded, stained and finished in a dazzling high gloss varnish. My dad didn't stop there; he Swiss-cheesed the impact area with one-inch-diameter holes so as to decrease air resistance, thus providing more velocity to the paddle as it sped toward my little white behind.

Neither of my parents was overly social, but where I grew up on Cleveland's east side, the houses were close together, so you really couldn't avoid your neighbors even if you wanted to. I mean, one step out our side door you were standing in the driveway, and the other side of the driveway was within three feet of our neighbor's house, the Vimmer's. I don't remember either of their first names, but as a kid in those days you didn't dare address, or even refer to, an adult by his or her first name, so I never made note of either. All I knew is that ol' Mrs. Vimmer didn't have much use for me or . . . me and my slingshot, me and my bow and arrows, me and my blow gun, or me and my BB gun. That was the order of progression for my weapons as I got older and moved up the bird-killing, ordnance- performance ladder.

I wasn't a favorite of Mr. Vimmer's, either. He and his wife lived by themselves, and they were both very old, but hell, when you're ten years old, every adult is old. They had emigrated from Czechoslovakia, just as my grandparents on both sides of the family had done sometime around the turn of the last century when it was still a part of the Austro-Hungarian empire. My parents, then, were first generation Americans, but they grew up in households that spoke Slovak, so they both could speak and understand the language. That's how the Vimmers preferred to converse, but they spoke enough English to be understood. They could, therefore, gripe about me in two languages.

On the other side of our house, thank god, was an empty lot, which when you're just a kid, was like having a veritable wilderness next door. It must have been . . . oh, twenty yards across that field to the neighbor's house. There the Piros family, who were Italian, lived, and their youngest boy, Sam, was one of my friends. No one seemed to know who owned the lot, and no one maintained it, so it was simply a neglected field with lots of high grass, thistles, and thick bushes. Even better, it was two lots deep, so it extended from our street, Benham Avenue, to the street behind us, Oakfield. There were two other such fields in the neighborhood, so if I got tired of exploring mine, there were other wild places to hunt and explore. To have such wilderness areas in the middle of a major metropolitan city was, indeed, a stroke of magnificent good luck for a young boy.

In those days neighborhoods tended to be clannish, with one or two ethnicities being dominant. Ours was Slovak/Bohemian and Italian. The Slovaks were always bad-mouthing the Bohemians—only among themselves of course—and the Bohemians belittled the Slovaks. When I was young, I could never figure that out because I knew they were both from the same country. It was only later that I realized this prejudice was a holdover from the old country: Bohemians looked down on the Slovaks as backward country cousins. On the other hand, they were united in thinking themselves superior to the Italians. Whomever it was the Italians disliked, I can't recall, but it was probably us. Seemed everybody had at least one nationality to look down on. Nevertheless, everyone in our neighborhood seemed to get along pretty well.

******

I was born in June of 1940, and can remember the air-raid siren, which was on a tower behind the police station three blocks away, being sounded in practice drills during my afternoon naps. I can also remember going to the corner grocery store, Rudyk's, with my mom, and her handing over little green or red cardboard discs that had something to do with butter and meat rationing. I remember my uncle Emil coming to visit us dressed in his U.S. Army Air Corps uniform, and the flags that hung in the front windows of homes that had sons and daughters in the military.

I also remember getting my first dart gun on Christmas Eve of 1946. As inconsequential as that may seem, it was a big moment in my life. The "dart" consisted of a round Popsicle stick with a rubber suction cup on one end. The "gun" was a pistol with a coil spring in the barrel. You simply inserted the shaft of the dart into the barrel and pushed it home, which compressed the spring and cocked the gun. I can only guess at the muzzle velocity—all I recall was that twenty-five to thirty feet was about as far as the dart would go, even if elevated to the maximum angle of departure. Still, at six years old, it impressed the heck out of me.

I also got an Erector set that same Christmas, or maybe it was my brother's; I can't be sure. Anyway, I built this little tower that looked like the old oil-well derricks that had a flat platform on top. I would then take a playing card, fold it in half so that it would stand on edge atop this platform, and, voilà, that was my target. I'd practice by the hour bowling the cards over with my dart gun. Tiring of that, I'd use the living room furniture to cover a stalk to my playing-card target, pretending it was some sort of dangerous beast.

It didn't take long for me to figure out that if I removed the suction cup from the dart, the stick that remained was far more aerodynamic. Now I had a lighter projectile, a higher muzzle velocity, and a flatter trajectory. Of course I couldn't actually articulate those thoughts then, but I did have a grasp of things mechanical and an intuitive understanding of elementary physics. Shooting just the stick I had greater range, but not much more. Lacking a stabilizing spin to what was essentially a tiny arrow without fletching, the thing started tumbling end over end just a few feet from the muzzle.

Nor did it take long for me to figure out that if I put my little arrows in the pencil sharpener, I would have some serious projectiles. This advance in technology became problematical because you cocked the gun by pushing the arrows into the barrel with the palm of your hand. Now I had to load my dart gun by placing the sharp point against something hard in order to push them into the barrel.

The minute my mom saw that I was now shooting pointed sticks instead of harmless suction-cup darts, well, that was the last I saw of my first gun. "You could take someone's eye out with this," she said, vigorously shaking the deadly projectile at me.

That is my earliest recollection of the ember that would flame into a strong hunting instinct and in anything that propelled a projectile of any sort, be it a stone, marble, ball bearing, dart, BB, arrow, or bullet. Televisions were not widespread until the 1950s, so my only exposure to such things would have been through magazines, but even if there were gun and hunting magazines, which there weren't, they wouldn't have been seen in my house. As for movies, until I was old enough to go by myself, the only ones I saw were those my mom took me to see, and they weren't exactly guy flicks.

My dad was neither a hunter nor a shooter—nor for that matter were my uncles, on either side of the family. You would think that because I didn't grow up in the kind of environment that nurtured such interests that I somehow developed those interests on my own. Yes and no.

That's not to say my dad *never* hunted; he just never hunted after marrying my mom in 1933. In the late 1920s he attended Ohio State University and during the summers he would drive to Wyoming, which was quite an adventure in itself back in those days, where he worked as a photographer in Yellowstone National Park. While out there he did, in fact, do a little hunting, which brings me to another seminal moment in my life. No, make that a seminal *object*.

Sometime between his marrying my mom and my birth seven years later, Dad had put together a photo album in which there were the usual family-type pictures. These were taken on a fairly regular basis chronicling his days at OSU, the four years he courted my mom, and the early years of their marriage. But in that album there were also quite a few photos of my dad taken during those times he spent in Wyoming. After all, he was a photographer. Among those pictures was one of my dad posed in front of his Model A Ford coupe with a bunch of mallards spread out on the ground and with him holding a Winchester Model 97 pump shotgun.

Also in that album was a fascinating picture of a mysterious man whom I can only remember my dad telling me was either a distant relative or a friend of someone on his side of the family. In any case, the picture was obviously taken in Africa, for it showed this fellow, whoever he was, squatted down between two very dead African lions with magnificent manes. I'm talking MGM lions. As I recall, this chap had a pipe clenched in his teeth and was holding what I much later determined was a 1903 Springfield with an aperture sight.

I'm not sure how old I was when I first became fascinated by that photo album, but I couldn't have been more than six or seven. It was like a magic carpet for me, for among those pictures of my dad out West and the one of the mysterious lion slayer, I was transported to a world of far-away places, of excitement and adventure limited only by the parameters of my own imagination. These weren't abstract pictures of strangers in a movie or magazine; they were of my dad and a relative or friend of the family, and that made it all so much more real, so much more possible.

The most important seminal moment in my young life occurred when at the age of twelve I saw the movie *King Solomon's Mines* starring Stewart Granger and Deborah Kerr. When I heard those haunting drums in the background as the credits rolled at the beginning of the movie, accompanied by a visual of an acacia tree silhouetted against the backdrop of the Serengeti, it just reinforced what I wanted to do with my life. To this day the opening soundtract to that movie moves me to tears.

******

So basically I knew what I wanted to do with my life—to hunt all over the world, play with guns, and write about it—for as far back as I can remember. I mean, to my mind, what red-blooded male wouldn't want to do that? But when I told my mom what I wanted to do, she got terribly upset.

"Don't you think your father and I would like to go traipsing off all over the world and doing exactly what we wanted? You have to realize that that's a pipe dream."

We had plenty of those kinds of conversations. My mom was simply doing what any good mom would do under the same circumstance. She was simply trying to get me to temper my expectations—to prepare me for what she thought would be inevitable disappointment. By the time we were having such conversations, I was old enough to appreciate how hard my parents were working to give us a head start in life. During the war my dad worked at two jobs: full-time as a policeman and part-time delivering ice—not everyone had a fridge in those days. Even my mom worked part-time as a secretary for the parish priest.

My parents were great, and I admired them, but there was no way I aspired to their kind of life.

I watched my dad spending his vacations painting the house and working around the yard. *How depressing*, I thought. To have just three or four weeks a year to do what you wanted and spend it on such banal pursuits was an anathema to me. I swore I'd blow my brains out if I had to live like that. Of course, I couldn't say that to my mom, so when she lectured me about what she felt was the inevitable disappointment I would have to endure, I just kept mum. I could never hurt her feelings like that.

OK, so I knew what I wanted to do. The trick was, how was I going to make it happen?

******

When I was graduated from high school, I didn't want to go to college, despite my parents' wishes. Whereas my older brother had been an honor student at the same Catholic high school I attended, Cathedral Latin in Cleveland, Ohio, I was kicked out after my junior year after failing to pass algebra, then failing to pass the same course again in summer school. How I hated school!

So after finishing my senior year and graduating from a public high school in Parma, Ohio—an accomplishment I was so proud of that I refused to have my picture taken for the year book—I took a job as a sweeper in the factory where my mom was secretary to the guy who owned the business. (Hey, it's who you know, you know?) By then my mom had given up on being a housewife and taken a full-time job.

Anyway, after a year there and my having attained the dizzying grade of machine operator, I moved on to a similar job sharpening industrial saws. It was the same story there as with my previous gig: I would figure out how to do a job better and faster than it had been done previously; my ideas would be implemented; but then the foreman would take credit for it. I got zip.

It took about three years of that for me to realize I was getting nowhere fast. As much as I disliked the idea of college, I realized I needed that silly sheepskin if I were to have any chance at all of achieving my dream of becoming a globe-trotting gunwriter. In retrospect, I've learned that is not true, but I believed it then.

And so it was with great reluctance that in 1961 at the age of twenty-one I enrolled in the Ohio State University. To say I was not your typical college student would be a galactic understatement. In my freshman year I ran a trapline on the Olentangy River behind the OSU stadium, and at night my buddy, Joe Pazourek, and I would climb the ten-foot-high cyclone fence crowned with barbed wire to get into the stadium so as to shoot sleeping pigeons by flashlight with our home-made blow guns.

All it took to make these guns was four feet of copper tubing, plastic golf tees, and some coat-hanger wire. With just a few thousandths to spare, the golf tees fit perfectly inside the copper tubing. With needle-nose pliers we'd take a five-inch piece of wire and form a tight loop at one end. We'd then heat the other end on the stove and push it through the center of the tee and stop it about the middle of the wire. We'd then heat the loop end and pull it into the tee where it would melt itself into the plastic. We spent hours making dozens of those expendable projectiles; they may not have looked as good as the commercial ones, but they worked just as well.

The problem was, although the darts were lethal, they weren't very humane; the pigeons would just fly off seemingly unfazed, and it often took hours for them to die, which they did with great flourish all over the OSU campus. So the days after our forays into the stadium there were pigeons flopping all over the place with these colorful plastic things visible on one side, and a thin wire sticking out the other. When someone finally figured what was going on, an article appeared in the OSU *Lantern* demanding that the fiends responsible be brought to justice. Given the liberal atmosphere prevailing in our colleges today, now they would have insisted on our execution.

The first two years I was at OSU coincided with my spelunking days. So when I wasn't checking my trapline or shooting pigeons, I would practice rappelling out of the third story window of our boarding house—98 East 13th Street as I recall—in preparation for exploring two of the most dangerous wild caves in the United States, Schoolhouse and Hellhole, both in Pendleton County, West Virginia. After Judith—who was my girlfriend at the time—and I achieved that goal, our cave exploring days came to an end.

When did I have time to study, you may ask. I didn't. On weekends I'd drive up to Cleveland to be with Judith, but after two years of that I decided to drop out of school to get married. We'd been dating for three-and-a-half years and I figured it was time. I also felt that two years of college would put me in a better job-finding position than if I had just a high school diploma. Wrong! I wasn't too particular as to what kind of job I'd accept other than I didn't want to work in another factory. I applied at a few gun/sporting goods stores because by then I was a veritable walking encyclopedia—at least I thought so—on modern rifles and cartridges, and was somewhat conversant about handloading as well, even though I had not yet gotten into metallic cartridge reloading.

Between the time I dropped out of school in March of 1963 to September when Judith and I were married, I failed to find a decent job. If truth be told, however, I only looked for about two months, because those two months of rejection convinced me I had to finish school. A college degree in those days meant a lot more than it does today.

So I returned to OSU that September a married man. Judith took a job working in a department store and waitressing on the side, and with a little help from my parents, I was able to concentrate on my studies for the first time. Those two years were pretty uneventful. We rented a house on Woodruff Avenue, which was just about one block off campus. It was a two-story house that was divided into four units, so all we had was a small kitchen, a bathroom, a bedroom, and a living room. That autumn I bought a Lyman Spartan reloading press and started reloading, first for a Marlin Levermatic in .256 Winchester Magnum, then a Remington 722 in .257 Roberts. The only place available in our apartment to mount the press was to a wooden chair. I would C-clamp it to the chair and then wait for Judith to come home so that she could sit on the chair for ballast while I resized cases.

We had a budget of twelve dollars a week for food, so I tried to supplement our meager income by hustling pool. I won more than I lost, but under the circumstances, I could only wager a few dollars at most. When I was flush, I'd buy the latest *Guns*, *Gun World*, *Shooting Times*, and *Guns & Ammo* magazines, but most of the time I just stood there in the store next to the display rack and read the articles. Back then, those were the only dedicated gun magazines being published. I read those magazines from cover to cover, along with the monthly columns of Jack O'Connor of *Outdoor Life*, Pete Brown of *Sports Afield*, and Warren Page of

Field & Stream. The idea that I would get to know these men personally was a fantasy at the time, but then fantasy would come to define my life.

I devoured those articles not just to learn more about guns in general, but to study the kind of writing and photography that comprised the typical gun magazine article. In addition to the above-mentioned firearms editors of the "Big Three" magazines, the major gunwriters back in the mid-1960s were Col. Charles Askins, Col. Jim Crossman, Maj. George Nonte, Elmer Keith, Byron Dalrymple, Bob Steindler, Bob Hagel, Les Bowman, Jack Lewis, Ken Waters, and Dean Grennell, to name most of them. These guys wrote for so-called "vertical" magazines, meaning they were devoted strictly to one subject: guns, and to a lesser extent, hunting. Nevertheless, each magazine tried to have something for everyone, so in each issue there'd be an article and/or column about rifles, handloading, black powder, handguns, shotguns, wingshooting, and big-game hunting.

******

It was fortuitous for me that about a year before I graduated, my brother, who was working as a chemical engineer for U. S. Steel, was transferred to Pittsburgh. As a boy growing up in Ohio, Pennsylvania was "big-game" country to me, a place where you could hunt deer and bear with a centerfire rifle, which was no small consideration for me because by then I was a hopeless rifle "nut." I figured that if I had to work at an honest job—just temporarily of course, until I became a big-time gunwriter—I'd rather it be in a state where I could indulge my passion for rifles and hunting. In Ohio you had to hunt deer with a shotgun and slugs, and as a rifle guy I had no interest in that.

So it was that upon graduating with a BA in English Literature, Judith and I moved in with my brother in Pittsburgh until the time I landed a job and could afford a place of our own. Adding to the urgency was the fact that Judith was pregnant with what was to be the first of our two sons.

I quickly learned that without a teaching certificate, a sheepskin in English literature was in the job market about as saleable as a degree in witchcraft or basket weaving. It took four long months before I was offered my first job; it was an inside sales job with James H. Matthews in Pittsburgh, a company that made all sorts of industrial printing machines. The salary was $400 a month, which was lousy pay even for a college grad back in 1966, but I figured that under the circumstances, I couldn't pass it up.

After settling in to my new job, a new home, and with a new son, Ian, I said to myself: *OK, John, there's some order to your life now. If you plan on being a gunwriter, you had better start writing!*

It wasn't like I was working at developing my writing skills prior to my taking that first job after college. In fact, other than the one course in creative writing that all English majors were required to take, I wasn't any more versed in putting words together than any other grad with a degree in Arts & Sciences. But I was told by my English teacher in high school that I was a good writer, and my counselor in college, who also happened to be my creative writing instructor, told me the same thing. The reason I chose English Literature as my major rather than journalism was that I didn't want anyone trying to teach me to write in ten-word sentences. If I truly did have a knack for the written word, I'd soon find out.

My Brief Flirtations
with Honest Work

The inside sales office at James H. Matthews consisted of three rows of desks, three desks to a row. Carl Hanley sat at one in the row in front of me, and one desk to the right. Though Carl and another associate went out for lunch on occasion, most of the time they brown bagged it, as I always did. During those lunch hours we'd talk about all sorts of things, but it didn't take long for Carl to learn about my plans to hunt all over the world and to make a living writing about guns.

Carl was one of those people who would look at a rose and only see the thorns. He was around forty-five at the time, and it was obvious his life hadn't turned out the way he wanted. I didn't know what his aspirations were, but he was not a happy camper, and he seemed to enjoy raining on my parade.

"Jon," he told me, "ten years from now you are probably going to be sitting at that desk, or some other desk, working at a job that's just as boring as the one you have now. You may even be more successful than I've been and climb the management ladder, but the kind of glamorous life you're talking about is a fantasy. Have you ever stopped to think how few people in the world do that sort of thing?"

It was like I was listening to my mom, but Carl's motives were hardly out of compassion.

It wasn't long after that Carl learned I was working on an article at my desk during lunch hour. He asked me if I had ever had anything published.

"No, but then I haven't submitted anything yet," I replied.

One day after a particularly spirited discussion in which Carl was even more dismissive and negative than usual, I told him I was going to hunt in Africa before I was thirty-five years old.

"You're dreaming, kid. That takes money . . . a lot of money. And you're what . . . twenty-seven now? One thing's for sure: You're not going to make that kind of money working here. I suggest you come live with us down here on earth and save yourself a lot of disappointment."

And become like you, I wanted to say, *a man with no dreams, no aspirations, living a life—as Thoreau so perfectly put it—of quiet desperation?*

As it turned out, it took me two years longer to get to Africa than I said it would. I was thirty-seven.

On My Way

I don't know how many lunch hours it took me to write that first article, but it had to be at least two months' worth, with dozens of rewrites. Every time I thought the piece was finally finished, I'd read it over again and want to make changes. Now making changes was no problem for me because I wrote in long hand, but it sure was for Judith, who had to type my handwritten manuscripts, a job she undertook for the next twenty-five years.

It was long before home computers and word processing, so every time I made a change other than to correct a spelling error, which Judith could simply white-out and type over, she had to retype the entire manuscript. It got to where I just couldn't ask her to retype that first article for the umpteenth time. That's when I knew the time had come for me to go with what I had, even though I wasn't quite satisfied with it. It would take me two decades before I got comfortable enough to submit a manuscript with just a couple of edits and without a guilty conscience. Being a perfectionist, I found it hard to let my work go, but then editorial deadlines have a way of interjecting reality. Then too, perfection is a decidedly subjective commodity.

Being marginally satisfied with the copy, I knew that photography was the other and no less important part of the editorial package. It was obvious to me that without good ones—photos that supported the copy and vice-versa—even the best-written and/or authoritative piece would likely be rejected. So I studied the kind of photos used to illustrate the typical gun-magazine article as much as I studied the writing style and content of the various publications. At the time I started that first job at Matthews, however, I knew nothing about cameras and photography, so one of the first things I did was to buy a Konica rangefinder 35mm camera.

After a few weeks of experimenting, learning the camera, and developing some idea as to the difference between good and bad composition, I was pretty cocky. Keep in mind that back then all gun magazine illustrations were in black-and-white, which in many ways makes photographing dark, yet reflective surfaces like blued steel, more challenging than color photography. Then too, a long, narrow object like a rifle presents special problems in composition; it's so much easier to photograph a handgun, which is square or nearly so instead of an object that's five times as long as it is wide. I quickly learned that my rangefinder camera was worthless for close-up stuff, so I traded it in on a Canon SLR and a set of close-up lenses

Anyway, the more I learned about photography, the more I realized how lousy so many of the photos that appeared in the various gun magazines really were. Close-up pictures lacked depth of focus because they were taken with wide apertures so that the author could hand hold the camera using faster shutter speeds. That's just being lazy. Some were taken in bright sunlight, which resulted in photos where blacks lacked detail and whites were bleached out. Or the author would use flash, which when photographing guns, netted results even worse than those photographed in bright sun. Others still had no idea about composition—how to photograph a rifle without shadows and how to obtain the most attractive angles to best illustrate the points being made in the copy.

In those days article submissions required eight by ten glossies, and it became obvious to me that the cost of film developing and printing would cut deeply into my profit should I be lucky enough to sell an article. Soon I was processing my own film and printing eight by tens in a makeshift darkroom in the basement of our rented home in Penn Hills, a suburb east of Pittsburgh.

My equipment was as basic as it gets. I had a Durst 35mm enlarger, a plastic film developing tank that held two rolls of film, and three developing trays—the first for a Kodak Dektol developer, the second for water with a little white vinegar as a stop bath, and the third for a Kodak Fixer to stabilize the print. I used Kodak Plus-X, which was a slower film than the Tri-X everyone else seemed to use, but it yielded less grainy prints. I learned how to "push" Plus-X, which had an ASA of 125, to 250, so that I gained an f-stop and still had more detailed prints and more depth of focus. I used that formula until publishing technology advanced to where even low-budget gun magazines began accepting color slides, which they could convert to black and white if they so desired.

It was a mixed blessing because, though it eliminated film developing and dark-room work, I never knew if I had usable stuff until my slides came back from the processing lab. It wasn't so bad when they screwed up the film processing if I could easily redo the photography, which was the case with a typical gun-review piece. It was a pain to have to redo my work, but it could and had to be done. With photos from hunting trips, however, it was a whole 'nother ball game.

Should the processing lab ruin some or all of the pictures from a hunting trip, you were, literally, up a creek without a paddle. I had that happen to me twice, which meant I had no story. Of course, the processing lab apologized and offered a free roll of film for every one they ruined. How magnanimous they were! Anyway, that was pretty much the drill for more than a decade until digital photography advanced to where it was good enough for magazine illustration. For me, digital photography would change my life even more than computers and word processing, but more about that later.

******

The day finally came to submit my first article. It had taken me a long time to get to that point—being a perfectionist meant that I rarely felt satisfied enough with either my article or photographs to submit them. Once I arrived at that point, however, the next question then became, "Where should I submit them?" *Guns & Ammo? Shooting Times? Guns? Gun World?* I considered all of them, but I felt the most prestigious publication of the day was not a monthly magazine but an annual—the *Gun Digest*. It was edited by John Amber, a veritable icon in the gun-publishing business with a wealth of knowledge, and many thought the *Gun Digest* to be *the* authority of the day. I figured if I could crack that one, there was hope for me.

Drawing upon my several years' experience hunting crows and ground-hogs using several calibers ranging from the .22 magnum rimfire to 6mm Remington, I used the working title "What Makes a Varmint Rifle?" for that first article. I also decided to use "Jon" instead of "John" for my pen name because back then it was unusual enough that I thought people might better remember it. Today, of course, that spelling is very common. As the title suggested, the piece simply affirmed the fact that there are highly specialized rifles/cartridges/optics for hunting groundhogs, but not having such a rig is no reason not to enjoy the sport. In summing up, I posed the question: "If circumstances allow the successful use of one's lever action .30-30 on groundhogs, who's to say it's not a varmint rifle?"

Once the article was in the mail, I began seriously to doubt if it had any chance of being sold. I mean, here I was, a twenty-six-year-old kid who to this day does not know how to diagram a sentence, submitting an unsolicited article without so much as a query to the editor to see if he was even interested in the subject. I was, however, perhaps naively, convinced it didn't matter who you were—your age, race, color, education, or who you knew—all that mattered was the quality of the work. The work stood on its own, and if it was good, someone would recognize it. My opinion hasn't changed.

******

I can't recall now exactly when I submitted that article to John Amber, but it had to be during the Christmas season of 1966. By mid-January I still hadn't heard from Amber, but I took some solace in the fact that, with the *Gun Digest* being an annual, the process might be slower than at a monthly magazine, especially around the holiday season. Still, after several weeks I was discouraged enough to have Judith retype the piece, while I put together another photo package. Of course, you can't query an editor or submit an article to a second publisher unless you're sure the first submission had been rejected.

Then, so help me, just as I was about to call the *Gun Digest* editorial office to see if, indeed, my piece had been rejected, Judith handed me a letter that arrived that day. "Congratulations," she said, a huge smile on her face as she handed me the opened letter. It was from John Amber, and it read:

> *Dear Jon:*
> *Your article is well done and we'd like to publish it in the twenty-third or later edition of the* Gun Digest. *A check for a hundred dollars will be forthcoming. Thanks for your submission, and we hope to see more of your work.*

17

My very first article was sold . . . and to the very first publisher I had sent it to! *(Take that, Carl Hanley!)* I could hardly contain myself. The check, which arrived several weeks later and was dated 12 April 1967, is framed and has been hanging in my office ever since. Ironically, though, I would have dozens of articles published before that first one hit print, as it was held for three years before it appeared in the 25th Silver Anniversary (1971) edition of the *Gun Digest*.

Flush with the success of my first effort, I immediately started on another article. This one was on the 6mm Remington, a cartridge I by then had had some experience with. The article covered the history of the round, and that of its archrival, the .243 Winchester, both of which were introduced in 1955. I went into why its original ".244 Remington" designation was changed to "6mm Remington," and why it never achieved the popularity of the .243. I also covered the comparative ballistics of the two, along with my experience with the cartridge in the field and at the reloading bench.

Like my first effort, the 6mm piece did not come easily, as I probably spent as much time writing it, rewriting it, and agonizing over both the copy and photos as I did with that first article. Again I realized that I had to stop revising at some point and just submit the thing, and, again, I was in a quandary as to which of the four major magazines I should submit my article. My plan all along was that if I sold a piece, I would send the next one to another magazine, figuring that if I was ever to make a living at this stuff, I'd have to sell to and develop a rapport with all of them.

I decided to send the unsolicited piece to the *Shooting Times*. I had come to favor the *Shooting Times* over the other magazines because I liked the format and content better, but I still studied all the competition. Then the agony of waiting for a response began all over again. One week, two weeks, three weeks . . . and still no response. Maybe I was being unrealistic in thinking that even an article submitted over the transom would be looked at within a week or two by *someone*, but I soon learned that unsolicited articles by unknowns have little priority at any magazine.

Anyway, after a month or so I was discouraged enough that all I was hoping for was that the editor would have the decency to return my work so that I wouldn't have to have Judith retype it and I wouldn't have to reprocess the photos in order to submit the package elsewhere. All it took was to slip the article and photos into the large, preaddressed stamped envelope I provided that was de rigueur if one expected the return of a rejected manuscript.

It had to be five or six weeks later that an envelope arrived in the mail—not the preaddressed nine-by-twelve manila one I had provided—but a regular business envelope with the *Shooting Times* logo and address in the upper left corner! *It had to be good news,* I thought. *Why would they take the trouble to send me a separate rejection letter when all they had to do was put a pink slip in with the returned article?* When I finally stopped staring at the envelope and opened the letter, I found that it was from the editor, Bob Steindler, telling me he liked the piece and planned to run it in the January 1969 issue! He also said that he'd like to see any additional story ideas I might have. Wow!

Selling those first two stories were big events for me, but an even bigger one was the day I actually saw my first article appear in a national magazine. As Steindler promised, it was the 6mm Remington story and it was in the January 1969 issue of the *Shooting Times*. Not only that, it was the lead article starting on page six. Normally, the *lead* article is authored by the editor or one of the staff writers—not a nobody—and that pleased me all the more.

Over the next eighteen months or so I had three rejections of unsolicited articles, two of which I put in another envelope and sent them unchanged to another magazine. Both were sold. The one that wasn't sold was a submission to *Field & Stream*, and it was about fishing in northern Pennsylvania on the opening day of trout season. It was the only fishing piece I ever wrote, and it was the only rejected article I've had in the more than fifty years I've been writing. I chose to keep that article rather than send it to another magazine. It sat on my desk for almost a decade as a reminder of how lucky I was.

By the time my first article was published in the *Shooting Times*, I had sold several others, and thoughts of actually making a living at gunwriting began to seem possible. First, though, I had to get out of my galactically boring job at Matthews, and it was just blind luck that I stumbled upon a tiny advertisement in the help-wanted section of the Pittsburgh *Post Gazette*. The notice was for someone to serve as an assistant editor to a statewide tabloid that was devoted to hunting and fishing; it was called *Outdoor People of Pennsylvania*. The only requirement was ". . . some writing experience."

As luck would have it, I interviewed for the job and was able to show the editor/publisher, Gene Shaw, that I had already been published in several national magazines. I got the job. Not that I wanted to be an editor, but I figured it couldn't hurt to have a couple of years' experience editing a state-wide newspaper. As it turned out, I did learn a thing or two about the writing business from an editor's perspective, which surely contributed to my development as a writer and my better understanding of the writer/ editor relationship.

In 1969 *Outdoor People* came upon hard times and my job there as editor dissolved. It was another seminal moment for Judith and me. A few months earlier, in May, our second son, Sean, was born, so with that added responsibility on my shoulders, I had to decide whether to look for another job, or give freelance writing a try. We decided to take a chance and go with the latter option. Judith took a job at a local discount store, while I took care of the kids and pecked away at the typewriter on a card table that served as my desk. Thank God for *Mister Rodgers* and *Sesame Street*!

By that point in time I had managed to hunt white-tailed deer in what was now my home state of Pennsylvania, mule deer in Wyoming, pronghorn in Montana, black bear in Ontario, and caribou in Labrador. With the exception of the caribou hunt, all were done on shoestring budgets with a college buddy of mine, Ed Notebaert. We couldn't afford to fly anywhere, so we drove my Chevy pickup. We slept in the back in a small camper that was only as long as my eight-foot truck bed and not high enough to allow us to stand. We lived on fast-food burgers and lunch meat sandwiches.

Our most expensive venture was a mule deer hunt in Wyoming in the autumn of 1966; it was the cheapest one we could find in the Where-to-Go section of *Field & Stream*. For a hundred and twenty-five dollars each, we got a three-day hunt out of a fleabag motel in Pinedale, Wyoming. The owner of the place was also our guide, whose idea of a "guided hunt" consisted of driving us to the top of nearby Moon Mountain before dawn, leaving us there for the day with a bag lunch of balogna and cheese sandwiches, and picking us up after dark. I believe the nonresident license was thirty-five dollars. As that was my first "guided-hunt" experience, my expectations for future adventures had nowhere to go but up. However, I have to confess that our shabby treatment was understandable, at least it became so the first morning of our hunt.

My Criminal Past

Chapter 4

Ed Notebaert and I were driving across southern Wyoming on our way to Pinedale. We were in Ed's 1966 Pontiac GTO, a gift from his father upon his graduation from OSU a year after me. We had taken out the back seat and piled up blankets on either side of the drive train/differential hump to make a fairly level and comfortable bed so we could spell one another driving. If memory serves we made it from Columbus, Ohio, to Cheyenne, Wyoming, in twenty-two hours, and that was long before the interstate highway system was complete. Most of the driving was on state highways that went through all kinds of little hamlets, cities, and towns. How we didn't get even one speeding ticket is beyond me.

Having driven all night, we crossed into Wyoming about an hour before daylight. As the sun rose, we began seeing antelope . . . lots of antelopes, on both sides of the road. It was my first trip out West, and I had never seen a pronghorn before. I pulled my binocular from my duffel and glassed them as we sped down the virtually deserted highway—until I got car sick.

I wasn't prepared to see so many of these fleet-footed critters just milling around without a care in the world, sometimes just yards off the side of the highway. They were behind fence, of course, but I was surprised they would honor just three strands of barbed wire the way they obviously did. Just as obvious was that antelope season hadn't started, so that explained their indifference to passing cars. The more pronghorns I saw, the more the hunting instinct welled up inside me.

"Ed, I can't stand this. How many trophy bucks have we seen—fifteen, twenty? They're just standing around like in a zoo."

"Yeah, it's really amazing. I'd give anything to have an antelope license!

I, of course, was thinking the same thing, but I was also contemplating breaking the law for the first time in my life . . . and the stage was perfectly set for doing so. It was still early morning and the road that would eventually become Interstate 80 was virtually deserted. The road was so flat and so dead straight you could see a car coming ten miles in either direction, and there were times when both were vacant.

As temptation would have it, we came to one of those places where there was a pull-off area on the side of the road where only a trash barrel distinguished it from the nothingness in every direction. Not a house, barn, or outbuilding of any kind could be seen, only sagebrush on either side of the road for as far as the eye could see. That was the scene when I told Ed to pull over.

You have to wonder why the good lord put so much white on the prong-horn antelope when the early morning sun will light them up like a neon sign. Their bits of white blaze in the morning sun for miles. Standing by the side of the road on that brilliant Wyoming morning, our eyes were drawn to ten radiantly lit goats in the distance. They weren't miles away from where we were, but they could have been five or eight hundred yards. We couldn't tell exactly because judging distance over flat, featureless terrain is very difficult. All I knew was that they were way beyond ethical shooting range. Still, this was the first time we had actually stopped the car to glass for these neat animals, and seeing there was a good buck in the bunch only made me want to collect one that much more.

"I know what you're thinking," Ed said, his eyes, like mine, glued to his binocular. "That is a damn good buck," he proclaimed. After a long moment of pregnant silence, he said, "If you're going to do it, this is the place."

"Yeah, that's what I'm thinking. You stay here with the car," I told him.

There's nothing unusual about a car pulled over at a designated area. He would beep the horn if a car approached, and all I'd have to do is stay flat on my belly in the eighteen-inch high sagebrush to remain invisible to any passing car or truck. And unless another car decided to pull over, even if my 6mm Remington was a 155mm Howitzer, there was no one around to hear it!

The odds were not on my side. As I said, the land was absolutely flat, with no features other than the sagebrush to cover a stalk. Assuming the goats stayed put, I figured they were at least six hundred yards away, meaning I'd have to crawl on my belly for at least three hundred yards to get within reasonable range for a 6mm Remington and my 100-grain Sierra handload.

I managed to get through the fence and into the sagebrush without spooking the pronghorns, and after only three warning beeps from Ed, I had made it about one hundred yards from the road. It was however, as far as I was going to go because I was being impaled by tiny ground-level cacti. My quarry was still out of shooting range, and I was just about ready to give the stalk up as a bad idea when I remembered an article I had read. The author had tied a white handkerchief to the muzzle of his rifle and, lying on his back in the sagebrush just as I was doing, waved his rifle to and fro. By so doing—according to his story—he actually coaxed a buck to come several hundred yards closer, close enough that he was able to make the shot.

So picture this: There I was, lying on my back with the butt of my rifle on my chest, waving the flag of surrender. Staring up at the sky, I couldn't see what was happening, so after about ten minutes of what had to be a truly comical scene, I lowered my rifle, rolled over, and took a peek over the sagebrush.

I couldn't believe it: The biggest buck of the group—the object of my coveting—had closed the distance between us by a couple hundred yards . . . and was moving closer! On my back again and no longer feeling like an idiot, I continued the ritual. After another ten minutes or so I again looked up to see that the buck was now within shootable distance—about 250 yards away, I hoped.

Now a fear arose from my subconscious thoughts. I had read of the supposedly binocular-like eyes of the pronghorn, and so I pondered: *If that's true, they will pick me up the second I raise my head and rifle above the sage to where I'd have a clear line of sight over the brush.* Well, that was the worry. It didn't happen. I was able to settle my rifle across two pieces of sage—one under the fore-end and one under the butt—to give me the kind of two-point support needed to steady the rifle enough to make the 250-yard shot.

By then the buck suspected something wasn't kosher, but before turning to beat a retreat, he stopped, giving me a broadside shot. I took it. He dropped literally in his tracks, disappearing from view. I looked back to see Ed leaning over the hood of his GTO glassing me and giving me the thumbs up.

With not a car or truck in sight, I ran over to my prize. My shot had impacted higher than I wanted, but I was lucky enough that it broke the spine, hence the buck's immediate collapse. Having had some taxidermy experience, I knew how to cape an animal for a shoulder mount and proceeded to do so as fast as I could. I severed the head at the base of the scull, and seeing there were no vehicles in sight, ran back to the car and threw my booty into the truck.

From that point until we arrived in Pinedale, we never drove more than a couple miles per hour over the speed limit—what with me being up to my elbows in blood and with an illegal animal in the trunk. Arriving at a real rest area, I was able to clean up, and before checking in at our guide's motel, we purchased a plastic ground cloth and ten pounds of salt.

On arrival Ed and I introduced ourselves to our guide, who I'll call Slim, filled out our mule deer licenses, and took in a quick lunch. Slim seemed to be a nice guy, personable and quite talkative. I, however, was anxious to get to our room and finish the caping job—such is the pressure of a guilty conscience. As far as I recall, Ed and I were the only occupants of the motel at the time, for we saw no one, and there wasn't another car in the tiny parking lot. The five or six cabins that comprised the place were joined by a continuous elevated wooden walkway just like you see in a typical Western movie. It was quite quaint, if not photogenic.

Anyway, after showing us to our room, Slim bid us a good afternoon, followed by "I'll see you boys at breakfast." His leather-soled cowboy boots made quite a racket as he walked along the wooden sidewalk on his way back to his office.

We waited a few minutes, then went out to the car, wrapped the bloody head in the ground cloth, and brought it back to the room where we spread the cloth out and I immediately began finishing the caping job. After a few minutes my hands were again bathed in blood and antelope hair when the distant *clomp* of boots on the wooden walk could be heard getting louder and louder. Ed and I froze, hoping it wasn't Slim, but whoever it was we hoped our door was not his destination. Of course we had the curtains on the window facing the walkway drawn, not that it really mattered. I somehow knew those footsteps would end with a knock on our door. Sure enough, it did.

"Hey boys, you forgot your licenses," said Slim.

Understandable I guess when you consider we had other things on our mind.

"Just a minute," I shouted, as Ed rolled up the ground cloth and its bloody contents and hid it in the bathroom while I washed my hands. All this took at least a minute, which is almost an eternity when you're in a room the size of a postage stamp with walls so thin you could almost hear someone breathing behind it. I opened the door to a strange look on Slim's face as he handed over our licenses without saying another word.

Determined to get this thing over with, I resumed my task and was maybe ten minutes into it when there was this awful sound of two steps on the walk outside and another knock on the door. *Oh hell*, I thought, *I don't believe this!* Slim had obviously walked across the dirt parking lot rather than use the noisy wooden walkway, so we had no warning at all.

"I forgot to give you boys the hunting rule book that goes with the license. Wouldn't want you breaking the law," he quipped.

Now picture this: Slim again hears the sound of muffled voices, of plastic folding, of feet hurriedly scurrying across the bare wood floor, and of water suddenly running in the sink. . . . Just as I was about to open the door, Slim says, "I'll just leave this leaflet outside your door."

Thankfully, there were no more visits from Slim, and I was able to complete the caping operation, saw the horns off the skull with the small bone saw that Ed had had the foresight to bring, and get the hide well salted. On a short drive to town we got rid of the skull and all the detritus of our nefarious deed. It was the perfect crime.

I can't believe we were that stupid, but it wasn't until the next morning at breakfast that we put two and two together. Slim was not the ebullient guy we first met, as he barely spoke to us at breakfast, or at any time during the long drive to the top of Moon Mountain where he dropped us off with four balogna sandwiches.

"I'll pick you guys up here at dark."

We didn't even get a "Good luck."

By then we knew: Slim was convinced he had a couple of guys on his hands who were light in the loafers, and he was obviously a guy who wasn't at all understanding about alternate life styles. To make a long story short, we both shot mediocre bucks that very first day so that we could get the hell out of there. Thus went my first out-of-state big-game hunt. It was the first and only time I ever broke the law, game law or otherwise.

******

I think it was the following year, 1967, when Ed and I went on a pronghorn hunt in Montana. In those days there were still ranchers who'd allow you to hunt on their property. All you had to do was simply to ask for permission or, at worst, pay a reasonable daily trespass fee. We bought our licenses at a gun shop in Miles City, the owner of which was nice enough to direct us to a couple of those ranches. I remember that Ed and I both took decent bucks by the second day.

By then I was using a 7mm Remington Magnum I had built up using a barreled action from Herter's, the big mail-order house in Waseca, Minnesota, which I glass bedded into a Fajen stock. Ed was shooting the new 6.5 Remington Magnum that had been introduced a couple of years earlier, in a rifle that we put together just as I had done mine—with a barreled action and an after-market, do-it-yourself, semi-inletted stock. By then I was quite familiar with handloading, and I could take a semi-inletted and rough-shaped stock and turn it into a really good-looking custom rifle. For the next twenty-five years or so I did virtually all of my hunting with handloads and rifles I built myself using custom-barrel actions and do-it-yourself gunstocks. As the years passed, however, the opportunities to use my own rifles and handloads became increasingly limited.

******

Nineteen-seventy turned out to be a big year for me, not only because I continued to follow my plan of sending articles to different magazines, but also because I started to write for *Shooting Times* on a regular basis. Bob Steindler, the editor of the *Shooting Times*, took me under his wing and kept me busy writing for him. Later that year, however, Bob left the magazine, and the job of editor went to Alex Bartimo, who also liked my work—enough to fly me out to Peoria to the offices of the *Peoria Journal Star* newspaper, which was also the publisher of *Shooting Times*. It was pretty heady stuff for a thirty-year-old kid, because in addition to flying me out there, Alex and the publisher, Jerry Constantino, met me at the airport and escorted me to a private helicopter, which then flew us to the roof top of the *Peoria Journal Star* offices. En route they explained that the *Peoria Journal Star* also published *Rotor & Wing* magazine, a publication devoted exclusively to vertical and short take-off and landing aircraft (VSTOL). If they were trying to impress me, they sure succeeded!

In the February 1971 issue of *Shooting Times* my name was added to the masthead as special assignments editor. And within a year or so after that I was asked to join the editorial staff of *American Firearms Industry*, and shortly after that, *Rifle and Handloader* magazines. *American Firearms Industry* was a trade publication that went to federal firearms license (FFL) holders, so it was not considered a competitor of the *Shooting Times*. The same went for *Rifle and Handloader* since neither was a newsstand publication. Though I never actually signed a contract, sometime in 1973 *Shooting Times* and I came to an understanding that I was not to write for *Guns & Ammo*, *Guns*, or *Gun World*. That was OK with me, for I had already sold articles to *Guns & Ammo* and *Guns*, so they were at least familiar with my byline. The only gun magazine I had not written for by that time was *Gun World*, and for good reason.

Now how I ever talked my way onto the editorial staff of a trade publication I'll never know. I didn't know squat about the problems of gun dealers and distributors, but I learned as I went by reading the magazine I was now writing for every month and by talking with dealers and industry people. Over the next twenty-five years I would serve two separate stints as marketing editor of *Shooting Industry* and two stints with *American Firearms Industry*.

Between the time I joined the staff at *Shooting Times* in 1971 and 1980, I was pretty much the favorite of the editor, Alex Bartimo, and we became good enough friends that we'd talk at least once or twice a week. Of my tenure there, I think I can say that I, along with John Wooters, Bob Milek, and Skeeter Skelton, pretty much wrote the majority of features and columns that comprised *Shooting Times* magazine.

One day I got a call from Alex—around 1975 as I recall—asking me if I'd like to accompany him on a trip to Cornell University to interview a new writer who had started doing some gun legislation articles for *Shooting Times*. His name was Dick Metcalf, and he was teaching political science at Cornell. We met Dick in the faculty restaurant and spent a couple of pleasant hours talking. Even though I had been writing for only six years or so, Dick was very deferential, saying that he'd been reading my stuff ever since I had joined *Shooting Times*. He then went on to say that his interests were parallel to mine, i.e., guns and hunting, and the political stuff less so. Nevertheless, he was doing a good job writing about Second Amendment and gun legislation politics. Before we parted, Alex asked Dick if he'd like to join the *Shooting Times* staff as our legislation editor and do a monthly column. Thus Dick began what I believe to be the longest tenure for any writer with *Shooting Times*, or for that matter, any other gun magazine—nearly forty years.

******

The next big change in my career came when I started to attend the annual National Sporting Goods Association (NSGA) trade shows in Chicago where I got to meet the VIPs of the various gun, ammo, optics, and related accessories manufacturers and their press-relations people. Back in those days the NSGA was the largest trade show of its kind; however, guns and hunting products had to share floor space with fishing, boating, archery, team-sports equipment, and sport-clothing manufacturers. By the early 1970s the show had gotten so big that the fishing-tackle industry felt they were lost amid the jock straps, pool cues, and ping pong balls, so they broke away and started their own industry trade show. The second to defect were the firearms people and, thus, was born the SHOT Show (Shooting, Hunting, and Outdoor Trade), the first gathering of which was in St. Louis in 1979.

The New Kid and Jack Lewis

Chapter 5

Even more important to me on both a personal and professional level was the invitation I received from Remington to attend its annual Writers' Seminar in 1972. It's an annual event usually held in late October where writers get to see and shoot all the new rifles and shotguns slated for introduction the coming year at the trade and NRA shows. Though I had gotten to meet a few writers and editors at the 1971 NSGA Show, this was my first opportunity to meet all my heroes—the guys whose articles I had been reading for so many years—all in one place, up close and personal. In the evenings the booze flowed freely, and it was in that hospitality suite environment that I was able to shed some of my innate shyness, an affliction I still suffer to this day.

That first seminar I attended was held at Remington Farms in Chestertown, Maryland, on the Chesapeake Bay. If memory serves, Remington flew us into Washington, D.C., where they then bused us to a nearby hotel where they had a hospitality suite set up. To my mind these gatherings were exclusive; after all, there were only about twenty of us invited from the entire country, so I felt being one of them was really cool.

I was among the first groups to arrive—they shuttled us in batches of three or four as we arrived at the airport from different parts of the country—and one of the few guys already there were Jack O'Connor of *Outdoor Life* and Warren Page of *Field & Stream*.

"Hi, I'm Jon Sundra," I said, offering my hand. Both barely acknowledged my existence—Warren with a weak handshake and Jack with a barely perceptible nod, one hand being occupied with a drink, the other with a swizzle stick on which three olives were impaled. The other fellow in the room was Jack Lewis, founder, publisher, and editor of *Gun World* magazine. I had always enjoyed reading Jack's stuff because he had a wry sense of humor and it always filtered through in his stories. In those days the *Gun World* offices were in Capistrano Beach, California, and one of Jack's favorite venues for testing new guns and cartridges was Catalina Island. To test those cartridges and guns he would seek out feral goats. Some of those articles were not all that informative, but they were always entertaining.

I had met Jack briefly at the previous NSGA Show, but I was surprised that he recognized me. As I approached, he was leaning against the bar, resplendent in a black cowboy shirt, black jeans secured with an obscene belt buckle from his rodeo days, and a black Stetson with a turquoise hat band. In front of him on the bar was a cup of coffee. Jack's drinking days were several years behind him, but I wish I knew him when he did drink, for the stories I heard about him over the ensuing years were legendary. I already knew of some of Jack's exploits when he was, by his own admission, a belligerent, ugly drunk who only stopped when he passed out or someone *made* him pass out. I learned a lot more of his exploits directly from Jack once we became friends, but that would take several years because we got off to a bad start.

"How are ya', Jon," he said, extending his hand, squinting from beneath the wide brim of his Stetson.

I soon learned that he was almost always squinting because he was almost always smoking. He had a Sherman cigarette in his mouth from the time he got up in the morning to when he went to bed at night—four packs a day. The human eye never gets used to smoke, and his brimmed hat kept the smoke lingering below, so it's no wonder Jack was always looking at you through slits. The constant presence of a Sherman in his mouth didn't help his articulation. I found his mumbling difficult to understand even though my hearing had not yet begun to deteriorate.

"I'm fine, Jack, and you?"

"I've been better . . . but then I've been lots worse, so I've got no reason to complain. I've been reading your stuff, Jon. I like it. How about writing for me?

At that time *Shooting Times* and I had not come to any exclusivity agreement, so I thought writing for *Gun World* would just be another feather in my cap. When I told him I'd be interested, he asked me to send him some story ideas. After I got back home, I penned a letter reminding him of our conversation and of his asking me to submit some story ideas, which I did.

Several weeks passed and no response from Jack. Giving him the benefit of the doubt, I resent the original letter with a note to the effect that I understood my query or his response could have been lost in the mail, or simply fallen through the cracks at his busy office. Again, several weeks passed and no response. By that point I was pretty annoyed, but I managed to write a third letter in which I politely reminded Jack that it was he who had asked me to submit ideas. Again, I heard nothing.

Now if there's one thing that gets my shorts in a bunch it's being ignored. So from that day forward and for the next several years, I avoided speaking or even greeting Jack Lewis at subsequent seminars, trade shows, and cocktail suites. After I learned how little Jack paid his writers, I decided that I wouldn't have written for him anyway.

So, as I said, this went on for several years until one day when we were both guests—along with two or three other writers—of Ithaca Gun Company at the famous Vermejo Ranch in northern New Mexico. Ithaca was importing and privately branding the Finnish-made LSA-55/65 bolt-action, centerfire rifle, and the company had invited us writers for an elk hunt to promote the rifle. After settling in and rounding up a glass of chardonnay, I claimed one of the three or four chairs that were out on the porch. It was a beautiful autumn day, sunny, and unseasonably warm. I wasn't out there five minutes when Jack Lewis came out and settled into the chair next to me.

Under such an up-close-and-personal circumstance, it would have been rude to ignore the guy, especially when he initiated conversation. I don't know what we talked about, but we did so very amicably through three or four glasses of wine for me, and as many cups of coffee for Jack. Then, suddenly, he turns to me and mutters through his Sherman, "You know, Sundra, you're not the son-of-a-b---- I thought you were."

To which I replied: "And you're not the pr--k I thought you were."

Having said that, I thought it appropriate for me to mention the reason I had been going out of my way to ignore him . . . just in case he didn't know. "Three letters, Jack, *three letters* and you never answered me! Can you blame me for thinking you were a jerk?"

I never saw Jack actually laugh, but he was close to it at that moment.

"Jon, I honestly don't remember, but I can't imagine ignoring three letters. Sorry it happened."

And that was that. We became good friends, at least as good as possible given that we saw one another only professionally a few times a year at various industry functions. Jack would always try to sit near me at dinners, and vice versa, where he would accept the glasses of wine poured for him, then promptly hand them over to me. I never saw Jack take a drop of alcohol as long as I knew him, and there were plenty of drops at the functions we attended!

As I got to know him better, Jack would regale me with tales of his drinking days. I'm sure some were apocryphal, but even those had some truth to them because I heard the same stories from other sources who knew Jack better than I. One was my friend Jack Mitchell, who had worked for Lewis as a staff writer at *Gun World* for twenty-some years.

Jack Lewis had been a correspondent in the Marine Corps, and according to him, was kicked out of that illustrious organization for punching a superior officer. As such, he claims he was one of only two guys to ever be thrown out of the Marine Corps and later accepted back. He also served in the reserves for many years, but to sustain himself he rode broncs in rodeos and was a Hollywood stuntman before he started *Gun World* and *Horse & Rider* magazines. Jack's most well-known performance as a stuntman was when the famous director, John Ford, hired him to drive the motorcycle off the pier in the movie *Mister Roberts*.

Among Jack's circle of friends was Lee Marvin, Jonathan Winters, and Richard Boone (of *Have Gun Will Travel* TV-series fame). According to Jack, the four of them would gather in Hawaii every year for the Bill Fishing Tournament. I'm not sure whether they fished or not, but according to Jack they always got rip roaring drunk and pretty much stayed that way for the duration. One year Jonathan Winters showed up and announced that he had quit drinking. After a couple days of "suffering" a sober Winters, as Lewis described it, Jack told him he was much better company and infinitely funnier drunk than sober. The comment didn't sit too well with Winters, and the group never met again after that.

Back in the mid-1960s when Winchester was both a firearms and ammunition manufacturer, the company formed a partnership with the Italian

Fiocchi shotshell people. To get some good public relations out of it, Winchester chose for its gunwriters' seminar to send the writers over to Italy in, I believe, 1964. The itinerary consisted of a visit to the factory and then a couple of days of leisurely sightseeing in Rome. According to Jim Rikhoff, who handled public relations for Winchester at the time, and Bill Talley, one of the company's honchos, they had a company man whose sole job was to watch over Jack Lewis every waking moment of the trip. Still, Jack managed one evening to wade into the Trevi Fountain with his cowboy boots on.

Jack often repeated the same stories, but the most consistent one was that he was an ugly drunk. "Jon," he'd say to me, "once I started, I never knew when to stop. I'd wake up not knowing where I was or how I got there, usually with no money, and often with bruises telling me I'd been in a fight. I finally came to the realization that it was ruining my life and that I had to stop." And he did. Cold turkey.

In looking back on that first Remington Writers' Seminar and the many similar events I've attended over the years, I have one regret and that is I never took pictures of, or had my picture taken with, the iconic writers I got to know. As near as I can recall, at that 1972 gathering there was John Amber, Elmer Keith, Charlie Askins, Jim Crossman, Jack O'Connor, Warren Page, Pete Brown, Larry Kohler, George Nonte, Les Bowman, Grits Gresham, and of course, lil' ol' star-struck me.

It may be due to my somewhat shy and introverted nature, but I always felt it rude and intrusive to take pictures of those guys, or to hand my camera over to one of them and ask that they take a picture of me with . . . whomever. I just couldn't bring myself to do that. As I look back, I really regret that I didn't because all of them have since passed on. I would think the pictures alone of those guys doing all the stuff we did and in all the venues we visited would have made one helluva interesting book.

******

If there was such a thing as the golden age of gunwriting, I'd say it would have to have been from around 1970, when I got into it, to the mid-1990s. Those were the days when Remington and Winchester tried to outdo one another with their annual writers' seminars. Sometimes these events took place at the factories that produced the guns and ammo for what was then the two giants of the industry, or at their respective firearms museums—Remington's in Ilion, New York, and Winchester's in New Haven, Connecticut, before it was moved to Cody, Wyoming.

Even when the seminars were conducted at the museums, we always had the opportunity to shoot the latest guns and any new ammo loadings in both shotshell and metallic. At the very least we got to shoot skeet, trap, and sporting clays. If there wasn't a rifle range as part of the sponsors' facilities, they'd arrange to bus us to the nearest suitable public or private gun club for a day. I don't think they were ever turned down; after all, it isn't every day that Joe Average gets to meet the writers they've come to know through their reading of gun and hunting magazines. There were always good turnouts of local hunters and shooters at these events.

The best seminars, though, were those where we got the opportunity to use the new guns on hunts. If the emphasis that particular year was on a new shotgun, the venue would be an upland game or waterfowl preserve. If the company wanted to push a new rifle or cartridge, it would be a big-game hunt of some sort. Because the expense of taking twenty or so writers on all-expenses-paid big-game forays is considerable, it has to be the kind of hunt where a high percentage of success is virtually guaranteed.

After all, if only a small percentage of writers are successful—which is the kind of stats that Joe Average reader is all too familiar with—there's either no story, or the article fails to live up to the sponsor's hope for its new product. There's nothing like a hero picture of a hunter posing with a nice bull or buck taken with the latest and greatest new rifle, or an existing model chambered for a new cartridge. The venues, therefore, are often ranches in Texas and New Mexico where exotic species like fallow deer, blackbuck, axis deer, mouflon, nilgai, and so on are hunted inside high-fenced tracts where success is virtually 100 percent.

I personally do not like that type of venue, but I will say that the quality of the experience can vary according to the size of the fenced areas and the quality of the guides. I've been on some "hunts" that could be characterized by "Hank, you take Jon over to paddock sixteen and have him shoot ol' Charlie." I abhor those kinds of "hunts." Sadly, such operations do exist, and as such are easy prey for the rabid antihunters wanting to portray hunting as sticking the muzzle of a rifle through a cyclone fence to shoot some unsuspecting critter walking toward you to be fed. In all fairness, though, I've been on some exotic hunts where the high-fenced areas were several thousand acres, much of which was scrub oak so thick you couldn't see a deer if he was standing ten yards away. Under such circumstances, you couldn't "corner" a critter if it was imprisoned in a ten-acre parcel, let alone a ten-thousand one.

In any event, accepting a direct invitation, or simply following the wishes of an editor to represent his magazine at an industry event, is a tacit understanding that if you avail yourself to be wined and dined by a manufacturer, you're expected to reciprocate with what he hopes will be a positive review of his new wonder gun. This is where one's journalistic integrity is sorely tested. Personal invitations issued by companies are no different; in fact, the commitment is even more explicit when you're part of a small group—say three or four writers on average—invited to go on an honest-to-gosh hunt in some really neat place. These events are different from the seminars, but the hoped-for results by the sponsors are the same. I've been on many more hunts of this type than I have industry-wide new-product seminars.

In either case though, the expectations of the sponsor are the same: *We're investing a lot of time and money here, so if there's a hunt involved and you're successful, we expect some positive publicity.* Fair enough, but for me at least I so often found myself ethically conflicted because I ended up shooting an animal I really didn't want to shoot.

To avoid that kind of situation as much as possible, I would take the host aside at the beginning of the hunt and ask straight out: Would you rather I not shoot anything than shoot an animal that wasn't at least an average trophy? After all, how much positive publicity would there be in my posing with a forkhorn buck taken with some new super magnum?

I have to say that in most instances I was told there was no obligation to shoot any animal I didn't want to shoot. Still, there you are, having accepted the invitation and all the hospitality that goes with it, only to end up passing on an animal that most hunters would gladly have taken.

So, was it always a matter of no animal, no story? Not at all. In fact, I almost always salvaged a story from an unsuccessful hunt by minimizing the hunting aspect and concentrating more on the rifle itself—what was new about it if it truly was a new rifle, or its evolution if it was simply a variation of an existing model. It was pretty much the same if it was a new cartridge.

In either case, I was always sure to use the best animal taken on that particular hunt—there's always *someone* who takes a good trophy—and use it as a backdrop for photographs. It became a virtual trademark for me: I'd set the rifle against the horns or antlers of the downed critter and use a caption like: "A fine X taken with the new . . . whatever."

Never in my life have I posed for a photo with an animal I didn't shoot. I wish I could say the same for all my colleagues.

******

If I may go into the weeds a bit here, I have always been a trophy hunter, a term that among the general public puts me somewhere between a serial killer and a pedophile. Somehow they see shooting an animal for a trophy to be "stuffed" and hung on a wall as being the absolutely worst reason for hunting, yet in truth trophy hunting is the highest form of the sport. For some reason these people assume that a trophy hunter simply takes the cape and horns and leaves everything else for the coyotes, which of course is rarely the case.

A true trophy hunter will go home with nothing rather than shoot a creature of less stature than he set out to collect. To have a shootable animal in the cross hair and decide not to shoot is what real hunting is all about. It is perhaps the greatest manifestation of personal freedom we have outside war. Every hunter is a trophy hunter the first morning, but to pass on an animal that the average guy would settle for in a heartbeat, and do so on the last afternoon of the last day, is a guy who has my utmost respect as a hunter and as a man.

The definition of a "trophy" animal can vary to some extent, but shooting a spike buck, even if it's one's first deer, is not a trophy animal—no matter how proud one has a right to be of the accomplishment. There has to be some standard of excellence, but it doesn't have to be those set by Boone and Crockett, Pope and Young, Rowland Ward, or even Safari Club, whose minimums are the least stringent.

Then there are those who are neither for nor against hunting; their take on it is "So long as you eat what you shoot." A magnanimous attitude to be sure, but I don't think that's the reason why most men hunt. The way I see it, putting meat on the table today is a byproduct of hunting, not a rationale. I've never been a big fan of game meat, and believe me, I've eaten everything from eland, elk, and caribou backstraps, to moose nose, buffalo tongue, and zebra. I don't care what it is, who and how it's prepared, to me there's nothing like a dry-aged, well marbled Angus rib eye. I don't think that makes me any less of a hunter.

Changing Times

As I write this, it's May 2017, a time that has long since seen political correctness gone amok. It's a time when a mere handful of people who object to the presence of a commemorative cross, a manger scene, the name of a sport's franchise, and even the use of the term "Merry Christmas" can change the laws and customs of the vast majority. These are people who simply cannot stand those who disagree with them. Nowhere is this insanity, this utter lack of tolerance and common sense, more evident than when it involves firearms.

Two incidents in the news fairly recently come to mind. One involves a first grader who during lunch hour took a bite out of a corner of a saltine cracker, leaving an L-shape, which to the fertile imagination of a six-year-old resembled a handgun. The kid grasped the cracker as if it was, and pointed it at his friend sitting across from him, and said "bang." The kid was thrown out of school under the guise of "zero tolerance" for violence! Zero tolerance? Zero common sense!

The other incident involved a fellow who lived in Washington, D.C., who was found by the police to have had a single shotgun shell in the trunk of his car. No shotgun . . . or a gun of any kind. He was a law-abiding citizen with no criminal record of any kind. He ended up making national news because he was arrested and is now awaiting trial . . . for having a shotshell in the trunk of his car!

When I hear of such incidents, which is often, I think back to another time—or maybe it was another world—when tolerance and common sense prevailed. When I was a senior in high school back in 1957, I took a course in salesmanship, and as part of our final exam each student had to bring an object to class and give a ten-minute sales pitch. I asked, and was *permitted*, to bring an H&R Model 922 9-shot .22 LR revolver. Let me emphasize, this was not some rural, one-room schoolhouse on the prairie, but a 5,000-student high school in the largest suburb of Cleveland. It was a 6-block walk to school for me through a densely populated residential community where cigar-box homes were crammed onto lots measuring 40x80 feet. In short, it was as urban as you can get.

Anyway, I walked to school that day with my trusty 922 in its original box, which almost made it look like just another one of the books I was carrying. When it came time for class, just to see what kind of reaction I'd get, I went to my locker and took the pistol out of its box and walked down the crowded halls with it in my hand. I got a lot of surprised looks, but no one—students or teachers—seemed to give it a second thought; in fact, I got a lot of "hey man, cool!" and hands up surrender gestures with smiles or laughs.

Fast forward ten years to 1968 and to an incident that I remember virtually every time I board a plane for a hunting trip. It was my very first international hunt, and a freebie at that. I don't recall the details, but somehow I had wangled an invitation from the Quebec Department of Tourism to hunt caribou in the Shefferville area of Labrador as their guest. At the time I had had only a handful of articles published, so I was far from being the kind of established writer a press-relations guy could count on to get some ink, assuming the hunt proved successful. I think the fact I was still working as editor for *Outdoor People* helped a little. After all, being just across from Lakes Erie and Ontario, Pennsylvania had more licensed hunters than any other state. The guy I dealt with went by the name of Rod Hunter (obviously a nom de plume, being the public-relations guy for the fish and game division), and he evidently thought I was worth a gamble that only cost his department an airline ticket and a 50 percent subsidy for the outfitter who agreed to host my hunt at his cost.

In any case, those were the days when some airlines—mostly those that served hunting destinations—allowed you to bring onboard a rifle (or shotgun) in a soft case, provided it was stowed up front in the cockpit. When I stated earlier that the hunt was a freebie, that wasn't quite true; I only had complimentary air fare from Montreal, so I had to get there at my own expense. Judith and I were struggling at the time, so to save precious money, I drove from Pittsburgh to Montreal a day early and stayed in a motel close to the airport, as the only flight servicing Shefferville left early in the morning.

When I checked in for my flight, I told the stewardess that I had checked beforehand and understood I could board the plane with my rifle as it was in a soft case. I also said I knew that it would then be placed up front with the flight crew. The stewardess then told me that there were several other hunters on the plane, that there was no more room for my gun in the cockpit, and that I should take it to my seat! So there I was, on a commercial jet from Montreal with a hundred other people, sitting with a 7mm Remington Magnum between my legs. I could just as easily had a box of ammo in that soft case, for they never asked when I checked in.

Can you imagine a thing like that happening today?

Elmer Keith

Of all the gunwriters who have come and gone, I'd have to say Elmer Keith was, for me, the most iconic. Among my colleagues, however, most of them revere Jack O'Connor, some to the point of sycophancy. To me Elmer was a more interesting person by far, friendlier, and downright modest compared to Jack, whose life experiences and challenges pale when compared to Elmer's.

As a writer, however, compared to Jack—or anyone, for that matter—well, Elmer just wasn't. When I was on the staff of *Guns & Ammo*, I got to see some of Elmer's original manuscripts because Howard French, the editor then, shared them with me on occasion. Elmer knew two forms of punctuation: a capital letter at the beginning of a paragraph and a period at the end. In between, rarely was there a comma to be found, and if there was, it was in the wrong place. A lot of work went into redoing an Elmer Keith article, but the information therein was golden and well worth the time it took to edit Elmer's material.

I can't say that I knew Elmer very well, but he attended at least four or five Remington and Winchester writers' seminars when I was present. I talked to him on several occasions and found him to be pretty candid. Almost every article I've read portrays Elmer and Jack O'Connor as being mutually respectful of one another, considering their diametrically opposing views on light/heavy bullets, but that's not quite the impression I got from one conversation I had with Elmer. Elmer didn't like Jack, but I know he respected him. Jack, on the other hand, neither liked nor respected Elmer, but that's a story for another time.

Anyway, the conversation I alluded to took place under circumstances I can't for the life of me remember. (It's times like these that I regret never having kept a journal!) All I can recall is the conversation itself and that it was at a Remington seminar. For some inexplicable reason, Elmer and I found ourselves separated from the rest of the group, all of whom were on a chartered bus. How or why that could have happened is a mystery because from the time we arrived at the airport to the time we returned to get on the planes to take us home, we were always moved around as a group.

In any case, we're on this street corner, just Elmer and I, and he proceeds to tell me how he recently had run his Cadillac into a ditch near Salmon, Idaho, and had broken his back in the process. "I'm wearing a body cast, Jon. Still hurts like hell when I move around!"

This is a guy who at the age of twelve was burned so badly in a boardinghouse fire in Missoula, Montana, in 1911, that he became the worst burn victim in medical history to have survived up to that time. He suffered third-degree burns over 85 percent of his body. When he came out of the hospital his right hand, which was little more than a claw as he described it, was virtually backward on his wrist, and his chin had been welded to his shoulder in the fire.

The story of his long and extremely painful rehabilitation is nothing less than awe inspiring. The doctors predicted Elmer wouldn't live to see twenty, so they refused to try to fix his grotesque disfigurement. So without anesthetic other than a half-bottle of whiskey, he had his father break every re-growing bone in his hand and wrist. He passed out from the pain, and when he recovered, his father reoriented his hand and fingers and taped them to a board.

The rest we all know: that he went on to become the legend that is Elmer Keith, the man who was the prime mover behind Smith & Wesson's development of the .357, .44, and .41 Magnum handgun rounds. He was the man who helped popularize handgun hunting through his many articles for the *American Rifleman* and *Guns & Ammo* magazines. He also was the most influential proponent of big-bore rifle cartridges pushing heavy bullets at moderate velocity. He was admired and respected by his readers and colleagues alike, me being no exception.

Knowing the story of his life, the fact he was walking around with a broken back at nearly eighty years of age didn't surprise me in the least! I can't recall what brought it up, but it was during that waiting-for-the-bus episode that the topic of Jack O'Connor came up.

"I don't understand why that guy keeps promoting that coyote cartridge as being a good elk killer," he told me. "It ain't true. I've seen plenty of elk killed in my day, and the .270 is not a good elk cartridge. It'll do in a pinch, but it's far from ideal."

Elmer did a lot of guiding in Oregon and Idaho for elk and mule deer in the 1920s and 1930s, so he certainly had empirical knowledge. The .270 wasn't introduced until 1925, but he was guiding long enough after that to have surely seen many an elk killed—or wounded—with the .270.

There's a story, perhaps apocryphal, about Elmer that has to do with his guiding days, one that I've heard told many times at various writer events back in the day. It seems Elmer had a client out on a wilderness elk hunt when a snowstorm hit and the temperature plummeted. Somehow, his client had struck off on his own and had gotten lost. When Elmer finally found him, his client was dead and frozen solid, his legs fully extended. Being alone, Elmer couldn't get the unwieldy package tied down to a packhorse, so as the story goes, he took a buck saw and sawed his client in two, making two panniers out of him. As I said, it may be apocryphal, but, then again, maybe not. I could see such a thing happening in the 1920s and people not getting too upset about it under the circumstances.

By the time the Winchester seminar convened in 1973, I knew Elmer from the Remington seminar of the previous year, and from seeing him at various industry hospitality suites at the NSGA Show. The venue that year was a plantation in South Carolina where we hunted whitetails and upland game. Most of us were bunked in the guest lodge that had a bar and a lounge area downstairs and some bedrooms upstairs. Elmer was sharing a room with Jack Lewis because Jack was as tight with Elmer as anyone. (We were always asked ahead of time if we had any roommate preferences.)

Anyway, Elmer and Jack were in the first room at the top of the stairs. It was a two-tier staircase in that there were three of four steps up to a landing, then and 90-degree turn up the rest of the staircase. Late into the first evening, Elmer was doing what he was so very good at: consuming heroic quantities of Chivas Regal. (He pronounced it *tchi-vis*.) For some reason Elmer went up to his room for a few minutes and on his return, fell down the stairs, putting his elbow through a low hung window on the landing.

"I thought I was on the last godd--n step," said Elmer, getting up like nothing had happened. Anyone who's ever done that—think they have stepped onto the floor when there was actually one more step . . . and we've all done it—knows that you lurch forward. That's what happened to Elmer. He lurched forward, put his elbow through the window, and then got up as if nothing had happened . . . and in the process he never even lost grip on the cigar he had clenched in his teeth!

I have another Elmer Keith story that took place at the Remington seminar held at the Vermejo Ranch in New Mexico in 1975—this was the same Ithaca-sponsored event I mentioned earlier where Jack Lewis and I made up. Elmer was bunked in with Les Bowman, one of the nicest, humblest guys I've ever met in my profession. During the 1920s Les lived in Hollywood when it was still a boomtown. He was a barnstormer, which was a popular form of entertainment during the Roaring Twenties, and I believe it was either his wife or girlfriend who did the wing walking.

Les then moved to Wyoming where he developed a thriving outfitting business. He was also a highly knowledgeable rifleman, handloader, and ballistic experimenter. I'm not sure how his relationship with Remington began, but I think it was through his guiding business that he met Wayne Leek and Mike Walker, two guys who worked on product development at Remington. Impressed with his experience as a hunter, his engineering background, and his knowledge of rifles and cartridges, Wayne Leek retained Les as a consultant on the development of the .280 Remington and 7mm Remington Magnum. Les also did a bit of writing for various magazines, so that, coupled with his consulting work, got him invited to the seminars.

As I said, Les was a gentleman, soft spoken, and never had a bad thing to say about any of his colleagues. I always made it a point to sit down to talk to him because he was such a nice guy and had led such an interesting life. It was so fascinating, in fact, that I tried to get him to collaborate with me on his biography because I knew he was too modest to do it himself. He said he would think about it, but he passed away before anything came of it.

Anyway, we were hunting elk that year, and Elmer—who was never one to concern himself with protocol—arrived at Vermejo in a pickup truck. Instead of flying on Remington's dollar, he was chauffeured down from Idaho by one of his adoring fans. Not only that, he brought with him a Winchester Model 70 chambered in his humongous .338/378. Only Elmer could get away with bringing his own rifle to a Remington writers' seminar . . . and a Winchester no less. The Remington people were not happy, but hey, it was Elmer, so they let him use it, even though at these industry events the sponsor always furnishes the guns.

Elmer had been experimenting with necking down the voluminous .378 Weatherby case to .338, his favorite rifle caliber—it still may have been a wildcat at that time. It was either shortly before or shortly after that seminar that Weatherby did, indeed, add it to their cartridge lineup. It is one of the most brutal cartridges I've ever shot, churning up 54 ft-lbs of recoil, or more than 2-½ times that of an 8½-pound .30-06.

Anyway, I believe it was the second day of our three-day hunt when, on the way back to the ranch that evening, Elmer's guide pointed out some cow elk that were grazing fairly close to the road. Having spent two days not seeing a worthwhile bull, Elmer told his guide that he'd take a cow, as he was more interested in meat than antlers. After all, he had shot plenty of trophy bulls in his life. So the guide brings the pickup to a stop, Elmer gets out, and using the hood of the truck for a rest, takes the shot.

Not only was it a clean miss, but the old man was bleeding from his eyebrow like a stuck pig. The foremost proponent of big-bore, powerful cartridges and a legendary shot had missed a cow elk from a steady rest, standing about 150 yards from the road and getting a Weatherby eyebrow in the process.

Well, Elmer was so embarrassed, so humiliated, that he accused Les Bowman, his roommate, of fiddling with his scope while he was out of the room, just to precipitate such an incident. As I recall, Elmer didn't want to face anyone at happy hour or dinner, so he left that evening without saying good-bye to anyone. Elmer never accused Les to his face, but expressed that opinion to one of the Remington people, probably Dick Dietz, who was their press-relations guy at the time. In any case, by the next morning everyone had heard the story.

I'm not sure, but I think that may have been the last Remington seminar that Elmer attended, not because of embarrassment but because of age. Elmer had to have been close to eighty at the time. He suffered a stroke and died at the age of eighty-two.

Howard French, the editor at *Guns & Ammo* during the time I was under contract at Petersen's Publishing, told me about another Elmer incident. Howard was a good friend and a good editor; we hung out a lot together in the evenings at the SHOT, NRA, and Safari Club conventions, along with Bob Milek, Todd Smith, who went on to become editor of *Outdoor Life*, and Dave Hetzler, associate editor at *Guns & Ammo*.

The incident took place at the Winchester seminar the year it was held in Italy in the mid-1960s. That was before my time, unfortunately. Seems the Winchester folks took the writers out to a fancy restaurant in Rome one evening. It was cold enough that a lot of the guys had jackets, which they self-checked in a small anteroom prior to being seated. At the end of the evening while claiming their duds, Elmer held his hat upside down as if he was looking for something inside. When one of the Winchester guys—I think it was Jim Rikhoff—asked what he was looking for, Elmer replied in absolute seriousness, "Hell, I just wanted to make sure it's mine." Now that had to be the only ten-gallon cowboy hat in Rome, let alone the only one in that restaurant! That was Elmer.

Another time Howard was sitting next to Elmer at a bar when Elmer ordered a mixed drink, even though he usually drank Chivas Regal. The bartender was a black man. After a couple of sips, Elmer looked over at the bartender and said, "You make a pretty good drink for a n-----."

Howard cringed and then exploded, "For Christ sake Elmer, we don't use that word anymore!

"Well I was just trying to compliment the son-of-a-b----!" Elmer replied.

47

Charlie Askins

Charlie Askins could be the most charming of men, but by all accounts he was a man you didn't want to get on the wrong side of. The stories of him when he served as a border patrol agent prior to World War II are legendary, and not in a flattering way. He described himself as a killer, and in his autobiography, *Non-Repentant Sinner*, he proudly claimed to have killed twenty-seven men during his border patrol days and while in the U.S. Army in WWII, with the caveat "not counting Hispanics and blacks." After his retirement from the army, Charlie became a gunwriter; his last stint was with *Guns Magazine* where he served as shooting editor. He is credited with having authored one thousand magazine articles and twelve books on hunting and shooting. I succeeded him as shooting editor at *Guns* in 1990 and served in that position for more than a decade.

Charlie described himself to me, as well as in his writings, as a pathological killer, and that the only reason he hunted animals was that he could no longer hunt human beings. One of his goals in life was to kill one hundred Cape buffaloes, and if he didn't achieve it, he came close. My first exposure to his bloodthirsty nature occurred when we attended a Winchester writers' seminar in Colombia in 1976.

It was my first taste of dove shooting South American style, meaning there were typically so many birds in the air that you could shoot until you were either sick of it or your shoulder screamed "stop"! Winchester really did it up that year, flying about twenty-five of us, along with at least ten or so Winchester people, to promote a new semiautomatic shotgun they either had just introduced or were about to introduce. I'm not sure what model it was because I have a group photo taken at that event and some of us are holding over/unders. We were given a case of shells each before every shoot, morning and evening; that's two times 500 rounds of 12-gauge shotshells or 1,000 a day.

A couple of hours into our first shoot—it was an afternoon affair—one by one the guys came straggling back to the vehicles. Most had shot all five hundred rounds, but some of us had not, having had our fill before shooting a full case of shells. I was among the first to quit, but within a half hour or so everyone was back at the vehicles . . . except Charlie. He was still blasting away, and he was doing it with shells he had mooched from the rest of us. I was on a stand two down from Charlie, and on the stand between us was Jack Lewis. Just as I was about to call it quits, a bird boy pitches up with a case that had a couple of unopened boxes of shells in it.

"No mas," I gestured, pointing to the box he was holding, thinking he was there to renew my shell supply.

"No, no," he said, shaking his head. He then said something to my boy who understood and could speak a bit of English.

"He wants the *cartuchos* [cartridges] you don't shoot."

I pointed to the case on the ground that still had maybe four or five boxes left and motioned he could have them. A big smile flashed across his face as he swooped up his booty and headed straight to Charlie's stand. Now ol' Charlie spoke fluent Spanish, and I'm sure he promised his boy an additional tip for any extra ammo he was able to scrounge. Jack had already left his stand and I assumed he was the donor of the few boxes the kid already had when he pitched up at mine. No sooner had Charlie's bird boy dropped off the shells than I saw him heading off in the opposite direction for the same purpose. I don't know how many additional shells the kid was able to glom, but it had to be close to a case, so Charlie shot nearly one thousand rounds that afternoon.

As I said, Charlie could be the most charming of gentlemen, and he was one of the few ol' timers who had made me feel welcome at the first few writers' seminars I attended. In fact, he kinda' took me under his wing, more so than any of the others; in fact, some of them seemed to go out of their way to ignore me, as if to say "You're too young to be here, boy . . . never even served in the armed forces. What the hell do you know about guns"?

Two conversations with Charlie stand out in my memory, both of which took place long after I had earned my wings and was an accepted member of the fraternity. The first one took place at one of the seminars and it had to do with writing style.

"Jon," he said, "you're a damn good writer, but you're too diplomatic. You don't want to hurt anybody's feelings. You gotta' be more controversial, like me with my 'junk' stories."

He was referring to the articles he'd write on a regular basis entitled "Let's junk the . . . " and of which I was very familiar. He, of course, would pick the most revered rifles and cartridges like the Winchester 94, Marlin 336, the .30-30, .270 Winchester, and the .30-06, saying they were obsolete and belonged in the dustbin of history.

"I can't tell you how many letters those articles generated, Jon. Half the writers were incensed, telling me I was a son-of-a-b----; the other half said "Right on, Colonel." They may not agree with you, Jon, but they won't forget you. And that's what I was after—a reaction one way or the other, and I couldn't care less which."

I took Charlie's advice and wrote several such articles over the years, two of which were entitled "The .30-06 Ain't So Hot," and "Now Take The .30-06, Please." I, however, was more diplomatic than Charlie. The implication in Charlie's articles was that if you didn't agree with him, you were a nitwit. I've always tried to respect divergent opinions, so even with my iconoclastic article on the .30-06, I pretty much got away with it.

The other incident occurred at the SHOT Show. Judith accompanied me to the 1981 convention in New Orleans, and it was her last show. After attending so many trade shows that most of the people in the industry knew her, she stopped going, preferring to stay home with the boys. The hassle of traveling and of my dragging her from one exhibit booth to another got old after a while.

When we checked into our hotel the day before the show started, the first thing I did when we got to our room was to turn on the news. The lead story was about a private plane that had crashed into Lake Pontchartrain. All they knew at the time was that the flight had originated in Grand Island, Nebraska. When we heard that, we looked at each other and simultaneously gasped, "Joyce," meaning Joyce Hornady, the founder of Hornady Bullets and our friend. Judith and I had made three African safaris with Joyce and his wife, Marvel, in South

Africa, Namibia, and Zambia in 1978 and 1979. We knew Joyce was a pilot and owned a twin-engine plane like the one described on the news.

As it turned out, Joyce, his engineer Ed Heers, and customer-service manager Jim Garber were killed that day. A terrible pall could be felt the next morning when the show opened, and it remained for the duration.

Anyway, that was the atmosphere when we bumped into Charlie on the show floor the next day. After exchanging pleasantries, he asked how we were doing. "Fine," I answered.

Judith, however, disagreed and said, "We're having an awful problem with a neighbor, Charlie, and it's gotten to where it's affecting Jon's work . . . and mine."

Without going into too much detail, suffice to say that this neighbor had threatened us when we tried to move an old dirt access road that diagonally cut across our twenty-eight-acres and that he used to get to his mobile home. We offered to move his access road to the edge of our property at our expense. Though it would be a better road and afford both of us more privacy, he thought we were somehow screwing him.

Upon hearing of our plight, Charlie looked me straight in the eye and said, "Jon, I could make that problem go away. Just say the word."

I really didn't know what to say, or for that matter, what he meant. If he was joking, he could have fooled us both. He seemed dead serious. I often wonder what would have happened, if anything, had I said, "Yes, make it go away."

Jack O'Connor

Jack was the greatest gunwriter who ever lived. All you had to do was ask him. I didn't know Jack very well because he stopped attending the seminars shortly after I started in 1972, but I did have a few conversations with him. Knowing what I know now, I find it amazing that he even granted me an audience, let alone deigned to have an actual conversation with me. I think his condescension may have had to do with an article I wrote on rifle-stock design that appeared in the January 1971 issue of *Guns Magazine.*

If I had met Jack before that time, it would have been at the NSGA Show, but I don't remember that happening. If I had, he certainly had no reason to remember me until he wrote the letter below and we met the following year at the Remington seminar. Maybe that's why he was cordial enough when we met, for by that time I had several more articles in print and, perhaps, he had made the association. In any event, I really didn't form my opinions about Jack until after his death and after I had hunted with guides and PHs both here and in Africa who had been on hunts with him and his wife, Eleanor.

Jack was very gracious with his fans, but that was not the case when it came to his fellow gunwriters. Frankly, Jack had little use for any of us, especially Elmer Keith and whippersnappers like me. I'm sure he thought it presumptuous of me to be writing about guns as a full-timer at the tender age of thirty. Acknowledging the very existence of a colleague either personally or through his writings for *Outdoor Life* where he served as shooting editor for thirty-one years, let alone extending a compliment, did not come easy for him.

So you could have knocked me over with a feather when I received a handwritten letter from Jack O'Connor on *Outdoor Life* stationery that read:

Dear Jon Sundra:

I enjoyed your exceedingly intelligent and well-written article on stock design in the January issue of *Guns*. I have said much the same thing myself, but I think you have said it better!

Jack O'Connor
Box 382
Lewiston, Idaho 83501

After his passing in 1978, several fawning writers began referring to him as the "Dean of Gunwriters" and "Mr. .270," for he more than anyone else was responsible for elevating that cartridge to iconic status. It just so happened that one of the few conversations I had with Jack was about the .270. He told me that he wished he wasn't so closely associated with the cartridge. He went on to say that, although he had written about it and used it in the field extensively, he liked the .30-06 just as much, and the 7mm Remington Magnum as well. But whenever he wrote glowingly about any cartridge other than the .270, many of his readers reacted as if he was committing heresy. It's as though he wasn't allowed to write about anything but the .270, and he said he regretted that. I don't know if he ever made that admission to anyone else, but I can't recall ever seeing anything to that effect in print.

When I say that Jack didn't have much use for other gunwriters, that's not just my opinion. He pretty much said so himself, publicly, in an editorial he wrote for *Petersen's Hunting* magazine around 1975. I say "around" because that issue, along with several hundred other magazines in which my articles appeared, I deep-sixed a decade ago. I simply had too many accumulated, so I tossed the oldest ones out.

When Jack retired from *Outdoor Life*, Robert Petersen saw an opportunity to launch a sister magazine to his *Guns & Ammo* around the highly popular O'Connor. It was a shrewd move by "Pete" because Jack had a huge following that would automatically translate into readers and subscribers. Thus *Petersen's Hunting* came to be in 1973, with Jack being named as the executive editor. It was mostly an honorary title, for Jack wrote just a few articles for the magazine before his death in 1978. I served on the editorial staff of *Petersen's Hunting* as its eastern field editor starting with the very first issue.

Petersen's Hunting was still relatively new when Jack wrote an editorial in which he castigated gunwriters as a whole, saying that most of them either didn't know what they were talking about or couldn't write . . . or both. I was shocked at its mean-spirited tone. The message was so astonishingly arrogant that I couldn't believe editor Ken Elliot actually allowed Jack's article to show up in print or to allow the magazine to be used in such a way.

The era in which Jack achieved his iconic status is long gone. It was a time when, if you wanted to read about guns, you read the shooting editors of the "Big Three" magazines: Jack at *Outdoor Life*, Warren Page at *Field & Stream*, and Pete Brown at *Sports Afield*. What you essentially had for a period of about fifteen years after the end of World War II was the world of guns and hunting being filtered through and meted out to several million hunters and shooters by three guys. Oh, guns were also covered by *Argosy* and *True*, the men's magazines of the day, but they didn't do it on a regular basis. In my opinion Warren and Pete knew more about guns than Jack, but Jack was a better writer, and that made all the difference.

Bob Milek

I f the term "good ol' boy" ever makes it into the dictionary, Bob Milek's picture should be displayed next to it. When I joined *Shooting Times* in February of 1971, Bob was not yet on the staff, and several other changes were in the works that year. By the end of the year Bob Steindler was gone as editor and in his place was Alex Bartimo. Skeeter Skelton was handgun editor; John Wootters came on as rifle editor, and George Nonte would be made tech editor. With the December 1973 issue, I went from special assignments editor to hunting editor, and Bob joined the *Shooting Times* staff in November of 1974.

The one thing that sticks out in my mind regarding Bob's stint at *Shooting Times* was his obsession with the top-break, barrel-switching Thompson-Center Contender pistol. It seemed that in every other issue of *Shooting Times* Bob would have an article on testing or hunting with a Contender. I'm certain Bob had every model and caliber iteration of the Contender ever sold, as well as many that never made it to production.

Even though Bob and I served on the *Shooting Times* staff for some eight years together, we were somehow never invited to the same industry events or hunts together, so the only time I got to spend time with him was at the SHOT Show, the NRA convention, and a few writer seminars. Bob spent most of his free time at shows with industry people, and in the evenings only rarely did he dine with Alex and me or other staff people.

That all changed after Bob left *Shooting Times* to join the *Guns & Ammo/ Hunting* group in June of 1979. John Wootters had been the first to jump ship in May of 1978, and I left in October of 1980. Apparently, my leaving was the proverbial straw that broke the camel's back. Losing three of their core group of writers, the *Shooting Times* folks were determined that I would be the last defection to the enemy. The staffers who were left—most notably Layne Simpson, Rick Jamison, and Skeeter Skelton—were given written contracts and a substantial rate increase.

I thought I had left *Shooting Times* under the best circumstances possible because when I told my friend and editor Alex Bartimo that I was leaving, he essentially told me he couldn't match Petersen's offer but that if it didn't work out for me at Petersen's, I'd always have a home at *Shooting Times*. Yeah, sure. I was immediately removed from the comp list, and I swear the staff there must have been told never to mention my name. Years later when *Shooting Times* published its 25th Silver Anniversary edition, they gushed over their writers past and current, including Wootters and Milek, but my name was never mentioned. Apparently, their leaving was OK; mine was not.

I digress.

Immediately upon joining the staff at *Guns & Ammo/Hunting*, I got along swimmingly with the in-house editors, particularly *Guns & Ammo's* editor Howard French, and associate editors Dave Hetzler and Todd Smith. So, too, did Bob. At the close of every day at a convention or seminar—SHOT, NRA, and so on—the entire group would always wind up in the hotel bar, which we often closed. We all qualified as heavy drinkers, but we all knew when to stop . . . except Bob Milek. He would religiously get absolutely blitzed, but only on the first night; after that he drank, but not to excess. Elmer was much the same way; he'd over-serve himself with his beloved Chivas Regal, but he seldom encored.

I have to say that Bob had the greatest recuperative powers of anyone I've ever known. More than once some of us would wind up literally carrying Bob to his room in the wee hours, yet at 7 A.M. he was like a chipmunk. It was impossible to tell if he was hung-over. If ever I was anywhere near as drunk as I've seen Bob at 3 A.M., I would have to sleep the entire next day to feel even half human.

Bob explained his tendency to end up blitzed on the first evening of every industry gathering. He said there wasn't a whole helluva lot to do in his hometown of Thermopolis, Wyoming, and that the few times a year he had the opportunity to spend time with his friends and colleagues simply made him happy. If there's a better reason for drinking, I don't know what it is! His dying at the age of fifty-nine was a tragedy.

Bob and I had some great times together, especially during our expeditions to visit a few European factories. The incidents that most stand out in my mind occurred on a Sako factory tour, followed by a Sako-sponsored moose hunt in Finland. If memory serves—and often it doesn't!—after touring the factory in Riihimaki, we were put up for a day at the Intercontinental Hotel in Helsinki before boarding a night train to the north of the country for the moose hunt.

Bob, Howard French, and I were passing time in the hotel lounge where we were taking full advantage of our free-bar tab. At the table next to us sat a young fellow, who we couldn't help noticing had pounded down three or four drinks in maybe a half-hour at most . . . and who knows how many more before we got there. Anyway, he started to mumble, at first at a low decibel level, but after a minute or so, louder. As I recall, we were the only people in the lounge, what with it being midafternoon, so the lounge staff didn't seem to be too concerned.

Suddenly, this guy started spewing explicatives as though he was reading them off a laundry list. I'm talking a litany of F-bombs, cuss words, and body parts, all in English, but with a thick Finnish accent. It wasn't directed toward anyone or thing; he was just staring off into space, glassy-eyed, as he rattled off one vile word after another.

Bob turned to him and said, "Hey, fella', what's the idea? Those are despicable words you're shouting, and this certainly is not the place for it."

"OK, I stop," was his reply. He was obviously very drunk, but his English was good enough that we learned he had just returned from the States where he had been playing semipro hockey, and he didn't want to forget any of the English swear words he had learned! He seemed harmless enough, and he did stop swearing. But after a minute or so of silence, he looked over at Bob and says, "You are a little sh--."

Bob ignored him, but it did no good.

"I said, 'You are a little sh--,'" the guy again declared.

Now Bob became miffed and responded, "And you, sir, are an idiot."

At that the Finn tried to rise out of his chair, but failed.

By now Bob was standing over him. "C'mon, get up," he said.

This time the Finn managed to rise out of his chair, all six-foot-four or so—blonde hair, blue eyes, definitely SS material and then some. Bob stood about five feet, seven inches as I recall, and would have been no more than breakfast for this guy.

Just as something regrettable was about to happen, two police came scurrying into the lounge to escort this guy out. The bartender had made the call. As they ushered the guy out, he turned his head and said, "I'm leaving now." Like he had a choice in the matter.

******

By the time we boarded the train that night for the moose hunt, Bob and I were feeling no pain, nor was the president of Sako, who was wearing a tea pot warmer, which he had pilfered at the train station, on his head. It looked something like a tiara, so we started to call him "Pope." He played right along as though he was born for the part.

All told, there were about eight of us, four Sako people and us, the fourth being a fellow writer, Clair Rees, who was a Mormon and not a lot of fun. At some point well past midnight on our several-hour train ride, the only ones of our group who were still up were Bob Milek and I. There were very few other people on that train, and most of them were also asleep, but of those who weren't, Bob and I managed to tick off most of them.

It was one of those drunks where both of us found everything the other said to be hilarious. Moreover, we each had a bottle of wine in hand as we went from car to car for reasons I can't remember. We did, however, try to behave whenever we saw the conductor approaching, but at one point he surprised us when we were, of all places, in the luggage car. He proceeded to open the sliding door, which faintly lit up the cold Finnish countryside that was flashing by. Without saying a word, he pointed to me, then to Bob, and pointed outside.

Bob cried out, "You want us to jump? You can go to hell!"

The conductor shook his head in disgust and said, "The wine, the wine!"

"Oh," was our collective response. "You want us to throw the wine out?"

"Yes!" barked the conductor.

Whatever wine there was left in those two bottles—and there couldn't have been much—we more than made up for on our arrival at our destination station. Either our hosts had had the foresight to stock up on wine or they had been forewarned about our proclivity for it, for we found on arrival that they had a few bottles on hand for the hour-long bus trip to hunting camp. Bob Milek was not a wine drinker, but he was when he was with me, and I guess my reputation proceeded us!

Bill Jordan
and Cheval Blanc

Bill Jordan was one of my favorite colleagues and I regret that I wasn't able to get to know him better. Like Charlie Askins, Bill treated me as an equal from the very first time we met, and in subsequent meetings as though I was one of his oldest and best friends. That's the one character trait that all really nice people seem to have in common. There was something about his deep voice and slow Southern drawl I found reassuring and . . . almost melodic.

In many ways Bill's history parallels that of Askins's. Both served in World War II and Korea, both retired with the rank of colonel, and both served on the border patrol. However, personality-wise, they could not have been more different. Even though Jordan received personal commendations from three U.S. presidents, and President Ronald Reagan conferred the Medal of Freedom on him, he was the most modest "gunwriter" I've ever known. That's saying something, for collectively we are not exactly known for modesty.

I either saw or overheard Charlie berate others on occasion. These were young editors especially who may have landed a job as editor or assistant editor on a gun or hunting magazine and who may not have known much about either. Nevertheless, their position warranted some respect since they did represent their publications.

"It's Colonel, to you son," I heard him say more than once.

Jordan, on the other hand, never mentioned his military history or rank, and when a "newbie" did address him as "colonel," his response was always, "Please, just Bill." While Askins actually bragged about shooting people in war and as a border patrol officer, Bill refused to talk about such things, even though he obviously had similar experiences. While Askins talked big, Bill Jordan was big, physically. He stood well over six feet tall and had hands the size of pie plates. A more modest man all around, Jordan did finally talk about his experiences in both the war and on the border patrol in *No Second Place Winner*, the best known of his three books.

When Bill retired from the border patrol, he took a job as the southwestern field representative for the NRA. That along with his part-time gunwriting got him invited to quite a few industry events and seminars.

His proficiency with a handgun is legendary and attested to by the fact that he held a long-standing world record for drawing a holstered revolver, firing, and hitting a target in .28 of a second! He gave many public demonstrations of that skill as part of his NRA affiliation, and also on several national television shows.

In his day his preference for revolvers over semiautos put him in the minority among his fellow handgun experts, and in the extreme minority today. Though I am far from being knowledgeable enough to write about handguns, I know which end the bullet comes out of and enough to have my own studied opinion. I have to side with Bill on the revolver thing.

I've just never developed the kind of confidence with a semiautomatic pistol that I have with a revolver. With a wheel gun, I know its status at a glance, and I have more faith in its reliability, whether that's statistically justified or not. I feel strongly enough that if it came to defending myself, I'd rather have six rounds in a revolver than sixteen in a semiautomatic. Call me crazy.

Anyway, my favorite story involving Bill Jordan revolves around wine, and it took place at the 1976 Winchester Writers' Seminar in Colombia that I mentioned earlier in this book. If memory serves, Winchester was introducing a new, more affordable version of its Super X-1 semiautomatic shotgun that year and a new member of their imported line of O/U shotguns from Italy. It was appropriate therefore that the venue be Colombia, for back then, before the drug cartels took over, it was just about the best place on earth for dove shooting.

It was the first day of our two-day shoot and after a morning of dove slaying we were having lunch in a small town in the only restaurant large enough to seat the thirty or so of us. Outside it was close to one hundred degrees and there was no air conditioning. I was somewhat surprised that they actually had wine on the menu, though the selection consisted of but a handful of reds and whites and all from Chile, as I recall. Obviously prepared in advance for our arrival, every table in the restaurant had been placed side by side so that we were all actually sitting at one table, albeit a helluva long one.

Anyway, the Winchester guys ordered several bottles of wine for the table, half red, half white. Sitting next to me was Jordan, with tee-totaling Jack Lewis strategically seated directly across from me so that he could easily slide his wine over to me. As my eyes wandered around the room, an unlikely sight caught my eye. There on a shelf above the restaurant's huge front window some ten feet above the floor were five bottles of wine sitting upright in a row, each spaced about two feet apart. One of the labels looked familiar, though I was too far away to see any detail.

Now it just so happened that I had a minibinocular in the little ditty bag I had with me, so I used it to check what I assumed were empty bottles put up there for decoration. Upon doing so I was absolutely stunned to see that the middle three bottles carried the label "Chateau Cheval Blanc!" Here in one of the most unlikely places in the world were three bottles—three *empty* bottles I assumed—of a Premier Grand Cru Saint Émilion!

I could not make out the vintage, but that really didn't matter: It was Cheval Blanc, one of the world's greatest wines! A thought flashed through my mind: I wonder who had the pleasure of emptying those three bottles and what was the occasion? I immediately motioned to our waiter, who apparently was the manager, if not the owner, and asked if he spoke English. Luckily, he spoke enough, so I asked him if those were empty bottles.

"No, not empty," he declared.

Still somewhat skeptical, I asked if there was any way he could fetch one of those bottles for me and open it. He nodded, asking if I wanted him to grab all of them.

Well, I thought, *since he asked*, "Yes" I said, adding "but just the three in the middle."

If any of the Winchester people noticed this guy climbing a ladder and pulling down three bottles of wine, I'm sure they couldn't have cared less. I mean, even if one of them did notice, I'm sure they would have assumed—and understandably so—that those bottles were there for decorative purpose, and even if there actually was wine in the bottles, it had to be worthless plonk. Were I not the wine geek I am, that's what I would have thought.

Putting the bottles on a side table, the waiter proceeded to open one and brought it over to me. Upon seeing the label in detail, my heart almost stopped. *Oh my God, it was a 1961*, one of the ten greatest vintages of the twentieth century! Not wanting to attract any attention from that point on—even though there were no knowledgeable wine people in that room—I grabbed the bottle from the waiter's hands and unceremoniously poured myself a sample—into what could have passed for a jelly glass—as if it were nothing more than the house wine.

Despite the fact I had one of the world's greatest red wines in front of me, my expectations were tempered. Here was a fifteen-year-old wine that had been stored upright for who knows how long, in daily temperatures between 80 and 90 degrees. Even though the wine was 20 degrees too warm, it was celestial. No way could it have been stored improperly and up on display for very long.

Now I knew Bill well enough to know that he liked wine, but he admitted he didn't know much about it.

"I think you'll like this," I said, pouring him a generous glass.

On the first sip his eyes lit up. "Damn, that's good. What is it, Jon?"

Not wanting to stir the curiosity of the others seated around us as to what we were drinking, I just said it was a wine I had heard of before and that it was fairly decent. Between the two of us Bill and I managed to get into the third bottle, though we did eventually have to share some of it with a couple of other guys who had no idea of what they were drinking. From that day on, every event where there was a dinner involved, Bill always tried to get a chair next to me, as if good wine somehow followed me.

Now I'm certain those three bottles of Cheval Blanc were included in Winchester's lunch tab, and I'm equally certain that the restaurant owner simply didn't know what those bottles were worth. Otherwise, I'm sure the Winchester people would have immediately brought it to my attention because it would have literally doubled the lunch bill for all thirty of us! Today, in 2017, the eight-year-old 2009 vintage of Cheval Blanc is averaging $1,150 retail; and it goes for two-and-a-half times that in a restaurant! What relatively few bottles of the 1961 vintage that still exist are seen only at exclusive wine auctions or in private cellars and are worth a small fortune.

The only explanation I can come up that makes any sense at all is that the restaurant had recently changed hands and that the new owner simply found a few bottles of wine stored in the basement or some other unlikely place that the previous owner just forgot about—though I myself could never imagine forgetting three bottles of Cheval Blanc! Seeing that the wine was from France, the new owner probably thought it would add some class to the place by putting them on display.

Believe it or not, I had a dream many years later about that incident. In my dream I was in the Winchester exhibit at SHOT and some guy dressed in a waiter's outfit presented me with a bill for $9,000!

Consulting

Chapter 12

For almost as long as I've been in the writing business I've been continuously active as a press relations/advertising consultant. While most of my colleagues have by necessity supplemented their magazine writing by authoring books, I took a different route.

In 1968 when I took the job as assistant editor of *Outdoor People of Pennsylvania* and moved to Bridgeville, Pennsylvania, it just so happened that Bridgeville was the home of the Small Arms Manufacturing Company, a gun-barrel manufacturer. Small Arms not only produced gun barrels for many American firearms manufacturers, but it also had a retail outlet called Federal Firearms that provided gunsmithing services. Customers could send in an action or barreled action and have it fitted with their Star barrels chambered in any caliber suitable for that specific action, and in their choice of barrel length and contour.

When I arrived in Bridgeville, it was the heyday of "sporterizing" military rifles like Mausers, Springfields, and Enfields, and Federal Firearms was one of the biggest in the business. With the retail store less than ten minutes from my house, it soon became a hangout for me. After I had had a couple of articles published, my credibility with the owners who ran the factory was established. The factory was where all the action was, and it was just a quarter mile down the road from the retail store. It was there that I was able to get a crash course in gunsmithing that would serve me well in the coming years.

At that time the only advertising Federal Firearms did was with *Shotgun News*, and because there was rarely a change in the ad, it was something a chimp could do. Federal was doing what many companies that didn't have complicated, multi-publication ad schedules did: It formed its own in-house agency and delegated someone within the company to oversee it. By appointing an in-house "account executive," the company avoided paying ad-agency commissions.

I don't know what precipitated it, but whoever was handling the simple job of paying the bill at the end of the month screwed it up to the point where the owners, who were shockingly unsophisticated about all things business, asked if I would take over as their advertising agency. After all, I was in the "magazine business," and that was good enough for them. The owners told *Shotgun News* that I was now their agency of record, and that made me eligible for the 15 percent agency commission. All I had to do was come up with a name for my "ad agency" and pay one-month's ad billing in advance to establish credit, which I had no problem collecting from Federal Firearms.

Initially I didn't realize that, in return for the 15 percent commission I received and whatever the ad budget was, I was now responsible for paying Federal's monthly bill. If for some reason Federal didn't pay me in a timely fashion, I was on the hook for, as I recall, around nine hundred dollars, which for me was a veritable fortune back then. As it turned out, there were no problems, and little ol' me was now a one-man accredited advertising agency.

As so often happens in life, one business enterprise can lead to another. Because I had established myself as an advertising agency, a company came to me with its advertising needs, and the unexpected consequences of that meeting resulted in the establishment of my consulting business. This is how it came to be:

In 1970 a new Swedish centerfire rifle debuted in the States under the Husqvarna name. Without going into too much background, suffice to say that Sweden's military armaments manufacturer, FFV, was in a slack period, and having to care for its employees virtually from cradle to grave in Sweden, the company had to seek out something to keep its workers busy. Toward that end, FFV purchased Husqvarna's sporting arms division and moved it to its sprawling military arms factory in Eskilstuna.

Younger folks may not be aware of the Husqvarna name as it relates to sporting arms, but the company produced beautiful rifles based on one of the finest commercial versions of the 1898 Mauser ever made. Indeed, it was right up there with the Belgian-made FN version used in the Browning Hi Power rifle. At that time, however, the company was in the midst of a changeover to a new bolt action of its design. It was a twin lug Mauser type, but it had the recessed bolt face and plunger ejector that we are so familiar with today.

What made this action unique was the shape of its locking lugs. They were pie-shaped, and by that I mean the base of each lug was narrower than the top so that in cross section each lug looked like a slice of pie. What did this accomplish? First of all, the lugs acted like dovetails within their raceways, providing lateral support for the bolt. Then, in addition to an incredibly smooth and wobble-free bolt, there was no bolt stop/release on the side of the receiver bridge, and the bolt shroud was nicely contoured to provide a pleasing silhouette. The net result was an exceptionally clean and remarkably smooth action. As for the stock, it was a time when the high gloss Weatherby-look dominated the marketplace, and the FFV people did a great job with their version of it.

Initially Tradewinds imported a small number of these guns to the United States under the Husqvarna name, and Smith & Wesson did the same with its own name on the gun. Those arrangements, however, were short lived. The FFV people decided they wanted to run the whole show, so they set up their own subsidiary company here in the States to handle importation and distribution of the rifle under the name FFV–Carl Gustaf, in honor of the Swedish king.

Long story short, I really liked the rifle and wrote several articles praising it. At the 1972 NSGA convention I met Wildey Moore, the guy who was running the show here for FFV. He was impressed enough with the articles I had written that, once he found out I was handling advertising for Federal Firearms, asked if I'd be interested in taking him on as a client to handle advertising as well as press relations. After giving it some thought, I told him I really wasn't interested in growing my advertising agency because writing was my primary interest, but I'd be interested in handling his press relations— the job of writing press releases and getting my fellow gunwriters to test and write about Carl Gustav rifles. He agreed, and that was the real start of my consulting career.

The FFV thing didn't work out as well as the folks in Sweden had hoped, so after a couple of years they dissolved the subsidiary company and decided to go with an established importer. They chose a good one—Stoeger Arms, a company known as "America's Great Gun House." Established in the 1920s, Stoeger was not only the largest importer of foreign guns of all types, but it also published the highly successful *Shooter's Bible*.

At that time Stoeger was importing Llama handguns from Vitoria, Spain, and Franchi shotguns from Brescia, Italy, so the acquisition of a rifle line like the Carl Gustav was both timely and fortuitous for Stoeger. It worked out well for me, too, because Stoeger's president, George Sodini, asked me to stay on as press relations consultant not only for the Carl Gustav line but for Franchi and Llama as well. I did, and for thirteen years thereafter those three companies numbered among my clients, along with IGA, a Brazilian shotgun manufacturer that Stoeger would also acquire.

Shortly after getting the Stoeger gig, I took on Zeiss, the iconic German optics giant, as consultant to its sports-optics division here in the States. That lasted ten years, followed by a five-year retainer with Leica, the other world-renown German optics company. My longest consulting gig, however, lasted twenty years, and it was with Rutland Plywood of Rutland, Vermont. On reading this, you may well be asking yourself, what's plywood got to do with guns, hunting, or sports optics? Well, it was Rutland that developed the wood laminate that's used in today's gunstocks.

My acquisition of Rutland in 1987 as a consulting client was rather serendipitous, and it came about as a result of my being an avid fan of wood laminate as a gunstock medium long before Rutland appeared on the scene. I began using laminates in the mid-1960s to make stocks for my own rifles, and at that time, the only sources were through mail-order firms like Fajen, Bishop, and Herter's. The blanks, however, from which those stocks were fashioned were never meant for use as gunstocks but for furniture. Nevertheless, I realized how much more stable a laminate was compared to a traditional stock of one-piece walnut, so I stocked all my own rifles accordingly.

Over the next ten years I wrote several articles about my preference for wood-laminate gunstocks, but no manufacturer saw fit to offer one on a production-line rifle. Then came the 1987 SHOT Show, and Ruger, Savage, and Winchester all had on display one or more of their guns sporting multi-colored stocks made of wood laminate, and all had been fashioned from blanks supplied by Rutland Plywood. The blanks were comprised of ¹⁄₁₆₀-inch thick sheets—veneers, actually—of color-dyed birch epoxied together under great pressure. On average thirty-two veneers comprise the average stock and . . . well, we all know what a laminated stock looks like. Within three years Rutland Plywood was supplying every major firearms manufacturer and gunstock purveyor here and abroad with their laminate blanks.

It was at that 1987 SHOT Show that Jack Barrett, the owner and CEO of Rutland, introduced himself to me. Being a hunter and gun enthusiast Jack related how he had read a couple of my articles and that's what prompted him to start developing a quality laminated gunstock. When he found out I was in the consulting business, he asked me to take him on as a client and help get the laminate story out to the gun-buying public. It turned out to be a great fit for me because shortly after taking on Rutland, I also got Boyds' Gunstock Industries as a client. Boyds was (and is) the largest gunstock maker and was one of Rutland's biggest customers. I say *was* because the Rutland factory burned to the ground in 2014.

In addition to the companies already mentioned, other consulting clients I've had over the years include Norma, Sako, Fajen, Gamo, Schmidt & Bender, Legacy Sports, E. R. Shaw, and probably a few others that fail to come to mind immediately.

So while my colleagues authored books to supplement their magazine writing, I had my consulting. It was a better fit for my personality. I have always liked the fact that with a magazine article, after fifteen hundred to two thousand words, you were done and could go on to another article, another topic . . . it simply took a lot less time than authoring a book. I just didn't like the sustained effort necessary to write a book. Is it any wonder then why I had no burning desire to write books? Consulting always just seemed the better way to go for me.

Consulting also gave me the opportunity to travel, which has always been a passion of mine. You might ask, "How is consulting within the firearms and optics industries synonymous with travel?" As a press-relations consultant, my job is to get my colleagues to write about my clients' products, and quite a few of my clients had factories in Germany, Spain, Italy, Sweden, Finland, Portugal, Brazil, and Yugoslavia. What better way to establish a good rapport with writers and editors than to take them on an all-expense-paid factory tour and/or hunting trip to Europe, Africa, South America, or wherever?

My modus operandi was simple: I knew all the writers; I knew all the editors; and I knew the magazines. I'd simply choose three writers or editors whom I thought were the best choice for the product I wanted to push, and then I would explain those choices to my client before actually extending the invitations. My choices were submitted only as suggestions, so if my client had a specific writer or magazine in mind he wanted to include, there was no problem. Rarely did that happen, however, and the choice of invitees was usually left to me.

It was simple, really. If we were going to visit the Llama factory in Spain, I'd invite handgun writers; I'd invite shotgun writers if we were going to the Franchi factory in Italy; and I'd invite rifle guys if we were going to the Sako factory in Finland. I always tried to time these trips with either the local hunting season or to festivals like the running of the bulls in Pamplona—which I've done three times—Oktoberfest in Munich, and so on. Whatever the itinerary, I always tried to keep the time devoted to business to a minimum. On all these events, once the initial arrangements were made, I had little if anything to do, so I was treated as just another guest writer and the host company took care of us from the moment we arrived to the time the guide put us on the plane for home.

On a typical Stoeger press event, for example, we'd fly into Madrid where we'd be met by someone from the Llama factory. That person acted as our tour guide of the city for two days. We'd then take the train north to Vitoria and the Basque country where the factory was located. After a brief tour of the factory we'd then head for Pamplona and the insane ten-day festival that's celebrated there every July. A couple days there and it was off for Milan, where we'd be met by someone from Franchi. From Milan we'd be driven to Venice, where we'd spend three days sightseeing. We'd then make the short trip to Brescia and the Franchi factory, followed by a trip to the Lake Garda area before heading home. In other words, these trips are 10 percent business, 90 percent pleasure.

It goes without saying that those who accept these invitations (and virtually everyone does) are expected to write (or if an editor, to assign) at least one feature article about what they saw at the factory, combined with a test and evaluation of the product. Most of the time we'd end up getting at least two articles from each guest over the course of a year, to say nothing of making my job easier in the future when there was a new gun or scope my client wanted written up.

It worked for the gunwriters, too. For many of them, those trips to Europe, Africa, or South America were their first international jaunts, so all was exciting and new. In many ways I was the travel agent of choice for my fellow gunwriters. Of course, not all such events were overseas. Depending on the client, product, and budget, some visits were to factories here in the States. If not, we'd host a deer or antelope hunt. No matter the location—either exotic or local—it was all good.

My consulting work allowed me to see the manufacturer's side of the picture, and I found that fascinating. To be involved in the designing and in the teething problems of bringing a new product online, then advertising and promoting it, gave me insights into the industry that few other writers have had.

The Complete Rifleman

I've enjoyed another unique niche in this business: Beginning in 1989 and for twenty-two years I was the sole author and editor of my own annual magazine, the *Complete Rifleman*. Harris Publishing of New York published many gun and hunting magazines, and Lamar Underwood, the editorial director for Harris's outdoor books division, thought an annual devoted entirely to hunting rifles could sell. Of course, the idea of an annual devoted strictly to rifles was nothing new; there were several such books on the newsstands at the time. What would make this annual unique was that it would be written by one guy—me—but that's not how it started.

The original idea was that I would serve as editor, write several pieces for the book, and assign the rest of the articles as needed to whomever. That's how Stanley Harris, the publisher, envisioned it. Lamar, however, thought differently. Anyway, Lamar convinced Stanley that it was worth a shot, telling him I had a lot of loyal readers, and in the more than ten years I had been writing for them, they rarely got Sundra hate mail from irate readers. "I think having Jon write the whole magazine would work," he stated with an air of finality.

I was already known throughout the industry strictly as a rifle and hunting guy. As such I was by far—and still am—the most narrowly focused gunwriter. That was OK by me. To write an entire magazine, however, would require expertise that I might not have. Those were my thoughts then, and, moreover, I frankly couldn't understand how so many of my colleagues could be expert at so many facets of the gun, hunting, and competitive shooting worlds and write about all of them with authority! I'm not that smart . . . or accomplished. I don't know about their lifestyles, but as a husband and father, I had the usual family obligations. Add to that my consulting activity, my passion for exotic cars, gourmet cooking, wine, travel, and golf . . . well, that left only so much time I could devote to playing with guns.

To me, just trying to be knowledgeable enough in modern rifles, cartridges, and hunting, and keeping up with all that was new and write about it with any authority, bordered on presumptuousness. How in god's name could anyone be expert enough in rifles, shotguns, handguns, ARs, competitive rifle and handgun shooting, handloading, and black powder and actually have a life? Truth is, you can't, at least not what I would consider a life. I learned early on that those of my colleagues who dazzled me with their breadth of knowledge had virtually no life outside the world of guns . . . but I digress.

While it was flattering to hear Lamar singing my praises to Stanley, I had my doubts that I could do eighteen more feature articles per year. I was, after all, shooting editor of Harris's *Guns & Hunting* magazine, field editor for *Petersen's Hunting*, plus I wrote for a couple of Harris's other gun/hunting magazines. I then thought about how when I was under contract to Petersen from 1980 to 1985, I had to do twelve columns and twelve feature articles per year for *Guns & Ammo* and the same for *Petersen's Hunting*, plus feature pieces for several of Petersen's annuals. That was as much as I wanted to do. Were I to take on this new gig at Harris, I'd be writing as much or more.

When I expressed some doubt as to whether I could take on that much extra writing, Lamar told me they wouldn't all have to be original pieces. "You can use appropriate articles you've done for us the previous year, as well as stuff from other magazines, so long as you can get permission to reprint. If you can do at least eight original pieces and the rest pick-ups, I'm OK with that."

So was Stanley.

At the time I was not writing for any magazine that bought all rights to my work, so I was pretty much free to reprint my articles elsewhere, as long as they ran at least a few months after their initial publication, and with the postscript: "This article originally appeared in the x issue of x magazine and is reprinted here with permission."

That was enough to make me think I could do it. Something else that helped to convince me was the thought: *How cool would it be to have my own magazine, with my name and picture on the cover, no less, and my biography on the inside front cover next to the table of contents?*

So it came to be. In the first week of November 1989, Vol. 1, No. 1 of the *Complete Rifleman* hit the newsstands. It was five months later in April that the final sales figures for that first effort came in. Sales were good enough that I would be doing a second *Complete Rifleman*. By then I had been offered the post of shooting editor at *Guns* magazine, replacing Charlie Askins. I accepted the post, and with that acceptance came doubts as to whether I would be able to continue with *Complete Rifleman* and still do a first-rate job at my new position.

Somehow I did manage to put together a second annual, and that was followed by twenty more until Stanley Harris pulled the plug in 2011. His rationale was that no one wanted to read about traditional rifles anymore! According to Stanley, all the shooting public wanted to read about was ARs, and I was not a big fan. Looking back now, however, I have to wonder if that was the real reason Stanley decided to ax the annual. Perhaps Stanley was reacting to the writing on the wall in print magazine publishing. What we all now know for certain is that in April 2016 Harris Publications shut down its operation for good, bringing its thirty-nine-year history to a close.

I have since changed, but that's how it was then.

It's an AR World

When it comes to hunting rifles, I've always been what you'd describe as *conservative, traditional*. If you're among the growing ranks of Modern Sporting Rifle (MSR) fans, you would probably call me *old fashioned*. I started my big-game hunting career more than a half century ago with bolt-action rifles and have pretty much remained faithful to them ever since. Oh, there have been lapses when either by choice or circumstance I've hunted with other action types—Ruger No. 1s in particular—but for the most part I've been a bolt-action guy.

I'm not alone in this preference, for I'm sure that in the game fields of the world the bolt gun still handily outnumbers all the other alternatives put together. That, however, is slowly changing, at least here in the States as more and more ex-servicemen and -women entering the hunting ranks are choosing the AR-10 and AR-15 platforms over traditional long guns. That, of course, is perfectly understandable because for many of them the M-16 was their introduction to firearms.

As for me, I was not a fan initially, but by the turn of the century, ARs had become so popular that as someone who makes his living writing about guns, I simply could no longer ignore them, though I did give it a helluva try. In fact, I'm convinced that my reluctance to get into ARs cost me my post as rifles editor at *Shooting Illustrated*, the NRA's newsstand gun magazine, a post I held for ten years.

Don't get me wrong, I wasn't completely ignorant about ARs. I was passingly familiar with the history of the gun and who the leading manufacturers were. I knew the components and how everything worked. I was even beginning to learn some of the silly over-the-top acronyms that AR people love to bandy about to intimidate the less enlightened. I just felt I didn't know nearly enough to presume the status of "expert" and write about them.

The hardest thing for me was getting past the looks of the gun; it was black and it looked to me exactly like what it was—a military weapon. Then there was the fact that, in the case of the AR-15 platform, it lacked the capability of handling true "big-game" cartridges, and being the hunter I am, that was a big thing. Its big brother, however, the AR-10, can digest any of the .308 Winchester family of cartridges—.243, .260 Remington, 7mm-08, .308, and .338 Federal—but it was no less military-looking than its smaller sibling, and it was heavier and bulkier to the point where I just couldn't see myself hunting with one.

Anyway, it didn't happen overnight, but the more I learned about them, the more I was exposed to them on seminars and industry hunts, the more I came to appreciate the genius of the design, the modular simplicity, and most surprising to me, the *accuracy*. While the basic geometry of the AR can never be changed without a complete redesign, eliminating the carrying handle/rear sight, pedestal front sight, adjustable buttstock, and fiberglass handguard and going to a flat-top, upper receiver, no sights, a tubular handguard, and a fixed buttstock, would make it look a little less "military." As for the "black-gun" thing, that can be addressed by simply sheathing them in colors or camo.

One of the few truly new guns to debut recently is the DPMS Gen II 308. In fact, it represents the first substantive design change since the AR-10 was developed in the mid-1950s by ArmaLite as a possible replacement for the U.S. Army's M1 Garand battle rifle. DPMS was one of several gun companies that at the time was under the Freedom Group umbrella, the others being Remington, Marlin, H&R, Dakota Arms, and Bushmaster.

Originally developed around the .308 Winchester (7.62x51 NATO), the AR-10 lost out in government tests to the M-14, which became the official U.S. service rifle from 1959 to 1970. The adoption of the AR-10, however, had been somewhat controversial since some military minds at the time were looking for a smaller cartridge than the .308. That prompted ArmaLite, which was just a small company of less than a dozen gun designers and machinists, to work on downsizing the AR-10 around a .22 centerfire cartridge. Remington was developing this cartridge, which was based on a lengthened .222 Remington case, at that time for the U.S. Army.

To make a long story short, Armalite failed to sell its battle rifle to Uncle Sam, and in 1959 the company sold the manufacturing rights of both the AR-10 and AR-15 to Colt. Colt, after developing and refining the smaller gun, succeeded in securing a military contract from the government. The result was the M-16 rifle chambered for the 5.56x45 M193 cartridge. The M-16 eventually replaced the M-14 as the official U. S. service rifle, starting with its adoption by the U.S. Air Force in 1964. That same year Remington, who designed the 5.56 military round, commercialized it as the .223 Remington, and Colt began selling a semiautomatic civilian version of the M-16 we all know as the AR-15.

By the way, in an effort to be "politically correct," there is a movement underway to change the reference of these guns to MSR (Modern Sporting Rifle) because most people think AR means "assault rifle," when in fact it was an acronym for Armalite Rifle.

Anyway, Colt had all the work it needed supplying M-16s to the military, so any plans to develop the AR-10 were shelved. By the mid-1990s, however, the patents had expired and other companies who were already producing AR-15s began building AR-10s. After all, as popular as the .223 Remington is, it lacks the power and range of a true game cartridge. The .308 Winchester, on the other hand, is essentially a .30-06 in a smaller package, which means it's fully capable of taking any game in the world save the dangerous kind.

I am still far from what I would consider to be an authority on ARs, but I'm now knowledgeable enough to be comfortable writing about them.

Some Thoughts on Hunting

Chapter 15

Has there ever lived a hunter who hasn't been asked why he hunts? I think not. I, myself, have been asked that question hundreds of times, by fellow hunters on the one hand to rabid antihunters on the other. For the former the venue is often among friends in a hunting camp or strangers in a bar, where in either case alcohol prompts people to wax philosophic. For the latter, it's usually when I've been unfortunate enough to be seated on a plane next to a PETA whacko or a vegan.

There was a time when I tried to answer that question, but I've long since decided it's futile to try to discuss such a personal and emotional subject. Maybe it's a cop-out, but my usual answer now is to paraphrase the Spanish philosopher, Ortega y Gasset, who said that man does not hunt to kill; man kills to have hunted. That just may be the most succinct yet most profound explanation I have ever heard. It is so thought provoking that it often ends the conversation then and there because in a way it turns the tables on the person asking the question.

Nevertheless, since this book will never be read by an antigun, PETA member, or a vegan, I do feel compelled to offer some personal perspectives on what has been such an important part of who I am.

Regardless of what motivates one to take up hunting—for instance, me finding my father's photo album—one passes through several stages as a hunter. As an example of the first stage I recall an experience I had in a hunting camp in Pennsylvania the evening before the opening day of deer season. There were about a dozen of us sharing a cabin, and one of the guys had his son with him. The boy was too young to hunt on his own, but was ecstatic at the prospect of his dad allowing him to sit on the stand with him.

If that kid could have been any more excited that evening, I think he would have exploded.

All the boy could talk about was shooting and guns—his dad's gun particularly, which was a Savage 99 in .308 Winchester. All evening the father squirmed with the uneasiness that goes with hearing his son relate "facts" about guns and ballistics he'd learned from him, knowing there were perhaps others present who knew a little more about those subjects than he did. He shouldn't have worried, for no one was about to undermine the boy's faith in his father by calling his facts into question. That was something the boy would do on his own and all too soon, for that is the fate of all fathers.

In those young eyes that sparkled with the promise of ten thousand tomorrows, I could see myself as a young boy. The only difference was that my passion for guns and hunting was for the most part developed on my own. Of course, being best buddies with the kid whose dad owned the local sporting goods store didn't hurt. The two of us would spend hours in the store eavesdropping on the hunting tales and gun lore spun by neighborhood experts, some of whom had hunted in as far away and exotic places as Wyoming and Colorado!

Anyway, during one of this youngster's ebullient descriptions of shooting his dad's .308, it occurred to me that he was about to embark upon the first of several stages he would pass through as a hunter. Because all of us who hunt did not necessarily take it up as youngsters, the way in which we pass through these stages, and the time we spend in each, differs. After all, the moral and ethical perspectives of a ten-year-old are going to be different from someone equally inexperienced but older.

Most of us, however, did indeed start hunting as youngsters and pass through what I'd call the "shooting stage" where we simply want to shoot at something other than paper targets. We want to be afield with gun in hand and to have in our sights whatever legal game happens to be in season. When you think about it, it's the most profound manifestation of personal freedom available in a civilized society—to own a gun and have the legal right to take an animal's life at one's discretion. It is for that reason we must jealously guard that freedom and stridently fight all those who would take it from us.

As a ten- or twelve-year-old, however, such profundities never cross your mind. You just want to shoot *something*, and hopefully it will be at whatever animal that you happen to be hunting at the time. Again making an assumption that for most of us our first days afield found us with a .22 in hand, or maybe a .410 shotgun, and that small game was the quarry—rabbits, pheasants, squirrels, or whatever. If the action's too slow or if a flock of blackbirds is flying too close overhead, a too-trusting chipmunk may well pay a price. In my case I *know* such innocents paid the price! In those days it wasn't necessary to actually *hit* anything; the mere act of pulling the trigger on legal game was a thrill. The muzzle blast, the recoil, the smell of powder—all were affirmations that you'd become a hunter.

Thankfully, the stage where the barometer for success is measured in decibels passes rather quickly. That leads us to the next stage of our development as hunters, a period where success is measured by . . . well, success. The primary goal now is to "fill out," i.e., bring home the limit of whatever it is we're hunting. We feel that our skill as a hunter is directly proportional to how full our game bag is. The guy who consistently limits out, whether it's on rabbits, quail, or by getting his buck every year, has our respect because that has now become the yardstick by which we measure ourselves.

We're now a bit more knowledgeable about hardware, but what Dad or Uncle Ed thought about guns and cartridges still has a strong influence. In any case, equipment is still very much secondary to the hunt and to success. This stage is also one wherein the quality of the trophy carries little importance. Obviously, we're talking big game now—anything that can be measured by its horns or antlers. Of course, every hunter wants to shoot a wall hanger, but we're at the stage where passing up a shot at a legal buck in the hopes of getting a better one wouldn't enter our minds. To be able to say: "I got my buck" is important, even if it's a spike or forkhorn. Anything is better than going home empty-handed!

The next stage we hunters pass through is less rigidly defined than the previous two because it can take more than one direction. This is the stage where the seasons aren't long enough; we want to hunt and shoot as close to year-round as possible. We take up varmint and/or predator hunting in the off season. Then the gun itself—the type of action and caliber, optics, and other ancillary equipment—take on importance in and of themselves. Though guns must obviously hold some fascination for every hunter, for some, guns become a passion. Chances are we also start handloading, at first because we know it will enable us to shoot more, but in the process it turns into a fascinating hobby, one that vastly expands our knowledge of guns and ballistics. For many, varminting, shooting for groups, and hunting become excuses for handloading.

This is also the stage where we simply can't get enough information, so we become voracious readers of magazines and insatiable viewers of cable network outdoor channels. Guns themselves often take on the same importance as hunting, and we're now knowledgeable enough to have developed strong opinions about them. Where in earlier stages we considered one or two rifles and shotguns sufficient, that's no longer the case. We now appreciate the distinctions that make certain rifle types and calibers superior to others, given a specific application. Versatility of gun and caliber give way to specialization. We go from the .30-06 or .270 we once thought would see us through a lifetime of hunting, to owning several rifles, each designed to excel at a specific task.

This fascination with equipment doesn't affect all who enter this stage of development because there will always be those to whom the tools aren't nearly as important as the work itself; nevertheless, the equipment has to take on greater importance if one is to become truly accomplished. It's like trying to be a great race driver without knowing anything about cars.

Hand in hand with our desire for higher quality and specialization in our equipment is the expansion of our hunting horizons to justify it all. Our financial commitment to our sport is now to the point where the prospect of traveling to other states—even countries—is real.

Just as there are no shortcuts to competency with rifle or shotgun, so too are there no shortcuts to becoming an accomplished hunter—dare I use the term "trophy hunter"? Even though I know full well the connotations that go with the term, I contend that trophy hunting is the purest and most ethical stage in the evolution of a hunter and of the sport itself.

To the true trophy hunter, the prospect of going home empty-handed is of little or no concern. Everyone's a trophy hunter at dawn on the first day of the hunt. To still be a trophy hunter at dusk on the last day is what makes the difference. For someone who watches a nice 8-point buck or a 5x5 bull elk through his scope and does not shoot because it's not the trophy he wants is, to me, a person worthy of respect and admiration.

It also takes experience to judge when to pass on an animal that you have dead-to-rights, especially if it's an animal that most other hunters would shoot in a nanosecond. It takes having been in that position many times before and having seen many different species. What does "different species" have to do with it? I've seen highly accomplished trophy whitetail hunters, for example, get buck fever at the appearance of a black bear and miss from a distance of thirty yards. No matter how experienced you may be, hunting a new species for the first time can be, nay, *should be*, a real rush for anyone. It should be like turning back the clock to the time when you had that first buck in your sights. At a time like that, it's difficult to be highly selective, and it's twice as difficult when you know the chances of your returning to hunt that same species sometime in the future probably may not be in the cards.

Unfortunately, there's also a black side to trophy hunting. That occurs when hunting becomes not a competition with oneself, but with others. I'm referring to those to whom the noblest aspects of hunting are lost or perverted along the way. I'm not talking about the healthy, friendly kind of competitiveness that stirs in all of us and makes us want to win, whether it be at golf, chess, or bringing in the biggest buck. I'm talking about when healthy competitiveness is corrupted to the point where winning and recognition becomes an obsession and hunting a mere means to an end.

Such a person is not above buying a trophy and even entering it in competition. Does he do it because he thinks he can get away with it? It's impossible to say. The sad fact of the matter is that there are enough pseudo-hunters in the world that an organization like Boone and Crockett has to spend inordinate amounts of time verifying the authenticity of some of the heads submitted for entry in its record book. Those in charge of judging record-book entries do this to ensure that trophies are taken under fair-chase conditions. In a perfect world those questions should not have to be asked, but alas, they must be.

There's also a dangerous aspect to this black side of hunting because it has the power to affect the longevity of our sport. I'm talking about the antigun/antihunting crowd. This group will latch onto anything that is negative in our sport in order to support its calls for the prohibition of guns and hunting, for make no mistake, these people detest guns and trophy hunting. To them, guns are the root of all evil, and trophy hunting is an abomination. They contend that while it's bad enough to shoot a deer or elk for meat, to do it with the idea of having it "stuffed" to hang on a wall is no different than displaying the severed head of one's enemy on a pike, or the taking of his ear or scalp as a token of victory. Pseudo-hunters—and I don't call them hunters—have the power to ruin the reputation of the sport of fair-chase hunting, and, at the very least, play into the hands of the antihunting groups.

Then there are those who unwittingly put themselves in a *professional* position where there is constant pressure to bring in not just one, but record-book heads on a regular basis. The Whitetail Cult is a perfect example. To my knowledge it is the only niche in the world of hunting where "experts" can actually make a living on the speaking circuit telling others how to get a trophy buck. The temptation to bend a rule is great, especially for those people—writers like me, outdoor show hosts, film makers, and outfitters—who would gain monetarily and professionally by bringing in a record head.

The way I see it, any "pressure" to bring home game was supposed to cease when it ceased being existential to life. Today we hunt because we choose to—for the thrill, the challenge, the competition within ourselves . . . whatever. Dead is dead, but the motivation for the kill and the spirit in which it is done is what makes all the difference.

I stated earlier that there are no shortcuts to competency with firearms, hunting skills, or field experience. It is ironic, therefore, that the more competent we become and the more knowledge and experience we acquire, putting game on the ground becomes less important. In short, the more skills we acquire, the less inclined we are to use them.

So where does it all end? I'm not sure, but surely it's different for each of us. I do know that *who* you hunt with and share a camp with takes on increasing import, as does *what* you hunt with. Sooner or later it will no longer seem "proper" to use a 12-gauge on dove or quail; you'll want a 20 or 28 . . . and no more than two shots. And that .300 magnum you would have used on a whitetail hunt a few years back now seems . . . well, superfluous. You'd now much rather use that little custom 7x57 or .257 Roberts you had built just for that purpose. You may even start hunting with a single-shot rifle. After all, you really shouldn't need or want more than one shot, should you? Not now. Not any longer.

"That boy of yours," as I was called by our neighbors, with my older brother, Richard.

My mom and dad the year they were married, 1933, and the year Dad joined the Cleveland Police Department where he served until his retirement.

Judith and I with our sons, Ian and Sean, Christmas Day, 1969.

My dad in his Wyoming days.

This picture of my dad circa 1930 was instrumental to my developing an interest in guns and hunting from a very early age.

Me, my dad, and my older brother Richard, 1959.

87

My wedding day with my parents, Jack and Ann, surrounding us, 7 September 1963.

My sons, Ian (left) and Sean, on a dove shoot in Argentina, 2002.

Judith helping out with a story I was working on about guns and loads for squirrel hunting.

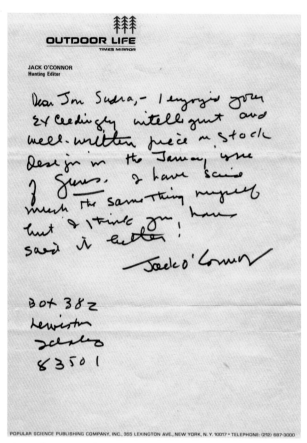

An uncharacteristic letter from Jack O'Connor commenting on a story I did for Gun Magazine *on rifle stock design.*

	INVOICE NO.	AMOUNT	DISC.	NET	DATE	INVOICE NO.	AMOUNT	DISC.	NET
				"What Makes A Varmint Rifle"					
12.		$100.00	Story Cost		(23rd Ed.	Gun Digest	or later)		

THE GUN DIGEST COMPANY
CHICAGO, ILL.

DETACH AND RETAIN THIS STATEMENT
THE ATTACHED CHECK IS IN PAYMENT OF ITEMS DESCRIBED BELOW.
IF NOT CORRECT PLEASE NOTIFY US PROMPTLY. NO RECEIPT DESIRED.

5128

The check stub from the sale of my first article to the Gun Digest, *which I submitted around Christmas, 1966.*

Charlie Askins at the Remington Seminar, 1972. Charlie kinda' looked out for me from the very start.

Remington's Nylon 66 semi-automatic is a true icon among .22 rimfire rifles. Several passed through my hands over the years.

Me with the father of the AK-47, Mikhail Kalashnikov at a Ruger party in his honor.

Other than SHOT, NRA and SCI Conventions, the only opportunity we writers get to see one another is at the corporate seminars, which are eagerly anticipated. This Remington bash was held at Bienville Plantation in Florida in 2013.

Me, Bill Ruger (center), and Grits Gresham at a Ruger event honoring Mikhail Kalashnikov.

One of the more memorable seminars was this one in Colombia sponsored by Winchester in 1976. In this picture are most of the gunwriting luminaries of the time: Jim Carmichael, Les Bowman, Russ Carpenter, Bob Steindler, Ken Warner, Elmer Keith, Grits Gresham, Hal Swiggett, Jack Lewis, John Wootters, Charlie Askins, Neal Knox, and George Nonte.

Standing at both ends are John Snow and Wayne Van Zwoll. The center two are Jim Zumbo and Scott Rupp. I can't recall the date or details but we were huntin' somethin'!

Me and J. D. Jones on a dove shoot in Mexico, circa 1985.

Me and Warren Page (right) of Field & Stream at the 1974 NSGA. The man in the center worked for the Swedish Carl Gustaf arms factory.

Rees, French, and Bob Milek in Germany at a Zeiss function. I'm standing in front, toward the right.

Petersen's Tom Siatos, John Wootters, and me with my first place shooting award at Zeiss' Binopticum, a word coined by Zeiss for this event, in 1976.

Me and Grits Gresham (right) on a Remington antelope hunt. The guy in the middle worked for Remington.

Me and Remington president Tommy Milner at a company event.

Me at the Sport/Varmint Nationals in 1973.

Me and Steve Hornady (right) on one of several hunts we've made together.

Me and Ernesto in the Mexican state of Sonora. Among others, we hunted jaguar in Yucatan and elephants in Malawi.

The only animal of mine that appears in a record book is my Namibian elephant that stood over eleven feet at t[h]e shoulders. It was entered in the Rowland Ward record book for its body size by my PH, Volker Grellmann.

This Gold Medal ibex was taken in the Gredos Mountains of Spain.

This black lechwe would have made No. 1 in the SCI record book at the time. With me is my PH Robin Voight.

Charlie Askins at an early SHOT Show. He took quite a shine to Judith and always sought her out.

Bob Milek, Clair Rees, me, and Howard French pose with my Finnish moose. Bob and I were almost thrown off the train on our way to the hunt.

Gun World's Bob Zwirz and Elmer Keith asleep at the Remington seminar in 1972. Elmer always caught up on his sleep at writers' seminars.

I was using wood laminates long before they came on the scene in the late 1980s. Here in this photo from 196_ I'm holding two of my personal rifles that I stocked in laminates. I later became a consultant to Rutland Plywoo_ who became the major supplier of laminates to the industry.

I was the sole author and editor of The Complete Rifleman, an annual I did for Harris Publications for twenty-two years, from 1989 to 2011.

Bill Jordan (on left) at a Zeiss function in Germany in 1976. Bill was one of the old guard who was very welcoming to the new kid on the block.

Here I used a Carl Gustaf rifle in 7mm Remington Magnum to take this nice Wyoming mule deer. I helped establish the company on these shores, but it was a short-lived venture.

Shooting prairie rats is an application for which an AR is ideally suited.

The uncanny accuracy of the AR is a source of constant amazement for me. Shown here is a 200-yard group fired with an inexpensive factory load.

Chambered for any of the .308 Winchester cartridge family, the AR-10 iteration shown here in the form of Remington's R25 is capable of taking the vast majority of the world's game.

After a while the camaraderie of good people becomes as important as the hunt itself. Here I am with Luis Sier of Sier Safaris, Argentina, a friend of more than thirty years and with whom I've hunted some twenty times over the years.

My old friend Ernesto Zaragoza of Guaymas took his Malawi elephant during the few weeks when hunting was opened in that country.

Joyce Hornady in Zambia, 1979. This was one of three safaris I made with Joyce and his wife, Marvel.

This was one of two leopards I've taken with my original Remington 700 chambered for my 7mm JRS.

I took this lion with a .284 Winchester. It wasn't planned that way, but that's how it worked out. I definitely would not recommend doing what I did.

Field testing the 7mm Remington SAUM prior to its introduction in 2001.

*Here I'm playing with a python in South Africa, 1978. The picture is blurred because my friend and the gu_
taking the photo, George Daniels, was so afraid of snakes he flinched when the snake struck.*

Me and Slim Pickens on a Winchester antelope hunt, September 1980. Slim enjoyed making Blazing Saddles *more than any other of the many movies he was in.*

As is so often the case, on the Winchester antelope hunt in September of 1980 there were no sighting-in facilities. Here Grits Gresham fights with a spongy mattress that's supposed to serve as a steady front rest. It was an exercise in futility.

Whatever hunting skills I have developed are the result of squirrel hunting with a .22 rimfire.

The two finest lever action .22s ever—the Winchester 9422 and the Marlin 1894M—are no longer made. Ditto for the Marlin 39A and the Ruger 77/22.

Me with one of the sixteen black bears I've taken over the years. I took this one in Quebec with a custom Ruger No. 1 chambered in .284 Winchester.

I shot this bear from a distance of about twenty feet as it came out of thick brush.

Not all shooters are capable of extracting all the performance potential of a given gun. A highly skilled benchrest competitor might have improved these groups substantially.

My 7mm JRS (far right) is the most efficient of the .280 Remington-based wildcats. From left is the .280 Remington, the .280 RCBS, and the .280 Ackley Improved.

116

Me and Norman Deane, one of the pioneers of South African ranch hunting.

The typical accommodations on a South African or Namibian hunt today are nothing short of luxurious.

The result of any "gun test" is valid only for that particular gun, load, and shooter.

My passion for exotic cars finally culminated when I got into Lamborghinis twelve years ago. I have been drivin them ever since.

I wish I had kept my original Browning T-Bolt, rust and all.

My best buffalo was taken in Tanzania in 2008 and measured 44½ inches, but he was the least satisfying.

Hunting Asiatic buffalo in Australia's Northern Territory is a great experience, but it's not the same as hunting its African cousin.

I traded my Ruger No. 1 chambered in my .375 JRS wildcat for a dinner for six and two bottles of 1955 Chateau Margaux. Big mistake!

One of the guns I will never part with is my original Remington 700 chambered in my 7mm JRS wildcat. Its wood laminated stock is comprised of horizontally stacked 5/16-inch thick walnut.

Having cleanly missed a buck ten minutes earlier, I killed this one that was standing in virtually the same spot, and I was using the same hold from the same dead-steady rest.

This buck was facing in the opposite direction I thought it was when I shot.

On my "fortunate hits" list is this 6x6 bull elk that jumped at the exact moment I pulled the trigger.

My last Bucket List write-offs was this Siberian ibex I took in 2008.

I consider the Javan rusa to be the most beautiful deer in the world.

Awaiting a jaguar.

Jaguar camp in Campeche, 1987.

The sitatunga made my Bucket List simply because it sounded exotic, it looked exotic, and it was found only in exotic places!

The tree stand from which I shot my two sitatunga

The highest priority on my Bucket List was a jaguar. This one was the last legal one shot in Mexico.

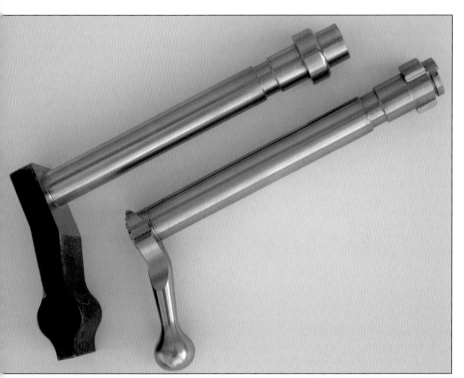

When the base of the bolt handle serves as a nonbearing auxiliary safety lug, it's best when it's integral with the bolt body.

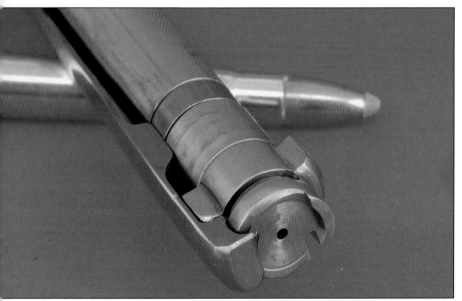

The controlled-round feed system of the Mauser is still my preference for a dangerous-game rifle. This bolt from a Montana Rifle Co. Model 1999 represents an improvement in that the left locking lug isn't bisected for passage of the ejector blade.

The most iconic rifle ever invented and the most copied—the military Model '98 Mauser. With minor changes it is still considered the closest thing to perfection in a bolt-action rifle.

Detachable magazines are gaining favor with an ever-increasing number of hunters. One of the best Browning's rotary magazine, found on the X-Bolt.

Europe has chosen another path in the evolution of the bolt-action rifle—the straight pull. This Merkel RX-Helix is a prime example. It, the Blaser R8, and a few other straight pulls are drastically different from our concept of what a bolt-action rifle should look like and operate.

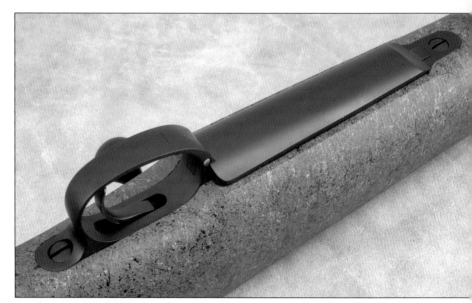

Another reason I prefer the Mauser system for a dangerous-game rifle is that it has a fixed magazine with hinged floorplate. Personally, I like the straddle type as shown here.

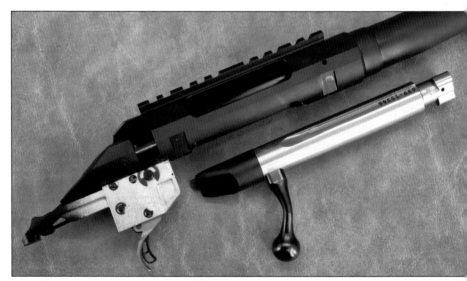

JRS-The Ever-Changing Perfect Rifle-06: The growing list of "fat bolt" actions like this Ruger American are easier and less expensive to manufacture, yet compromise nothing in the way of functionality or accuracy.

I Get Mail

Over the fifty years now that I've had this gig as a gun/hunting writer, I've gotten my share of reader mail. Some letters have been laudatory, others castigating, and still others were from folks who simply wanted to express their points of view, which may or may not have been different from mine.

I can recall several conversations with my old friend and colleague, Charlie Askins, who made of career of being a contrarian. Every two or three years he'd write an article entitled: "Let's Junk the .30-30" or "To Hell with the Lever Action," then sit back and watch the fur fly as incensed readers would write to the magazine, venting their wrath on the man who had the temerity to blaspheme their favorite rifle or cartridge.

Charlie never cut his readers slack. There was never any gray area with him. The good Colonel couched his opinions in a way that everything was either black or white; you were either with him or against him. I recall a couple of conversations with Charlie on that very topic.

"Jon," he'd say to me, "every time I'd write one of those articles, it just made me more unforgettable with the readers. Sure, some hated me, but a helluva lot more wrote to say they agreed and commended me for having the chutzpah for saying what I did. You're still young enough to start doing the same yourself. It's worked for me."

Well, Charlie's advice, well intentioned though it was, just isn't my style. I like to think that the people who read my stuff know that I definitely have opinions, but I've always tried to present them diplomatically enough that those who don't agree aren't offended to the point that it prompts them to take pen in hand. Conversely, those who do agree with me seldom feel inspired enough to write and say so. The bottom line is that, relatively speaking, I don't receive what I'd describe as a lot of mail, but as I said, over the span of fifty years it still amounts to quite a pile!

What follows are distilled, paraphrased forms of some of the more entertaining letters I've received over the years. I believe they accurately capture the flavor of the originals without distortion.

> *Mr. Sundra: I'm just getting into handloading and I need your help. I own a .223, a .270, and a .30-06. What I need is the most accurate handload for every bullet weight in each caliber, using every powder available. Also, I need to know what range to zero each load, and the downrange trajectories from 50 to 500 yards. Oh, and I need this information right away if you don't mind. Signed: In a Hurry*

> *Dear Jon: I inherited a rifle from my uncle that's real interesting. It's got this real short barrel and most of the markings appear to be filed off. All I can make out is "7-something" and a couple of marks. One looks like an upside down hat, and the other is what looks like a crown with the tiny letter "C" or "G" under it. Can you tell me who made this rifle, when was it made, how many were made, the caliber, and what it's worth? I know you're busy, so I've included a self-addressed stamped envelope. Signed: Curious*

A lot of the letters I get are from folks who believe that whatever appears in print is gospel. If it's there in black and white, and your by-line is on the story, you own it for the rest of your life, so if there's a mistake anywhere, you own that as well. What they don't realize is that the photo captions we send in are often rewritten, even switched sometimes, by an art director or an assistant, and not caught in the proofreading. Sure, I've made mistakes on occasion, but usually it's as I've described.

> *Jon Sundra: You're an idiot. In a picture that appeared in the June issue of BLASTER magazine, you identify the .280 Remington as the 7mm Rem. Mag, and vice versa. Any moron knows the difference. Four years ago you did the same thing in a picture showing a Model 70 and a Remington 700. Hell, if that's all it takes, I think I'll become a gunwriter. Signed: Judgmental*

Some of the mail I've gotten over the years deserves to be shared!

Then there's the reader who simply will not allow an author to change his mind, and that whatever opinions he expressed twenty-five years ago must be chiseled in stone for all eternity. This type of reader, no matter how much time has elapsed or what new products or technological changes have come about to change the players or the playing field, simply won't accept the fact that the one constant in life is change. Here's a letter from a reader who refuses to allow for a change of opinion:

Dear Mr. Sundra: In a recent column by you in PLINKING magazine, you stated that there's "virtually no difference" between a 130-grain .270 Win. and a 140 gr. .280 Rem. Well, that's not what you said 28 years ago when you were the shooting editor of FUSILADE. I came across a copy the other day and in it you said that "the .280 Rem. is a tad more versatile than the .270, particularly if you're a handloader." Well, which is it? If it weren't for guys like me willing to do the research to expose so-called "experts" like you, well, God help us. Signed: Gotcha'

Then there's the expert, the guy who knows everything there is to know about some arcane aspect of rifle or cartridge history and is just waiting for some poor gunwriter to make a false step that will open the door so that he can enlighten us all. These are the guys who dare (or plead with) the editors to run their letters in the "Readers Write" department.

Dear Mr. Sundra: I enjoyed your recent article in BARRAGE magazine on the '98 Mauser. However, you failed to mention the Balzano Conversion by which the '98 can be successfully converted to full auto. Obviously, you are unfamiliar with young Guiseppi Balzano, born in 1881 in the village of Chianti, just north of Florence. The son of a gunsmith, Guiseppi wanted nothing more than to be a shepherd, but the elder Balzano would have none of it. Young Guiseppi would be a gunsmith or nothing! As it turned out, Guiseppi bowed to his father's wishes, and history has shown we're all the better for it. By the way, at the time of his death in 1955, Guiseppi was working on converting the Dardick pistol into shooting round bullets. Why are the gifted among us always taken so young? Signed: Top That!

Unlike the other letters I've paraphrased thus far, which represent a synthesis of many similar letters, this one is not a restatement but an actual letter that I received.

Dear Jon: My uncle Fern always told me the .30-06 shoots harder than any .300 magnum. Is that true? I've checked the ballistic tables and it looks like the magnum has the edge. But my uncle says that's all BS designed to sell guns. He says he has the proof. One day when he and a hunting buddy were checking their rifles for the deer season, they tacked a target to a tree trunk that he said was about 15 inches thick. Uncle Fern swore his .30-06 came out the other side every time, while his buddy's .300 magnum never did. Does the fact that uncle Fern's bullets were real pointy and didn't have lead tips like the .300 magnum have anything to do with it? Signed: Thirsting for Knowledge

This next category is very similar to the letters I received from "experts," except that in this one the author demands an answer. Of course, the answer must be a verification of his superior knowledge, which is often wrong. These letters go something like this:

Dear Mr. Sundra: I am about to embark on a rifle-building project and would like your opinion. I will be basing my rifle on a military Mauser action, for as you know, they are the very best examples of the genre. However, I'm torn between the 1909 Argentine and the VZ-24. Each has its strong points, but I'm concerned primarily with metallurgy. The '09 is simply case hardened, but the VZ-24 was hardened using a new process for that time whereby photometric ions and veebelfetzer molecules were vapor infused, then homologated into the tempering flux. If you had to choose, which do you think would make the safer action?

Now this guy, in addition to having a Ph.D. in metallurgy, is an expert on the Mauser action. He can tell you which arsenals, in which countries, turned out how many rifles, when, and for what armies. He's forgotten more about Mausers than I'll ever know . . . and he knows it. This is one you can't win, so you politely answer by saying something to the effect that he's much more qualified to answer his own question than you are. If that doesn't satisfy him, at least he won't be writing another letter.

One topic that generates lots of mail deals with cartridge and chambering confusion. Here's one that will send chills down your spine.

> *Dear Jon: I have a friend, a real gun expert, who has a Remington rifle stamped "7mm Express Rem." but he uses .280 Rem. ammo in it because he says it's the same caliber. It made me think of something I read in* ENFILADE *or maybe it was* BARRAGE *magazine, where the guy said the 7x57, 7mm Mauser, and a .275-something-or-other all use the same ammo because they are the same caliber. Now I have a .30-06, which is a .30 caliber, and the other day when I tried shooting .300 Win. Magnum ammo in it, I couldn't get the cartridge to chamber. And I really tried! I thought the .300 magnum was a .30 caliber? Is there something wrong with my gun? Signed: Really Confused*

If I've given the impression that letters like these are typical of reader mail, that's certainly not been my intent. Indeed, the vast majority of letters I receive—and I'm sure I'm speaking for my colleagues as well—are thoughtful and incisive, and very often we, the editors, are the ones who learn in the process. Letters from readers represent the only bridge between us; they provide valuable feedback as to what kind of job we're doing, and I, for one, enjoy reading them.

Let me close with a letter I received very early on in my writing career. This would go back to the late 1960s, and it came from what I assumed was an old cowboy living in rural Montana.

> *Dear Jon Sundra: I live out in the sticks and don't get into town very often. But I like to shoot . . . been doing it all my life. But .30-30 shells are getting expensive, so I'm thinking about taking up handloading to save money as I am on a fixed income. Now I don't know much about it. My neighbor handloads and says it's not hard, but I've never seen him do it. What I don't understand is how guys like you who shoot a lot, have the time to load all those shells. My neighbor,*

for example, said he used a load of 60½ grains of a certain powder. Now my eyes ain't what they used to be, and I've seen gun powder. Some of it's as fine as sand, and I'm not sure I can accurately count all those tiny grains. What if I go over, say like 62 or 63 grains. And what about that half grain? How do you do that? Do you use a razor blade or is there a special tool for that? Or could I just round it out to an even 60 and to hell with the half grain?

Not only did I have the pleasure of writing for a living about subjects that I cared passionately about, I also had the opportunity to meet and interact with icons of the industry. The icing on the cake, however, was the mail I got from my readers. Did I have the best job ever, or what?

The 7mm Guy

O ver a lifetime of hunting one can't help but develop certain affinities. Even for those who are not the least bit sentimental about guns, it's just human nature to favor a particular cartridge or caliber, especially when it's brought you nothing but success.

I like the 7mm, not any one specific cartridge but the caliber in general. Between the 7x57 and 7mm-08 at the one end and Remington's 7mm Ultra and the .28 Nosler at the other, there's been a .28 caliber that to me always seemed just right for the job. I will, however, admit to a few exceptions. I wouldn't, for example, recommend using a 7mm of any kind on lion or buffalo—though I have done it—on the big bears, and, of course, on elephants. Any other soft-skinned game on earth can be taken quite handily, thank you very much, with a bullet measuring .284 of an inch.

The 7mm has a long and storied history, but it wasn't launched on these shores until sixty-five years after the caliber debuted in Europe. The first 7mm of consequence was the 7x57, a cartridge of Mauser design that first appeared in the Spanish Model 1892. It is essentially the German 7.9x57 martial cartridge originally developed for the commission rifle of 1888, necked down to 7mm. The shoulder on the 7mm version is pushed back a little, resulting in a slightly longer neck and shorter body, but see the two side by side and it's obvious they share the same case. For that matter, our own .30-06 is based on what is just a slightly lengthened 8mm Mauser case.

During the tenuous periods of peace prior to and after World War I, the 7x57—or *7mm Mauser*, take your pick—established itself as one of the most popular sporting cartridges in the world . . . except here in the States. Oh, it was well known enough among serious rifle cranks, but to the majority of

America's hunters and shooters, the 7x57 remained a "foreign" caliber and was chambered here only on a very limited basis, most notably in early Model 70 Winchesters and in the Remington Model 30. Another 7mm that enjoyed great popularity in Europe is the 7x64, a cartridge designed by Wilhelm Brenneke in 1917; the .280 Remington, which would surface here forty years later, looks suspiciously like the 7x64.

In retrospect, our slow and grudging acceptance of the 7mm was perfectly understandable. After all, we had the .30-06, a cartridge that was more potent and more versatile than any foreign military caliber, and until quite recently, versatility was the most sought-after attribute in a cartridge. No more, but that's another story.

It wasn't until 1957 that the .28 caliber got its foot in the door here, and then it was something of a fluke. As it was told to me many years ago by Remington's Mike Walker, who was at the center of this caliber's development, the company wanted to chamber its then two-year-old Model 740 autoloader for the .270 Winchester but was encountering a problem. The company found that the pressure levels to which commercial .270 ammunition was loaded was too punishing on the action. The Remington folks decided that if the Model 740 couldn't handle the .270, they'd design a cartridge as close to it as possible that *would* work. The .280 Remington that debuted that year, therefore, represented what was essentially the company's "Plan B."

The solution was a no-brainer: neck-up the .270 Winchester a mere .007 of an inch to the long-established 7mm bore and load it to a maximum of 60,000 psi. (The .270 is loaded to 65,000 psi.) However, to foil the inevitable dimwit who would sooner or later try to cram a .280 Remington into a .270 Winchester rifle, Remington increased the head-to-shoulder dimension on the .280 by some .051 of an inch. The result was a case that had a slightly larger combustion chamber than the .270, enough so that the .280's ballistics virtually matched those of the Winchester round at slightly less pressure.

As good as the .280 looked on paper, however, it couldn't deliver its claimed velocities in the Model 740 autoloader. Moreover, Remington had chosen, at least initially, not to chamber its Model 721 bolt-action rifle in the .280. Unfortunately, the gunwriters of the day were only too happy to point out these shortcomings, so when the initial dust settled, the .280 failed to capture the imagination of America's hunters. The .270 Winchester was still the long-range champ among nonmagnum cartridges.

That all changed when Remington in 1962 had another go at the .28 caliber, this time with a belted number called the 7mm Remington Magnum. Why the "7 Magnum" struck such a responsive chord when just five years earlier the .280 bombed, is open to speculation, but surely the biggest reason was performance. Here was a cartridge that was clearly superior to the vaunted .270, never mind its foreign designation.

It was the announcement of the 7mm Remington Magnum that began my fifty-year odyssey with the .28 caliber. I was 22 at the time, and in my second year of college. (Yes, I was a slow learner.) To say I was a budding rifle crank back then would be putting it mildly! I still have a class notebook from English Lit wherein the margins are filled with my drawings of cartridges, most notably ones looking like Remington's Big 7. Come to think of it, perhaps that had something to do with my being a twenty-two-year-old sophomore.

Maybe it was the iconoclast in me, but I just couldn't get excited about the .270, the .30-06, or any other established cartridge. I wanted something new, different, and *hot*, and it seemed to me Remington's 7 Magnum was what I was looking for.

Shortly after graduating in 1965, I acquired my first 7mm magnum; it was a BSA barreled action that I had ordered from a Herter's catalog, which I stocked and glass bedded myself. I think it was in 1967 when I took that rifle on my very first out-of-country hunt, a trek to Quebec's Labrador region for caribou. I had that rifle for a couple of years, and though I did not slay a lot of critters with it—a few whitetails, mule deer, black bear, and pronghorn—everything I pointed it at expired without ceremony. I was hooked. After all, isn't it how most of us come to favor a particular rifle or caliber? We all develop faith and confidence in a specific rifle or caliber based on our successful experiences.

By the time I made my first African safari in 1977, I had gone through three more bolt-action 7 magnums and was now using a Ruger No. 1. I had also become disenchanted with belted cases, so when I returned to Africa the following year, it was with a custom Ruger 77 in .280 Remington. The year after that it was with another custom Ruger 77, this time in .284 Winchester. Though neither matched the ballistics of the 7 magnum, everything I shot with those nonmagnum 7s still fell over, and I'm talking big animals like kudu, gemsbok, wildebeest, roan, sable, zebra, and eland, to name a few. Now I was more of a 7mm nut than ever.

For a twelve-year period from 1979 to 1991, I used my own wildcat, the 7mm JRS, almost exclusively. It is essentially a blown-out .280 Remington case with a 35-degree shoulder, a .300" neck, and a body taper of .015" from head to shoulder. The 7mm JRS increases the .280's capacity from 63 grains of water to 70. On a magnum-length action that allows seating the bullets to where they don't infringe on powder space, I get 3,100 fps from a 150-grain bullet in a 24-inch barrel. That's an average among three rifles that I've shot extensively.

Since those first three safaris, I've made many more treks to Africa. Add to that, I've taken about a hundred other hunting trips on foreign soil and who knows how many more here in the States. Regardless of where I've hunted—from Alaska to Zambia, South Africa to Siberia, the South Pacific to the Arctic Ocean—there's been a 7mm in my hand most of the time. I've had no regrets.

Now I'm not about to try to make the case that a 7mm is in some way superior to the .30 caliber. Push a .308" bullet of similar sectional density and ballistic coefficient, and it'll shoot as flat as a 7mm, and it will arrive with more authority. A good illustration would be to compare the two most closely matched bullets in each caliber—the 140-grain 7mm with the 165-grain .30 (both have the identical sectional density of .248), and the 154-grain 7mm with an SD of .273 to the 180-grain .30 with an SD of .271. In other words, the 140 and 154 grain bullets are to the 7mm bore what the 165 and 180 are to the .30.

Hornady is the only manufacturer of 154-grain bullets, so we'll use its figures to compare its flat-base, spire point with its .30/180 of identical profile. For comparison of the 7mm/140 and .30/165, we'll use Nosler's Ballistic Tips, also having identical profiles. The ballistic coefficients for these pairings are also very close. The 7mm/140 has a BC of .485, while the BC of the .30/165 is .475. For the heavier slugs, the 7mm/154 has a BC of 433, while the .30/180 rates .425.

Pushing both the 7mm/140 and .30/165 at 3,300 fps—realistic velocities for middle-of-the-road magnums like the 7mm Weatherby and .300 Weatherby—a 300-yard zero will have the 7mm impacting 6.2 inches low at 400 yards while the .30 hits 6.3 inches low. Shove the 154/7mm and .30/180 out at 3,100 fps—again, realistic velocities—and our points of impact are minus 9.9 inches for the 7mm and minus 10 inches for the .30.

If we average the retained energy at 400 yards, we're looking at roughly 1,860 ft-lbs for the two 7mms, and 2,150 for the .30s; that's 14 percent more energy for the .30s. The downside is that the 14 percent greater energy comes at a cost of *30 percent more recoil*. For those wishing to double check my figures, I used the Barnes Ballistics Program as my source.

Again, there's no denying the numbers; the .30 has the advantage. I've just never felt that the increase in retained energy was necessary, certainly not at the cost of 30 percent more recoil. If I did consider those extra foot-pounds necessary, it would be because I was shooting at critters I shouldn't be shooting at with a 7mm in the first place! Believe me when I say I'm not recoil shy; I can't afford to be. I don't have to like it, either.

To me, the .30 caliber, especially when you get into the magnums, always seemed to be more gun than necessary for the vast majority of game, and not enough for the rest. The only big game in North America that to my mind warrants more than 7 magnum performance is the big bears, and for them I want something with a short barrel and a big hole in it . . . like a .375. It's the same with African game. With the exception of leopard, if it's dangerous game I'm after, I want a bigger hole than a .30 caliber!

The foregoing differences apply regardless of what class of cartridges we're comparing: the 7x57 and 7mm-08 to the .308 Winchester—the .280 Remington to the .30-06—the 7mm Remington or Weatherby Magnums to the .300 Winchester—the 7mm STW to the .300 Weatherby—the 28 Nosler to the 30 Nosler—or the 7mm Ultra Magnum to the .300 Ultra Magnum. Take whichever of the foregoing pairings you like, you must pay a price of around 25 to 30 percent more recoil to get as flat a trajectory with a .30 as with a 7mm. This is for a margin of retained energy downrange that experience has shown me to be unnecessary.

Another immutable fact is that the less recoil we have to contend with, the better we shoot. Take a hundred shooters or take a thousand shooters, and then hand them rifles having 30 percent less recoil. They're going to shoot better. The differences increase when you go from magnums to super magnums. Ask any competitive shooter why he wants every last legal ounce of rifle weight coupled with a cartridge having the least amount of recoil. Ask any experienced guide or professional hunter about clients showing up with rifles they can't shoot. I guarantee you it happens more when there's a .30 caliber involved than with 7mm.

The simple fact is that 7mms are easier to shoot well and they are fully capable of taking all but a handful of the world's game *without compromising*, which is why the .28 caliber keeps gaining in popularity. Remington, for example, now has its name on five 7mm cartridges, and loads for two more, the 7x64 and 7x57.

It should come as no surprise, too, that there is as wide a range of component bullets available in .284" as there are in .308", and in more weights. Consider this observation: Among the various manufacturers, handloaders can choose 7mm bullets of 100, 110, 115, 120, 125, 130, 139, 140, 145, 150, 154, 160, 162, 168, 170, and 175 grains. If you've got a particularly finicky rifle with regard to its shooting a specific bullet weight better than others, you've a better chance of finding it if you've got a .284" hole in the barrel.

If I had to sum up my more than fifty years of intimacy with the 7mm, I guess I'd have to say that I've never been one to compromise when it comes to my rifles, and I've never had to with a 7mm of one kind or another.

Stupid Is as Stupid Does

Chapter 18

W e've all heard the expression "It seemed like a good idea at the time." That's because when you are doing something stupid, you're not aware of it; if you were, you wouldn't be doing it. So much for profundities.

I once waded out crotch-deep into the Luangwa River, one of the most croc-infested waters on earth. It was at night, and I had nothing but a flashlight on me. Why you might ask? I was trying to catch "a small one" alive to take back to camp to show the wife. To understand such galactic imbecility requires some background.

As a young boy, guns and hunting in far-off places were not my only daydreams. Until about the fourth grade I was intensely interested in dinosaurs. In that respect I was pretty normal. When I was growing up, we lived in Cleveland. I attended Holy Family School on 131st Street, and right across from the school was a public library. By the time I was ten or so, I had read not only every book on dinosaurs in the children's section, but I was such a fixture there that the librarian allowed me into the adult area as well, and I read everything there, too.

When I was about ten, my interest in the big lizards waned and I became increasingly interested in snakes. I must have concluded there was no future in critters that died seventy million years ago. I'd never see one and I'd never hunt one. But snakes? They, too, were really cool, and they were things I could catch, hold in my hand, and collect. Of course, there were no snakes in my immediate neighborhood in urban Cleveland, but a half-hour bike ride away was Garfield Park, with its few acres of woods, fields, and a small stream that fed a lake in its center. It was there, in an area of small sandstones left from some long-forgotten construction project that I caught my very first snake. In fact, I caught two species that day: a dekay and an eastern ring-necked snake.

Both were no more than a foot or so in length, but to me had they been twenty-five-foot pythons I could not have been happier.

By the time I was a sophomore at Cathedral Latin High School, I was a walking encyclopedia on snakes. When in biology class we came to studying reptiles, my instructor handed the class over to me. To make it all the more interesting, I was permitted to bring to school that day several of the snakes I had in my collection, including a five-foot blacksnake. I commuted to and from school using public transportation and I used an ordinary pillow case to carry the snakes.

On the way home that day a couple of seniors from my school were on the bus. One of them asked me what was in the sack. I told them.

"Oh bull," one of them said, as he grabbed it from my hand. That kid must not have liked snakes because upon undoing the knot and peering in, he literally tossed the sack up in the air and headed for the front of the bus . . . as did everyone else. The minute the sack hit the floor the snakes were out, with the big blacksnake leading the way.

I'll never forget the scene: It was on East 116th Street and we were in front of St. Luke's Hospital. The driver was black, as were about half the people on the bus. When it became known there were snakes loose onboard, it was instant bedlam. The driver screeched the bus to a halt right in the middle of the street and was the first to exit. A fire alarm could not have emptied that bus quicker. In a matter of thirty seconds I was the only person on the bus.

I never did recapture all the snakes, but the two or three I didn't were small enough and had apparently found hiding places under or beneath seats. When I assured everyone the snakes were harmless and that I had caught all them, most passengers re-boarded, but there were about a dozen or so who refused. I was never so relieved to reach my stop and get off that bus! I believe the incident made the papers, but I can't say for sure.

I was still into snakes after having graduated high school, so my buddy Joe and I, along with another buddy who would become my brother-in- law, Tom Krivanek, drove down to the Okefenokee and the Florida Everglades on a snake-collecting expedition for the Cleveland Zoo. I mention all this merely to establish the fact that I obviously had no fear of snakes, or reptiles in general. I didn't mind being bitten by any nonvenomous variety, which happened hundreds of times in the course of grabbing them anywhere on their body as they tried to escape capture or during routine handling. I did, however, try to avoid being bitten if the snake was more than four feet or so, for their needlelike teeth would be long enough to produce a little bit of pain for a few moments and draw tiny beads of blood at every puncture. Again, being bitten was no big thing.

On my second African safari to South Africa I was fortunate enough to come upon a large python crossing the dirt road in front of us. It was stretched out as it crossed the road, and we estimated it to be about fifteen feet in length. In the Toyota with me was my PH, Norman Dean, and my friend George Daniels, who was not particularly fond of snakes.

"C'mon, George, I want you to get a picture of me with that python."

"You're outta' your mind," came the expected response.

"Ah, don't be such a wus," I said, handing him my camera, which he was quite familiar with. "I'll protect you," I quipped.

Meanwhile, the python was moving slowly, but by the time I and a protesting George reached it, it was about halfway into the bushes at the side of the road.

"George, I'm going to grab its tail and try to get it to strike. See if you can get a picture."

Sure enough, as I tugged at its tail, it coiled up for business. Now snakes can only strike over a distance about a third of their length, so I knew how close I could get and still be out of range. Believe me, I did not want to get bitten by a fifteen-foot python! As good luck would have it, George tripped the shutter at the perfect moment when the critter's open mouth was about a foot or so from my face. Because George feared snakes so much, he flinched when it struck and the picture is a little out of focus. It is still sharp enough.

As unlikely as it may seem, the following year in Zambia when the safari was over and we were leaving the concession on our way to the airport in Lusaka, the same thing happened. A python was crossing the bush road in front of us and George was again in the car with me. As Yogi would say, it was déjà vu all over again.

"George, let's get a picture."

"Not again!"

"Why not, last year you got an incredible picture. Let's see if you can do it again."

Damned if he didn't. Again I got the snake—about the same size as last year's—to strike, and again George snapped the photo at the exact right moment. Looking at the two pictures side by side, the timing and coincidence are extraordinary.

So, the fact that I had no fear of snakes and was confident in my knowledge of them might help explain my galactic imbecility mentioned earlier. It was 1979 and when my PH, Eugenio Bidali, suggested we wade out into the Luangwa at night to capture a small crocodile, I was all for it. As I said, it was colossal idiocy. Reinforcing that decision was the fact that Eugenio had been a professional crocodile hunter for twenty years before import restrictions in the States and other countries made his job no longer profitable. Given his past, he easily qualified for a professional hunter license and was working for Zambia Safaris.

Our camp was in the Luawata concession of Zambia on the banks of the Luangwa. To get there we had to raft the Toyota across the river at Chibembe because there was no bridge anywhere in the concession. Nowhere before or since have I seen so many hippos and crocs as there were on that stretch of river. Just looking a couple hundred yards up and downstream from camp you could see dozens of crocs sunning themselves along the banks, many with jaws agape, as if wanting to get a tan on their tongues.

Hippos were always in sight, with as many as forty and fifty in a group, *onk onk-ing* and playing like kids in the river. They'd take turns getting sideways with the current, letting it roll them over and over. Watching them slowly revolve and seeing their stubby feet come out of the water as they rolled over on their backs remains one of the most comical antics I've seen in the animal world.

At night the hippos would come up the riverbank to forage and would travel as much as a half mile from the water, often going right through our camp to get there and passing within a foot or two of the thatched, open-sided *sitenge*s we called home. One night as I was about to get up to make my way to the toilet, I heard this strange staccato sound against the side of our hut. In the morning I described the event to Eugenio. Seems hippos when on dry land have this unique ritual of defecating while spinning their tail, which acts very much like a manure spreader. Sure enough, when I walked back to our hut, the side was splattered with hippo doo-doo.

148

Anyway, on the night in question, I don't recall the circumstances that brought it about, but the only people in camp that night were Eugenio and his wife and Judith and I. Of course the camp staff was there—cooks, trackers, skinners, etc.—but they were through work for the day and had retired. It was a beautiful evening . . . as most in Africa are, with just enough chill in the air to make sitting by the perpetual campfire all the more inviting.

I'm not sure what time it was, but it had been dark for maybe two hours, so it was around nine o'clock or so. What I do know is that all four of us were pretty blitzed, having wrapped ourselves around several sundowners apiece, plus three or four bottles of excellent South African Shiraz. That, of course, is what prompted our decision to go down to the river and try to catch a small croc. I figured if this guy, who had hunted these things for twenty years, didn't know what he was doing, nobody did. I'll never forget Judith's reaction when we announced what we were about to do.

"That's nice, hon. Have fun . . . and don't get eaten."

Eugenio was now handling the flashlight, the only one we had, as we eased our way down the rather steep bank to the water some fifteen to twenty feet below. For some inexplicable reason, neither of us thought to bring a rifle. But then why would we? After all, we didn't want to shoot a *croc*; we just wanted to catch one. There was no moon as I recall, so it was very dark.

When Eugenio said he could tell the size of a croc by the distance between the eyes, it sounded reasonable to me. Boy were there eyes . . . lots of them, and they glowed an ominous red in the white light. Within minutes we were crotch deep in the Luangwa, slowly working our way upstream. The water was warm and felt good. By the time we had gotten a hundred yards from the still-visible campfire, we had spotted at least twenty pairs of eyes, some gliding by as close as twenty feet from us with nary a ripple. It was surreal.

"To big . . . too big . . . too big," Eugenio pronounced every time the beam settled on a pair of those emberlike eyes.

It went on like that for another hundred yards or so when, suddenly, I felt the ground begin to shake, literally, and I instantly knew what was happening. We had gotten between a herd of hippos that had been foraging in the veld above and for some reason panicked when they heard us talking. Being between them and the safety of the river was the wrong place to be.

Now the riverbank at that particular point was quite steep, so a seven-thousand-pound animal descending it would work up quite a head of steam upon reaching the bottom, which of course is where we were. In a matter of seconds we had what seemed a stampeding herd of hippos less than fifty feet away coming straight at us, or more probably straight at the flashlight beam Eugenio had trained on them. Still up to our crotches in the water, there was absolutely nothing we could do but to freeze in place while expecting the worst.

What happened next was just another reminder of how I've been blessed with more lives than a cat. I'm just guessing, of course, but there had to at least twenty-five animals—that's around one hundred and fifty thousand pounds of hippo rushing straight at us.

"Kill the light," I screamed, even though Eugenio was little more than five feet away.

He needed no reminder as we stood there, up to our fannies in the Luangwa in the dark, hoping not to become bowling pins. Those massive bodies entered the water, and in their panic they whipped it to a froth as they forged ahead to get to safety. They surged all around us, even between the few feet that separated Eugenio and me, yet neither of us was hit head-on. They could just as easily have centered us on one of their huge noses, and who knows what could have resulted? Knocked unconscious, trampled, bitten in half, and drowned were all realistic scenarios, yet we were both unscathed.

I never sobered up as quickly as I did that night. "I think I've had enough fun for one night, Eugenio," I said as I waded ashore.

We could still see the ladies sitting by the campfire, which at that moment looked awfully inviting.

"Well?" was the first word out of Judith's mouth as we reclaimed the same chairs we had left a short half-hour before.

"Nothing," I said matter-of-factly. "We didn't see a croc Eugenio thought was small enough. It was fun anyway."

Until the day she died, I never told Judith what happened that night.

Blazing Saddles and My Longest Shot

Chapter 19

Ohe of my favorite movies is *Blazing Saddles*. Not the one that's occasionally shown on TV or even cable, that's so heavily edited for purposes of political correctness that it's not worth watching. I'm talking the original, uncut version with all its hilarious vulgarity and general irreverence of everything human. Among the stars of the movie—Mel Brooks, Harvey Korman, Cleavon Little, Gene Wilder, and Madeline Kahn, was Slim Pickens. So when I got an invitation from Winchester to hunt antelope with Slim, I gladly accepted.

It was back in the late 1970s that Winchester was somehow affiliated with Weaver scopes, and Slim was contracted as a spokesman in a series of Weaver ads. Also on that hunt were Grits Gresham and, I think, Jim Carmichael, though I can't be sure. I mean, it was nearly forty years ago!

Anyway, Grits was the shooting editor at *Sports Afield*, and Jim Carmichael occupied a similar slot at *Outdoor Life*. As for me, I had just signed on with Petersen Publishing as either hunting or field editor of *Guns & Ammo* and *Petersen's Hunting* magazines. At the time I had been on the staff of *Petersen's Hunting* since its inception, but I was no longer under any sort of exclusive contract. I had just left *Shooting Times* after a ten-year stint there. John Wootters was first to defect to Petersen's from *Shooting Times*, followed by Bob Milek, then me. Skeeter Skelton started his writing career with *Shooting Times* after his law-enforcement days and stayed with the magazine until his death in 1988.

As I said, this was primarily a Winchester-sponsored hunt, with Weaver supplying the optics. As is so often the case, when we showed up in camp we were handed what we were to use on the hunt—Winchester Model 70s, of course—all chambered in .270 Winchester.

"They're all sighted-in guys, two inches high at 100 yards."

Well, we all had heard that kind of assurance many times before, so based on past experiences all three of us asked if we could shoot a few rounds ourselves just for confidence. After all, with antelope hunting there was a good chance we'd be faced with some very long-range shooting, and I wanted to be sure my rifle was indeed shooting where they said it was.

You'd be surprised how many times I've been on industry hunts where the sponsors spend huge sums of money on high-priced outfitters and posh hunting camps, yet don't make sure there are adequate sighting-in facilities—like a solid shooting bench or a bipod/tripod with sandbags, and decent targets. Often it's a cardboard box with a rock in it and a crayoned bull's-eye of sorts scribbled on one side. As for a rifle rest, it's a rolled-up jacket placed on the hood of a pickup. You can usually count on there being a brisk wind blowing to make sighting-in even more frustrating.

Such was the case on this hunt. No bench, no rifle rest, no sandbags, and a cardboard box for a target. The solution? One of the guides brought out a foam mattress from the bunkhouse and doubled it at the front to support the fore-end for us to shoot from prone. Combine a spirited wind with a spongy, one-point support for the rifle and you're lucky to shoot 3-inch groups, even if you had a 1 MOA rifle. Four or five shots were enough for me to conclude that the 3-inch "group" I was looking at was approximately two inches high, and that told me little other than I hoped I wouldn't be faced with any shot longer than about 250 yards.

As for Slim, he chose not to check zero on his rifle, but I suspect it was because he was so fat that lying on his stomach would have been difficult for him. It didn't take long, however, to determine that Slim was one helluva nice guy, as modest and unassuming as he could be. And funny!

Everyone was pretty tired from traveling all day, so we all retired fairly early that first day. The next morning we each had our own guide and vehicle, and Slim and I got back to camp before everyone else, not having seen anything worth going after goat-wise. Now it so happened that an acquaintance of mine who was a custom knife maker found out I would be hunting with Slim Pickens and wanted to make a knife for him. As the two of us sat at the fire waiting for the rest of the guys to return, I thought it an opportune moment to present the knife to Pickens. It was a really cool knife and Slim was genuinely pleased to accept it.

I don't recall how the subject came up, but I remember asking Slim which of the many movies he had a part in was the most fun for him. Without hesitation he said "Hell, that's easy, *Blazing Saddles!*"

Then I, also without hesitation, told him that it was one of my all-time favorite movies. Whether he believed me or not, thinking I was perhaps just blowing smoke, I couldn't say, but I immediately blurted what I considered to be one of the funniest lines in the movie; it was by Harvey Korman.

"My mind is aglow with whirling, transient nodes of thought, careening through a cosmic vapor of invention."

He guffawed, slapping his thigh and saying "Ditto," which was his responsive line in the movie.

"Well I'll be damned, you aren't kidden." You musta' really liked the movie to remember that!"

Pleased that he was pleased, I instantly went into another Korman moment in the movie: "My mind is a raging torrent, flooded with rivulets of thought, cascading into a waterfall of creative alternatives."

Laughing almost hysterically now, Slim managed to again counter with the correct line from the movie: "Oh, Mr. Taggert, you speak prettier than a two-dollar whore."

"Jon, we could have made a second movie with the amount of out-takes we had. Between Mel Brooks, who was starring and directing the thing, Gene, Cleavon, Harvey, Madeline, and me, we ruined so many scenes because one or more of us just couldn't keep from laughing. It was the same making *1941* with John Belushi but not so much with *Dr. Strangelove*.

We spent the next twenty minutes or so talking about movies, and how much fun he had in making *Blazing Saddles* and *1941*, another of his movies that's not as well known yet almost as funny. By then the others were back in camp for lunch and regrettably that was the last movie-related conversation Slim and I had.

That afternoon and the next morning I had yet to take a shot at an antelope. There was no shortage of them, but the ranch where we were hunting was as flat as a pool table and stalking to get within a reasonable shooting distance was extremely frustrating. Thus far I had seen only two bucks that my guide Dirk and I thought were worth stalking. Neither was successful. Since only two full days had been allotted for hunting, by the second afternoon the pressure was on.

With daylight waning, Dirk spotted a buck that he said was worth going after.

"He's no Boone and Crockett, but he's a pretty good one."

At that point in my life I had shot maybe a dozen pronghorn bucks, two of which scored an identical 79½, which was just 2½ inches shy of the record book. It came down to the old dilemma of not wanting to shoot anything but a real trophy, yet feeling obliged to shoot *something* to get the story that Winchester had every right to expect of me. I knew they'd be perfectly OK if the only opportunities I had were on immature bucks or ladies, but to turn down a decent representative buck, well, that would not be cool in their eyes, and understandably so.

"Instead of trying a stalk," Dirk opined, "let's see how close we can get with the truck."

Antelopes will usually let you get a lot closer to them if you're in a vehicle rather than on foot, so I thought it was worth a try. It's when you try to get out of the vehicle that spooks them. You never drive straight toward an animal or herd; rather, you angle off about 30 degrees, which to the critters appears like you're driving off, but you are actually getting closer to them all the time. Dirk angled the truck to the right so that if we got close enough to try a shot, I'd be getting out of the truck on the off-side to mask my movements better. Two sandbags were already sitting on the hood to provide the two-point rifle support necessary for serious shooting.

Our buck-of-interest was with two younger studs, yet they appeared less concerned than he as we started our four-wheel stalk. The trio let us get to within about 250 yards or so, but when we stopped the truck, they spooked. Uncharacteristically, however, they only ran about 250–300 yards and stopped.

"How far," I asked.

Dirk was glassing them. "God, I dunno," Dirk said, "a long way, maybe 500, maybe 600 yards."

Back then the idea of an affordable, compact laser rangefinder was the stuff of science fiction. You had to guess distance, and flat, featureless ground made it more difficult than usual. If memory serves, U. S. Army testing has shown that the average margin of error for a soldier guessing the distance of a target placed 300 yards away is plus or minus 95 yards! And at 500 yards, the margin of error is double that.

"We're already losing light, Jon. I don't know if we have time to find another band. You wanna' give it a shot?" Dirk asked.

Even if I wanted to, I figured getting out of the truck and setting up across the hood would probably spook them anyway, so it didn't really matter. Then again, I thought about the Winchester and Weaver people and their hoping I'd get a story out of their investment.

"Yeah," I said on second thought, "I'll have a go, but I doubt they'll stick around once I try getting out of this thing and setting up."

Surprisingly, when I got out of the truck, they didn't spook, even though they were obviously nervous. I was fairly familiar with the trajectory of a 130-grain .270 Winchester zeroed 2½-inches high at 100 yards, but based on the casual gathering of bullet holes I got two days before, I couldn't tell within two inches of the actual point of impact. To make matters worse, there was a brisk wind blowing maybe 10–15 mph right to left, and the buck was quartering away, his nose into the wind.

So, with very little confidence and guessing the buck was about 500 yards away, I put the cross-hairs what I guessed to be about 40 inches above the midpoint on his shoulder, and about 20 inches in front of his nose. In other words, completely off the critter. Almost reluctantly, I nudged the trigger. The buck was far enough away that the gun recovered from recoil and I could see through the scope both the impact of the bullet and the collapse of the buck.

"What a shot!" Dirk yelled enthusiastically. "Fantastic."

I, of course, acted as though I expected no other outcome. I knew full well that it was 90 percent pure luck that my target was, indeed, 500 yards away; that 40 inches high and 20 inches into the wind was the correct hold; and that everything was based on the assumption that my rifle was, in fact, zeroed 2½-inches high at 100 yards. Truly, it was 90 percent luck.

As it turned out, Dirk, who was about six feet tall, paced off the distance across the dead-flat terrain and came up with 530 steps, which he said was an honest 490 to 500 yards. With today's laser rangefinders, if I'm shooting my own rifle and handloads and if I have a steady-enough rest, I'll take a shot out to 400 yards, but no farther.

That antelope was the longest shot I've ever made on a game animal. Varmints, however, are another story. The longest shot I've ever made was approximately 1,200 yards on a woodchuck back in my Pennsylvania days. Again, it was long before laser rangefinders, so my saying it was 1,200 yards was based on the fact that my 110 paces equals 100 yards.

Unlike the antelope, I didn't hit that woodchuck on the first shot . . . or the second . . . or the third. Nope, I got him on the twenty-third attempt! I was shooting a .25-06 that I had just finished building on a Sako barreled action in a Fajen Regent wood-laminated stock. The groundhog was on an opposing slope and the conditions were dry enough that my buddy, who was spotting for me with his binocular, could see where the bullets were landing, thus allowing me to make the necessary hold adjustments. At 1,200 yards and on the twenty-third shot, luck still had a lot to do with it.

Me and the .22

Rare is the hunter whose rite of passage was not made with a .22 rifle in hand. I know that certainly was the case with me. From the time I was old enough to be trusted with a Daisy Red Ryder B-B gun—a point in time my parents and I strongly disputed—I dreamed of the day when I'd get a *real* gun—a .22. My dad eventually relented and upon my attaining the ripe old age of thirteen, my parents presented me with a Winchester Model 47 single-shot.

It was the most beautiful thing I'd ever seen, but I saw precious little of that gun over the next couple of years because my dad kept the thing locked up. You see, I grew up in a big city—the east side of Cleveland where my dad was a cop—so I didn't really have any place to shoot my beautiful new acquisition. Because my dad was not a hunter or shooter himself, the only opportunity I got to spend with the little Winchester was when my best bud's dad—who *was* a hunter—took us out to the country. Needless to say, that was never often enough.

With a driver's license and a car at the age of seventeen came the freedom to hunt and shoot pretty much as time would allow. By then I had gone through several .22s by means of various gun trades. Among them were a Mossberg bolt action, a Marlin semiautomatic, and another Marlin bolt gun chambered in what was then the hot new .22 magnum (WMR). In fact, my two buddies and I all purchased .22 magnums as soon as they appeared on the market in 1956. Of the various small game we had available to us in northern Ohio, hunting squirrels with a .22 held the most fascination for us, and we figured the .22 magnum would make the ultimate squirrel cartridge.

During that first year, however, all we could find in stores was hollow-point ammunition, which proved too destructive. The following year when

40-grain solids became available, they did a better job. They extended our effective range a bit compared to the .22 LR, and they imparted enough energy to knock a fox squirrel off even the largest limbs—something a regular .22 wouldn't always do.

I used the .22 magnum only for those two years before I came to the conclusion that it was unnecessarily powerful for the likes of a fox squirrel. I then went back to the standard long-rifle cartridge; it just seemed more "proper." When I look back on those days, perhaps it was then that I developed this thing I have about matching the cartridge to the game. I always want an *adequate* caliber for whatever I'm hunting mind you, and for the longest distance I'm likely to be shooting, but only to a point. I wouldn't, for instance, use a .300 Ultra Magnum on white-tailed deer . . . or even a .300 Winchester Magnum, for that matter. It's just a thing I have about not using any more cartridge than necessary.

Anyway, where I found the .22 magnum to really shine was as a varmint rifle for potting woodchucks. The truck and dairy farms of northern Ohio where I hunted weren't all that large that they required shooting beyond, say, 100 to 125 yards, which on those large rodents is the maximum effective range of the WMR. On those occasions when I was faced with too long a shot, I'd simply sneak around to where I could make my approach from another direction.

Sneaking up on woodchucks and squirrels as a youngster taught me most of what I know today about stalking game. Whether the quarry is a fox squirrel or a Cape buffalo, those lessons learned so long ago in northern Ohio with .22 in hand are as valid and as universal today as they were then.

Of all the .22s that have passed through my hands since my teenage days back in Ohio, several hold particularly fond memories for me. One such gun was a Browning T-Bolt. If memory serves, I got mine in 1966, the year after the gun was introduced. It was a seminal year for me because it was that same year I moved to Pennsylvania where centerfire rifles were allowed for hunting and the same year I sold my first article to the *Gun Digest*.

Those of you as long in the tooth as I may recall the T-Bolt; it was the first straight-pull action of either rimfire *or* centerfire persuasion seen on these shores since the 6mm Lee-Navy rifle of the 1890s. In recent years we've seen straight-pull actions in the form of the Blaser R93 and R8, the Mauser 96,

Browning Acera, Merkel RX Helix, and Heym SR-30, centerfires all. But being a .22 rimfire, the T-Bolt was a unique rifle and one that lit my fire. I had to have one.

Now, I'm not one who is sentimental about guns. As one who has been writing about them for fifty years, too many have passed through my hands for that. That T-Bolt, however, was special, and with it I took my limit of fox squirrels not just once, but just about every time I took it afield.

Unlike the straight-pull centerfires, all of which have rotary bolts of some sort, being a rimfire the T-Bolt didn't have to contend with such high operating pressures. As a result, the design of the action was such that the locking lug was circular and fitted flush with the contour of the receiver. Upon pulling straight back on the bolt handle, the locking lug was cammed outward from the battery, allowing the bolt to be pulled rearward. A straight push on the handle reversed things by stripping a fresh round from the "clip" and, upon fully chambering the round, the circular locking lug was cammed back into its locked position, flush with the sides of the receiver.

As I said, I acquired my T-Bolt just prior to the start of my writing career and before it became a necessity to take photographs of virtually every gun I touched. In rummaging through my photo files, I was able to come up with only two pictures of that rifle. Regrettably, I sold that gun only because it fell victim to rust.

My T-Bolt had been produced during the infamous time in Browning's past when the company's stock wood supplier used some sort of drying process that involved salt. The result was that after a few years any surface contact between the barreled action and receiver resulted in rust. I, of course, knew nothing of this problem that plagued Browning in the late 1960s and early 1970s. It was only when I noticed slight signs of corrosion along the barrel channel that I removed the barreled action to find the underside of the barrel and receiver were badly pitted. I simply thought it had been my fault for not taking proper care of the gun after a wet outing. It was a couple of years later that I learned what really happened.

As successful as I was using that T-Bolt, I wanted something a bit more accurate, so I bought myself a match rifle with the idea of converting it into the ultimate squirrel rifle. I wasn't about to hack up an Anschutz, mind you, so I looked around for an economical rifle having enough wood in the right places that would enable me to carve out something resembling a sporter stock. I settled on a Savage. I don't recall what model it was, but it was an entry-level match rifle, single-shot, with a target-style stock having the rail and hand stop in the fore-end. Savage no longer makes that particular rifle, but I suspect that back in the early 1970s when I started that project, the gun I was working with was basically the same gun Savage is offering today as the Mark II target rifle.

With a hacksaw and assorted wood rasps, I reduced the bulky, target-style stock to something as close to a high-combed sporter as the original would allow; I then had the target-weight barrel cut and crowned at twenty-two inches. With CCI hollow points, that rifle would shoot half-inch groups at fifty yards all day. With match ammo, it shot even better, but solids didn't have the shock value to always knock a big fox squirrel out of a tree, especially if the squirrel was in a crotch of a tree or lying on a large limb. That converted Savage single-shot proved to be every bit as good a squirrel rifle as I had envisioned . . . alas, it too is gone, traded for some gun I can't even remember.

My next "affair" with a standout rimfire actually occurred before I had completed my ultimate squirrel rifle. It was with Remington's ill-fated 5mm magnum, a terrific cartridge that was unveiled in 1970 and represented the only real excitement to hit the rimfire world since the WMR of 1955.

The test gun I received from Remington was a clip-fed Model 591 bolt gun. It had a multiple lug—six in two rows of three—rear-locking action that had all the strength necessary to handle the higher pressures of this hot little .20 caliber that pushed a 38-grain bullet at 2,100 fps. Not only was it faster than the WMR and had better downrange performance due to its more streamlined jacketed Core Lokt HP bullet, but it was also more accurate by far than any .22 magnum I'd ever shot. Though it turned out to be too potent for squirrels, it made a better groundhog cartridge than the WMR and extended the effective range out to 150 yards, which was really saying something for a rimfire in those days. It would also have made a terrific round for ground squirrels and for those dumber prairie rats that show themselves at close ranges—ranges that would be a waste of a centerfire.

Despite its terrific performance and outstanding accuracy, the 5mm went the way of the dodo bird, and it took only three years to do so! By 1974 it had been dropped from production. The reason? Would you believe that the ammo, which after the first year was priced at $4.00 per box of 50 and about a buck more than .22 WMR, was deemed too expensive! That at a time when the Remington 591 rifle chambered for it cost $64.95! Go figure! Talk about another gun I wish I had! Had I even *suspected* it would be dropped from production, I would never have sent it back to Remington!

Other .22s that I consider true classics as well as benchmarks of their respective types—all of which I still own—are the Winchester 9422, the Marlin 1894-M, and the Ruger 77/22. To my mind it borders on travesty that these three fantastic guns are no longer in production.

From the moment I first picked up a 9422, I thought it was the finest lever-action .22 rimfire ever. I still do. What impressed me all the more was that it was introduced in 1972, a time when the old Winchester Repeating Arms Company was still reeling from the effects of what it had done to its guns in 1964.* Even though Winchester by then had started to implement improvements to enhance the quality of its guns, I found the 9422 to be head and shoulders above other Winchesters of the day. For me, the 9422 was as though it was being made by someone else!

To my mind, a lever action .22 is not as "serious" a gun as a bolt action. By that I mean it's more of a fun gun, the kind you grab when you just want to bum around the woods and shoot at targets of opportunity. Much the same can be said of a semiauto. Like any traditional-style lever action, the 9422 had hand-carry qualities that were so outstanding that it almost made you not want to mount a scope.

I feel the same way about my Marlin 1894-M in .22 WMR It's not as refined a gun as the 9422, but if you want a .22 magnum in the one uniquely American rifle type, this was the one. Like the 9422, it was just plain fun to shoot and a joy to carry.

---

*Winchester redesigned and cheapened its most iconic models—the Model 70 bolt action, 94 lever action, and the Model 12 shotgun—and in so doing, alienated what had been the most loyal customer base of any firearms manufacturer.

The Ruger M77/22 was rolled out in 1983, and here was a rifle that broke new ground for a rimfire in that it utilized two massive, midmounted, twin-opposed locking lugs that engaged recesses in the receiver bridge. It was obvious from the strength of the action that Ruger had bigger plans for this gun. Sure enough, a few years later the .22 magnum chambering was added, followed by a conversion to centerfire that also made it adaptable to handling the .22 Hornet and the .44 Remington Magnum pistol cartridge.

The 77/22 was one of the finest, most technically advanced .22s in the world, and I still can't believe that it's no longer being manufactured. It's such a shame, really, but I guess when its MSRP went to $999 in 2016, it priced itself out of the market. It was replaced with the Ruger American Rimfire, which is a very good gun, but it's a far cry from the 77/22.

Today we have, of course, the .17 HMR and the .17 Winchester Super Magnum, both of which leave the older rimfires in the dust. It was those older rimfires, however, that played such an important role in formulating my love of firearms and what I wanted to do with my life. As I look back today, it's with sadness I acknowledge that, as I grew older, and my hunting horizons widened to big game and the kind of rifles needed for such pursuits, my .22s got relegated to the back of the gun cabinet. That's also a shame, really, because so much of what aspirations I had as a young man, and to whatever degree of success I've had in achieving them, were formulated with a .22 rifle in my hands.

Bear with Me

Of all the hunts I've made over the years I've had more interesting and humorous experiences hunting black bears than I've had hunting any other critter. I've made twenty or so such hunts over the years and have taken sixteen bears, so that represents a lot of time in tree stands and ground blinds, though not all of my bears were taken over bait.

My first hunt was a stinker, and I mean that literally. I was just out of school and a buddy of mine told me about a couple of guys he knew who had driven up into Canada in a pickup camper and had shot their bears in the garbage dump of a lumber camp. That meant no outfitter, guide, meal, or accommodation expenses—our expenditure would just be a relatively inexpensive nonresident license.

Hell, I figured, I've got a little camper on the back of my Chevy pickup. If those guys could do it on the cheap, so could we.

It was an easy day's drive from Pittsburgh to the backwoods of Ontario. Sure enough, finding lumber camps was no problem, for there were logging roads everywhere. Getting permission, too, was no problem. The loggers even welcomed us since they considered bears pests.

As it turned out, the camp we settled on had a dump that was quite large, covering maybe six to eight acres, and in order to observe the place where they were dumping the fresh foodstuff, we actually had to park right in among the garbage. It was late May and unseasonably warm—hot actually—and the smell was enough to gag a maggot. After a short time though, the smell seemed to disappear. It wasn't gone really; it was just that our olfactory senses had been so utterly defiled that we just couldn't smell the odious odor anymore. We spent three days there, and if there were any bears coming in, it had to have happened after dark because we saw nothing.

On returning home, I pulled into my driveway to find my wife and about a dozen other ladies seated on the rear patio just a few yards from where I had parked. As bad timing would have it, I had returned home during a Welcome Wagon party. The ladies were outside because we had just moved into this house a few days earlier and all the rooms were still full of unpacked boxes and yet-to-be-placed furniture.

No sooner had I gotten out of my truck than my wife came rushing toward me, pulling me aside. "What is that awful stench?" she whispered.

Apparently, even the five-hundred-mile drive home hadn't diminished the stench that I was just beginning to detect. It wasn't five minutes before all the ladies were gone. I got a short "Hello, welcome to the neighborhood," and that was it. I mean, what could I have said? Should I have told them that I had spent the previous three days parked in a garbage dump in Canada?

******

My next interesting experience came the following year on a September hunt in Quebec. This time I booked an outfitter. It proved to be my first successful bear hunt, but one that I'll always remember.

Like so many bear hunting operations in eastern Canada, most outfitters like to put their bear hunters on a stand three, and even four hours before dark, on the slim chance that a bear will come to the bait in midafternoon. It didn't take many more bear hunts for me to conclude that 90 percent of all bears taken over bait are taken in the last half-hour of daylight, so I have long since insisted that I not be taken to my stand more than ninety minutes before dark.

When hunting over bait, hunting in the morning is so futile that it just isn't done, at least not in the many bear camps I've been in. The guides use that time to check baits to see which ones, if any, had been worked the previous night. Out West, on the other hand, where bears are spotted and stalked, mornings are just as productive as evening hunts.

Anyway, I'm up in this tree stand about twenty feet above the ground and some fifty yards away from the bait that had been messed with the previous evening. Like most greenhorns, I believed that bears were super smart, and that any movement, alien sound, or man scent within a mile would guarantee you'd never see a bear. Well, having been on this platform for more than two hours, I had to urinate badly.

I had been too stupid to have thought to bring a bottle, and I didn't want to climb down for fear of chasing off some bear that might be just out of sight and about to come to the bait. So, with an about-to-burst bladder, I stepped to the edge of the platform and proceeded to do what was necessary. While doing so, I took a quick look toward the bait. When my eyes focused back to the business at hand, I suddenly found myself urinating on a bear. Honest!

Normally, baits are put at the edge of thick cover, and that is the direction from which bears usually approach. This bear had come to the bait from the exact opposite direction, so I hadn't expected him to be right underneath my blind. It's also why bears just seem to materialize—one second there's nothing there and the next second there's a bear. It can be very exciting, especially when for two or three hours nothing has happened, and you're in a semistupor thinking nothing is ever going to happen.

That bear simply stopped for a moment, shook, and then padded over to the bait, where I shot him with my 6mm Remington Ruger No. 1. A single shot with a 100-grain Sierra handload dropped him within 20 yards from where he was hit. He wasn't a big bear—maybe 150 pounds —but he was my first bear. That golden shower hadn't bothered Br'er Bear in the least, but it made him unforgettable to me.

******

It was a couple of years later—around 1970 as I recall—and I was again hunting black bear in Quebec. This time I was in a prepared ground blind across a narrow ravine and some forty yards from the bait. It was the most stupidly conceived blind I'd ever seen, for it was nothing more than a dense bush in which a pocket had been pruned out. It provided cover on both sides and behind, but none in front! Were a bear to show up, I'd be in plain sight and any movement on my part would be seen.

After about an hour it started to rain quite unexpectedly, and I had no lens caps for my scope, nor did I have waterproof clothing. So, in an effort to keep my scope dry, I tucked my rifle—another Ruger No. 1, but this one custom barreled in .284 Winchester—inside my shirt. So there I was, seated on the ground, my legs tucked in, with my torso leaning forward as much as possible to protect the scope. It wasn't a heavy rain, but within a few minutes my arms, legs, and back were soaked.

Staring at the bait through the rain, I suddenly saw a large black form emerge from the brush. He was immediately behind the barrel of fish heads, and I could see that this was a nice bear, maybe three hundred pounds. I was excited. He was so close, however, that I couldn't chance movement until he faced away.

At the first such opportunity, I brought the Ruger to my shoulder, only to find that my body heat trapped inside my shirt had caused condensation to form. Both the ocular and objective lenses were so dripping with water that I couldn't see well enough to risk a shot. It was still raining, it was getting dark, and I didn't have anything dry to wipe the lenses with. Then it occurred to me that my hunched-over position might have kept at least the front portion of my jockey shorts dry. The problem was that I couldn't determine if that was the case in the cross-legged sitting position I was in. So, I inched forward until I was clear of the bush and lay down on my back, all the while moving only when the bear had his rear end toward me.

I almost broke out laughing when I realized what that scene must have looked like! There I was on my back in the wet grass with a section of my Fruit of the Looms pulled through my open fly while I frantically tried to dry off the lenses of my scope. Miraculously, the rain had stopped just minutes before. In what seemed like an eternity, I was able to clear the scope, roll over on my stomach, and shoot the bear from a highly unorthodox prone position.

******

Another time I was hunting in Maine, again out of a ground blind, but this time I was on a long-abandoned logging road. As always, the bait was placed in a clearing surrounded by thick brush to provide cover. The considered wisdom of bear hunters is that bears don't like to cross open ground on their way to dinner, so any good bait location will have thick brush cover next to it. If it's an established bait area that has been productive over time, it will also have well-defined paths through the forest and brush immediately behind it. That's the considered wisdom. I was just about to find out that not all bears get the memo!

So there I was, sitting well hidden in a blind with a good view of the bait, which was about sixty yards away. It was a bit uncomfortable because although it was the best vantage point, there were no trees to lean against. After an hour or so I was in a semistupor listening to the drone of mosquitoes outside my head net when I got this weird feeling I was being watched. I turned around to see a huge bear standing erect not more than ten feet behind me! There was no way I could turn 180 degrees from a sitting position and bring my rifle to bear—no pun intended. Luckily this guy was just as scared as I was—he obviously hadn't gotten the memo! He let out a loud wuff and was gone.

******

The next episode found me in New Brunswick. I was on the left side of a long-abandoned logging road, and if sitting on the ground with your back against a tree could be called a ground blind, then I was in a ground blind. Fifty yards down from me on the right side of the road was a small clearing where the bait was in an overturned fifty-five-gallon drum. On both sides of the road was underbrush so thick you couldn't see more than, maybe, twenty-five feet into the forest.

After about a half-hour a bear appeared. By using the bait drum for size comparison, I could see he was too small to shoot. Now watching the antics of a bear on a bait can be highly entertaining, so I did just that for about fifteen minutes until suddenly a larger bear emerged from the brush behind the bait. One look and Papa bear immediately gave chase—so intent was he on claiming the prize that he wasn't satisfied with just running the youngster off; he chased him right into the forest. The forest floor was dry enough that, although I couldn't see them, I could hear them running full tilt. At first it sounded as if they were going away, but then as the rustling started getting louder and louder, it became obvious they were circling and heading back in my general direction.

A few seconds more and I was certain they were no longer headed in my general direction; rather, they were headed straight at me! Judging from the racket, the bears couldn't have been more than thirty or forty feet away and they were closing rapidly. At that point the thought of having to defend myself never entered my mind, but I did feel a mite vulnerable and helpless just sitting there on the ground, so I instinctively brought my .444 Marlin 336 lever action to my shoulder.

It was a good thing, too, because a moment later a blob of black exploded out of the underbrush directly across the narrow road and headed straight for me! I didn't have time to think about Papa bear. All I could think about was that in another second I was going to be run over by a bear in full-panic mode. It didn't matter how small the bear was; he was still dangerous. The .444 barked like it had a mind of its own. The handloaded 240-grain Hornady XTP bullet turned that bear backward in midstride, and it died almost instantly some five paces from where I sat.

Now that bear had absolutely no idea that in another two seconds he'd be blundering smack into a human. Had I had the presence of mind to have waited another second or two before shooting, the bear would have realized what was happening and gotten out of there, in an even more frightened state than it already was. I never meant to shoot that bear; it was a matter of us both being in the wrong place at the wrong time.

******

You figure a point-blank episode with a bear like the one in New Brunswick is never going to happen again, but in the years following it did, and more than once. The first of these déjà vu incidents occurred on the fifth week of the black bear season on Vancouver Island in 2004. I and a couple of other writers were hunting as guests of Linda Powell, who for a decade handled press relations for Remington. Linda has this thing about hunting bears; she absolutely loves it and has done it enough times and in enough places to know where and with whom to book. At last count Linda had twenty bears to her credit, several of which are real monsters.

On our arrival after a short flight from Vancouver, we were met at the airport by Darren DeLuca who headed up Vancouver Island Guide Outfitters. On the flight over were a couple of other hunters who were booked with another of the island's several bear-hunting operations. They must have been greenhorns because both of them had gun cases the size of coffins, and each of their duffel bags could have held a Harley. I couldn't help but watch with some amusement as their meet-and-greet guy struggled to get all their luggage on a dolly and out to the parking lot.

"They'll learn," I said, turning to Linda.

"They will if they're smart, but some guys never do," she replied.

After a short drive we arrived at camp. Actually, "camp" doesn't quite paint an accurate picture. This was an elegant, eight-bedroom A-frame log chalet straight out of House Beautiful, complete with a lovely young chef by the name of Kristi who I would have put up against any Cordon Bleu graduate.

As we gathered on the porch the following morning, Darren issued our marching orders. "Jon," he said, "you go with Glen," pointing to a gaunt-looking chap leaning against a green Toyota that sat about six inches higher on its chassis than normal. I figured there couldn't be many places we couldn't get to in that rig, and if there were, I wouldn't want to go.

I was really looking forward to this hunt because it was to be a new experience for me. Up to that time all my previous bear hunts had been over bait, which wasn't allowed here. Here the modus operandi was to drive along the old logging roads while glassing opposing hillsides and clear cuts for foraging bruins. It was spring, and after a couple months of hibernation, bears are hungry. If they're not eating fish down at sea level, they're up on the mountainsides eating berries.

Within thirty minutes we were in hunting country, and what magnificent country it was. Snow-capped peaks rising over seven thousand feet from the surrounding ocean loomed in the distance. As rugged and steep as these mountains are, none apparently was too precipitous to preclude logging, the sole industry that has sustained Vancouver Islanders for over a century.

We would be hunting on just a tiny fraction of the huge island, but of the many square miles of it I did see, virtually every mountain bore the scars of clear cutting. Treeless tracts of one hundred acres or more dotted the flanks of every mountain, like huge scabs that are slow to heal. Every mountain had access roads carved into its flanks that from a distance looked like huge gray serpents. It's the combination of these old logging roads and the clear cut areas on opposing slopes that makes the spotting and stalking of bears feasible. As to how many bruins inhabit the island, it's estimated there's one for every square mile. That, Pilgrim, works out to twelve thousand bears!

Glen and I hunted till midmorning and then went out again around four o'clock and kept at it till dark. All told, we hunted about seven hours that first day and saw ten bears. Of course seeing a bear is one thing; being able to see it long enough and well enough to assess its size and sex—they don't shoot sows—and get within shooting range, was quite another. Of the ten bears we saw, only two had Glen's OK, but there was no way we could have gotten to either one because they were too far away.

169

I find it very difficult to judge bears, so I was perfectly content to leave that chore to Glen, especially after he told me he had taken one hundred and fifteen black bears over the ten years he had been guiding part-time. I wasn't holding out for a giant, but based on the number of bears that were on the island, I felt there was no reason to settle for anything short of a really good one.

The gun I had chosen to use was Remington's Model 673 Guide Rifle, which the company had just introduced that year, chambered in .350 Remington Magnum. It caught Glen's attention the moment he saw it, and with good reason, for you don't often see a 20-inch-barrel carbine with a ventilated rib and a huge, rearward-sweeping front sight that looks like a shark fin. Further distinguishing it is its wood laminated stock comprised of 5/16-inch-thick, alternating layers of blonde and walnut-colored birch.

As for the .350, it would be hard to come up with a better cartridge for black bear. For one thing, it makes a .35-caliber hole going in, and that's good. If the 200-grain Core Lokt expands as it always does, that hole opens up to around three-quarters of an inch in diameter, and that's better. Exiting the muzzle with 3,420 ft-lbs of energy, this cartridge is one that, well, ain't no bear gonna' laugh off! It does all that in a light, fast-handling short-action carbine. Unfortunately, the 673 was unappreciated to the point where it was discontinued in 2007 after just three years in production. You just never know what the public wants.

Day Two saw Glen and me back at it just after dawn. We had barely gotten into the hunting area when coming around a turn we spotted a bear feeding on the grass at the side of the elevated road about 250 yards ahead.

"That's a good one," said Glen, without even raising his binocular.

As we watched from the Toyota, he grazed for another minute or so and then exited stage right into the bush.

"I don't think he saw us," said Glen. "He sure didn't seem all that concerned. C'mon, let's take a walk up there. You never know."

The road made it possible for us to silently approach the spot where we had last seen him. The ground fell off sharply at the edge of the road, and we were standing about fifteen feet above a dense thicket that gave way to black timber about fifty yards away. Bears can move through brush with amazing silence when they want to, but they can also make an incredible racket when they feel there's nothing to fear. We couldn't see him, nor he us, but the moving bushes betrayed his position and the direction of his movement.

Without saying a word, Glen pulled a predator call from his pocket and gave it a couple of toots. Damned if those moving bushes some twenty-five yards away didn't start moving toward us! Steadily and with enough noise to wake the dead, the shaking brush got closer and closer until finally, at the base of the embankment not twenty feet below us, a huge black head appeared. At that point I'm sure the bear had not yet realized the situation as he stalked up the bank straight for us.

Even though I had my scope cranked down to 3X, at that distance the bear's head nearly filled a very fuzzy field of view. Using his eyes as the only reference point I could make out, I put the reticle just to the side of his snout and a couple of inches down. I loosed the 200-grain Core Lokt, and the bear did a backward somersault, collapsing in a heap not twenty feet below where we stood. The bullet had entered his brisket, penetrated his entire length, and was recovered at his hip joint, perfectly expanded and weighing 161 grains, or 80 percent of its original weight. Even Glen was impressed with the .350's performance. The skull measured 18⅞ inches. It was, and still is, the best black bear I've ever taken.

******

So far my encounters with "charging" bears were simply a matter of a hapless bear blundering into bad luck. I have to admit, though, if they had, in fact, been actual charges, how would the last couple of seconds of both incidents looked any different from the real thing?

I've had other run-ins with bears where their actions were as deliberate as they were bizarre. The incident that immediately comes to mind is the bear that wanted to join me in the tree stand. The first time it happened I was again hunting with Linda Powell of Remington, this time with W&S Outfitters near the town of High Level in central Alberta. There I was, sitting quietly in my elevated stand minding my own business and watching the antics of a too-small-to-shoot bear. I had been watching him for some fifteen minutes rummage about a fifty-five-gallon drum filled with molasses and oats when suddenly this jokester decides to climb into the tree stand with me.

My stand was about fifteen feet above the ground, but less than twenty yards from the bait. I hate being that close, but bear outfitters tend to do that in deference to their bow-hunting clients. Hell, with a rifle a hundred yards wouldn't be too far, and you wouldn't have to worry about scent, noise, or motion . . . within reason of course.

You would think that when you're twenty yards away, it would be hard to miss as big a target as a bear, but I have yet to be in a hunting camp where at least one bear wasn't missed and/or wounded and lost. Some outfitters have told me their hunters either miss or wound 15 to 20 percent of the time, and I can believe it. I was in one camp where over four days seven hunters missed or wounded six bears. Most of the time it's attributable to plain ol' "buck fever," but sometimes it's because the hunter aimed too low. When the baits are so close and when the hunter is in an elevated stand, it's all too easy to fail to take into account the rather steep downward angle of the bullet.

Anyway, judging the size of a bear can be tricky, but when you have a fifty-five-gallon at the bait site, well, that's how I knew this one wasn't a shooter. All of the sudden, this bear I had been watching stopped what he was doing and looked straight up at me, like he knew I was there the whole time. He then very deliberately walked over to the base of the three closely growing trees that supported my platform. Once he got directly beneath me, the wood floor of my perch hid him from sight, but I didn't have to see him—I could feel and hear that he was climbing the ladder.

Standing now, I moved to the edge of the platform, which consisted of two-by-fours nailed across two of the supporting trunks, to see my little visitor on the ladder about eight feet below me and closing. Holding my Marlin 444 like a pistol in my right hand, I lowered it to where the muzzle was just a few feet from Br'er Bear's nose. I was fully prepared to kill him had he gotten any closer, but it didn't come to that. I don't know if it was seeing me so close-up or the obscenities I was shouting, but he thought the better of it and backed down the ladder. I'm sure that bear was only being curious rather than aggressive, but still, you don't want to share a tree stand with a 150-pound bear.

Thinking such an incident had to be an anomaly, I soon learned that it wasn't. Two days later another and more worrisome episode happened when I was in a stand about twenty miles from where I had been that first evening. This second bear was the same size as the other one, but he had a small white patch on his breast whereas the other one had been solid black. The stand was a half-mile or so from the road where I was to be picked up, but I had forgotten my flashlight that day, so I wanted to leave my stand a few minutes earlier than usual. It was about twenty minutes before dark and I was just about to climb down from my perch when White Patch showed up.

Now I found I couldn't leave because I had a bear feeding fifty feet away. Whether it was a small bear or not, I didn't want to climb down, so I let out a shout, figuring that would have him outta' there like a shot. Not a bit! Instead, he just looked up at me. So I stood up and started waving my arms and shouting, "Get outta' here, you dumb SOB."

That didn't work either. In fact, he padded over to the base of my stand, circled it a couple of times, and then started up the ladder.

Christ, not again! I thought.

White Patch had suddenly become worrisome. He had seen me, he knew I was there, and despite all my noise and movement, he still wasn't afraid. When he got to within about six feet of me, I did the same thing as before: I one-handed the Marlin and lowered it to where the muzzle was within about three or four feet of his nose, but this time I pulled the trigger.

You would think that such a horrendous muzzle blast just inches from his face would have had a more dramatic effect, but all it did was stop him from climbing any higher. That damn bear hung there for at least fifteen seconds, staring up at me the whole time before slowly backing down the ladder. It was as if it was something he did every day! Once on the ground, he sat for a minute or two looking around, and then he lay down directly below me.

At that moment I remembered the bottle of Cognac I had in my rucksack. Why I thought that hitting him with a bottle would have any effect when a .444 exploding in its face didn't, I can't say. So, making like a bombardier, I lined up my precious but almost empty bottle of Metaxa 7-Star and dropped it. It was a perfect hit, landing squarely on his noggin with an audible and satisfying thud. So help me, all that bear did was shake his head. He then walked over to the bait, lay down, and faced me.

It was getting fairly dark now, and I wanted to get out of there. So as a last resort other than shooting this bear, I fired a shot aimed about six inches in front of his snout, which had to sting him, as his head was resting on the ground. That did it, but just barely. He jumped to his feet, regained his composure, and calmly walked into the forest where after maybe twenty yards, he sat down again. I could still see part of his blackness through the foliage as I climbed down the ladder, but I figured he was far enough away for me to react if he tried anything funny once I was on the ground.

Before that hunt was over, another hunter in camp had a big bear try to climb into his stand. He shot it in the mouth with a .270 that left powder burns on the bear's face!

******

In May 2006 I was again hunting with Wally Mack's W&L Guide Services out of High Level, Alberta. That being a two-bear area, the first evening on stand I shot an average bear just to have one on the ground for article-writing purposes. I could then spend the remaining four days trying to collect a really big one. Nothing showed on the second evening, but the third day made up for it. In some ways the events of that evening were just as bizarre as those that had happened to me two years earlier.

As is customary with Wally's operation, clients are driven in ATVs right to the base of their tree stands, a policy that is quite the opposite of most outfitters that hunt bears over baits. Most guides feel that any bear that's working a bait is usually napping somewhere nearby during the day, so the less disturbance in the bait area the better. Outfitters and guides of this persuasion, therefore, will drop you off a quarter mile from your stand with instructions to enter the area and get into your stand as quietly as possible. The bold bears of High Level obviously didn't get the memo!

So help me, not thirty seconds after my guide dropped me off at my stand, I looked down from my platform that I had just reached to see one helluva big bear already approaching the bait! I hadn't even sat down or chambered a round, and the putt-putting of the departing Yamaha was still loud and clear! That bear had to have been no more than a lob wedge from the bait when I was dropped off.

Despite the noise and movement I was surely making as I was settling in, the bear never looked up. He passed the bait barrel of honey-laced oats and went straight for the other bait—beaver carcasses hung from a pole lashed between two trees. The rodent cadavers were no more than thirty feet from the base of my stand and had been hung nearly seven feet off the ground, so if a standing bear could reach them, he had to be a shooter. This one was.

With the evening having barely begun, I decided to just sit quietly and watch for a while. After all, bears can be highly entertaining. But not ten minutes had passed before a second, smaller bear shows up. Knowing its place, it stayed at the bait drum, which was a comfortable distance from where the big one was grappling with the dangling beavers. This went on for several minutes, with neither critter seeming to mind the presence of the other.

Suddenly, the smaller bruin began running toward my stand, passed underneath, and climbed a tree about ten yards behind me. He didn't stop until he was about twenty feet higher than I. So there he was, looking down at me and I up at him. After staring at each other for about a minute, he scrambled down the tree, walked over to my ladder, and started climbing. I didn't want to frighten the big one away, so when the climber got within a couple of feet from my platform, I literally punched him in the snout with the muzzle of my Remington Model 798 .30-06. He dropped to the ground, pawed at his snout a moment, then started up another tree, this time one that was about three feet to the left of my platform. When he got to where he was literally eyeball to eyeball with me, I again hit him with the muzzle of my rifle. He scrambled down the tree and went back to the bait drum like nothing had happened.

All the while this was happening, the big bear had been feeding utterly unconcerned. I decided that before some other bizarre event occurred, I'd better take the shot. Just as I was about to pull the trigger, my target padded over to the bait barrel and chased the smaller one off. He then tipped the drum on its side and rolled it around as though it were a Campbell's Soup can. When he offered me a perfect broadside shot, I took it. He ran about forty yards and piled up.

He was a beautiful bear with no rubs whatsoever. He squared 7 feet, 2 inches, yet he was only the third largest of the 10 bears taken by the five of us that week. The bigger ones squared 7 feet, 3 inches and 7 feet, 5 inches. As nearly as we can figure, we saw over 50 bears on that 5-day hunt, and only one of us hunted every day. If there's a better place to hunt black bears over bait, I don't know where it is . . . and if there's another place where bears are less afraid of humans, I don't know where that could be, either.

The Truth about Gun Tests

A significant percentage of hunters/shooters who read gun magazines on a regular basis do so because they're interested in "gun tests." Why? Well, there are several reasons, all of which fall under the umbrella of curiosity, but the three major ones are:

- You already own the basic model in question and are looking for reinforcement.

- You're shopping for a new rifle and want to make an enlightened decision.

- It truly is a new design, in which case you're interested in learning what makes it so.

Let's expand on the first reason why readers are interested in gun tests. When a new variation of "your" gun is introduced, it's natural to have an interest in reading what writers have to say about it, and you're looking for affirmation that you made a good choice. But let's face it, the vast majority of gun tests consist of reviewing minor variations of existing models.

Think about it: The major domestically produced bolt-action centerfire rifles have been around a long time. The Savage 110 and Weatherby Mark V, for example, have been with us since the late 1950s, and the Weatherby Vanguard/Howa for almost as long. The Remington 700 recently celebrated its fiftieth anniversary, though in reality the basic action goes back to 1948. As for the Winchester Model 70 Classic, the current version surfaced in the early 1990s, but the basic design goes back to 1936. The bottom line is: What are touted as "new models" differ from others in their respective product line-ups in only minor detail.

Reason two needs little further comment other than to say that most of us want to make our buying decision knowing what the alternatives are. Unless we've already made up our mind as to what we want, comparison shopping simply makes good sense.

Reason three needs no further comment.

So then, just what is it that readers expect to learn from the typical rifle test and evaluation (T&E)? Well, if you're not familiar with the gun in question, you really can learn a great deal about it by reading an article, presumably written by a credible authority. There are some things, however, you cannot learn, and those things just may be the most important of all.

Gun tests, if not unique, are quite different from reviews of most consumer products because each firearm is a law unto itself when it comes to performance. Take, for examples, a toaster, a camera, or a television. If we were to buy the same product that we read about, we know that it will perform exactly as described by the reviewer. The toaster will toast, the camera will operate exactly as described and render pictures of the same color and sharpness, and the television will have the same picture quality as the one reviewed.

A rifle, on the other hand, is a different story because there are so many variables involved that affect its performance, not the least of which is the person shooting it. We'll discuss that factor later, but for now let's start by looking at those things we *can* learn about a rifle from a typical gun test.

I'm not sure how many rifle evaluations I've done over the past half century, but it must be approaching one thousand, so I've long since developed a somewhat formulaic system, as I'm sure have most of my colleagues. The first thing I check the moment I pick up the gun is its weight. I've never encountered a rifle that didn't conform to its printed specifications except in the weight department. I've reviewed rifles that were as much as a pound off its specification, and it's always been on the optimistic side. In other words, I've never seen a gun that was *lighter* than the maker said it would be!

Among the many things that can be checked before going to the range are cartridge feeding and extraction. Sometimes I'll use dummy rounds—no powder or primer—to check functioning, but it can also be done at the range with live ammunition. If a rifle has a tendency for its bolt to bind, it will manifest itself when the action is cycled from the shoulder. That's because the pressure on the bolt handle comes from a different direction when the action is operated in a port-arms position compared to when the gun is shouldered. In the port-arms position, the bolt handle can easily be pushed in the direction parallel to the bore, which induces very little torque to the bolt. When operated from the shoulder, however, there is a tendency to push upward on the handle, which applies torque and that, in turn, has a tendency to bind all but the smoothest of bolts. Generally speaking, if the bolt on the test rifle has a tendency to bind, so too will all other examples of that rifle.

Other functions that can be assessed prior to a visit to the range is trigger tension, smoothness, and creep, as well as the effort required to cock the action (upward pressure to achieve handle lift). I've encountered some rifles that required so much effort to cock that they could not be cycled with the rifle shouldered. All the aforementioned functions can vary among rifles of the same make, model, and caliber, though it's usually within fairly narrow parameters.

Whether a barrel is free-floated or pressure-bedded is a fact not usually found among the manufacturer's specifications, but it can easily be checked. If you can't slip a piece of paper between the barrel and fore-end tip and slide it all the way back to the receiver, you know the barrel is pressure bedded. I've encountered some test guns that had large gaps along the sides of the barrel, and no pressure band at the fore-end tip indicating that they were *supposed* to be floated, yet they wouldn't pass the paper test.

If the gun in question is *really* new, we want to see what makes it tick, so taking it apart to see its innards is mandatory. Lifting the barreled action from the stock reveals all kinds of things a reader would want to know. Is the receiver pillar bedded, partially glass bedded in the receiver ring/recoil lug area, or sitting on a metal bedding block? What about the fire-control system? Is it a two- or three-position safety, and when engaged, does it block the trigger, the sear, or the firing pin?

How is the magazine designed? If it has a hinged floorplate, is the magazine box integral with the floorplate frame or is it a separate unit? Is the trigger-guard bow a separate unit? Are cartridges stored in a staggered column or in a straight row? If the former, are cartridges fed from a central position in alignment with the chamber, or from alternating sides of the magazine? If it has a detachable magazine, can it be loaded or refreshed through the ejection port when it's in the rifle? Most cannot.

Potential problems with the receiver bedding can be determined in the reassembling of the rifle. Once the action screws begin to tighten, they should come to a sudden stop within a quarter-turn. This applies to synthetic stocks, be they injection molded or laid-up fiberglass, as well as one-piece and laminated-wood stocks. If while tightening either the front- or rear-action screw, it begins to resist to the turning of the screwdriver (or an Allen or Torx bit) yet continues to allow further tightening with increased torque on the screwdriver, something is wrong with the bedding. In other words, if it feels like the screw is *almost* snug yet continues to tighten with a mushy feel, that means the stock or the receiver tang and/or the stock is bending. In either case, there are serious strains being induced to the bedding dynamics between these two critical components that can (and usually do) affect group size and consistency.

If there are obvious bedding problems with a test rifle, should they be addressed before going to the range? That's a tough call, but if the writer does fiddle with the bedding, is that rifle still representative of that make and model? One thing is sure—if I do any tuning of the rifle, I always mention it. It it's minor stuff, however, the kind that any owner can address, like shimming the receiver ring to float what was not but should have been a free-floating barrel, or shimming it at the fore-end tip to apply dampening pressure where there was none, I'll do that.

It's almost a given that if we were to take two identical rifles of the same make, model, and caliber, the best-shooting load in one will not be the best-shooting load in the other. As already stated, that's due to many factors, the barrel being the starting point. Though both barrels are ostensibly identical, each of the various operations of drilling, reaming, rifling, turning to contour, hubbing, and threading is done to within certain dimensional tolerances. So long as each operation is within those tolerances, it's acceptable. As close as the two barrels are to being exactly the same, they are not. Neither is the granular structure of the steel, nor the harmonics of the barrel as a bullet accelerates down the bore. Harmonics can be changed by altering the bedding or shortening the barrel slightly and recrowning the muzzle, but these certainly are not things that should be done to a test rifle.

There are other factors that can vary from rifle to rifle that can only be checked by a machinist. One of these is the concentricity of the chamber/bore and the "squareness" of the bolt face relative to the bore line. Receivers can warp in the heat-treating process and as a result, the bolt, hence the bolt face, will not be square. When such is the case, there can be uneven contact between the locking lugs and their abutment surfaces. I've seen twin-lug actions where one lug was barely contacting its bearing surface, even after several boxes of ammo were put through the gun. Again, these conditions can be present in a rifle that passes its manufacturer's tolerances. Rectifying these conditions is part of what they call "blueprinting" an action.

Another condition that can occur in one rifle but not the next one off the assembly line is the uneven bearing of the recoil lug. Generally speaking, if it's a wood stock, recoil forces of the first few boxes of ammo will compress and seat the lug so that it's bearing across its entire surface. However, with a synthetic stock or one with a metal abutment surface, the condition is not likely to rectify itself.

There was a time when I worked up handloads if a test rifle didn't perform as well as I thought it should, but I no longer do that. The only thread of commonality between the rifle I test and the rifle you buy is factory ammunition. Even though you may get better or worse accuracy than I got, we at least can try the same load(s). And even then, chances are you'll be using a different lot (manufacturing run) of ammunition, even though it's the same load. It's not much, but that's about as close as we can get to duplicating conditions.

With handloads there's a nearly infinite number of possible combinations of bullets and seating depths, powder type and charge weight, primers, and differences in case preparation. Any one or more of these combinations can make a rifle a stellar performer . . . but only that *particular* rifle because, remember, every rifle is a law unto itself.

Last but not least, we come to that variable alluded to at the outset: the man behind the gun. Say we have a genuine half-minute rifle. How many of us can shoot it to its potential, especially if we're talking a big-game rifle in the

.300 magnum class or more? Having fired a couple hundred thousand rounds from the bench, I'm a fair-to-middlin shot, but I'll be the first to admit that I can't match what an accomplished benchrest shooter could probably wring out of that same rifle if it's chambered for a mild-recoiling benchrest cartridge. I might have an edge with larger and heavier recoiling calibers because I test all of them, from .17s to .470s, but it wouldn't be much of an edge.

There are a few rifle companies that guarantee accuracy, mostly it's MOA (1 inch at 100 yards), but some even guarantee one-half MOA. If the consumer gets reasonably close to what the maker claims, he's usually satisfied because he knows the sample target sent with the rifle was probably fired in an underground test tunnel where there's no wind and mirage to contend with; that the scope used was probably of a much higher magnification than the one he's using; and the guy doing the shooting was a professional.

Still, there's always a few who will send the rifle back to the maker because they can't duplicate the accuracy that was guaranteed. In some cases it was because the buyer didn't use the same control factory load or handload. In other cases it was due to a change in the bedding dynamics of the rifle, be it the result of "tinkering" or simply climatic changes. In still other cases it could be due to the fact that the customer simply couldn't shoot well enough. In the latter case, if a returned rifle is checked out and it does indeed pass the maker's guarantee, it brings about the awkward situation where the buyer has to be told as diplomatically as possible that he can't shoot.

What it all boils down to is that there are many things one can learn about a rifle by reading a T&E, but when it comes to accuracy, it only applies to *that* rifle. I've shot groups with test guns that were so small that I hesitated to report them, for fear some reader would buy that same gun and not get the same results. Such is the nature of this gun-writing business. With today's rifles and premium ammunition, a buyer can expect the sporter-weight rifle he buys to shoot—and I'm sticking my neck out here—1¼-inch, 3-shot groups at 100 yards with fair consistency with at least one- in-five factory loads tried. Many will do better, much better, especially if it's a heavy-barrel varmint/target rifle.

Last but not least, the writer has an obligation to express his subjective analysis of the gun's design. By this I mean, he should state what are its good and bad features and how the gun's overall quality and mechanical performance relate to its price. The latter is important because you can't expect a five-hundred-dollar rifle to be of the same quality as a fifteen-hundred-dollar one. Other than that, however, as for all the other elements—the fit, finish, mechanical performance, etc.—the consumer has every right to expect the same should he purchase that same gun.

******

Another aspect of gun tests—or the review of any consumer product for that matter—has to do with readers and how much faith they have in the reviewer's objectivity. There is an understandable cynicism on the part of many readers as to how objective a writer can be when evaluating a given gun for publication. I'm talking full-time writers now, whose livelihood depends on maintaining a good rapport with the press relations people who we must rely on to get the stuff we write about.

This is opposed to the part-timers who can afford to annoy a manufacturer because they have real jobs and write only as a hobby. (I've never considered what I do as a real job.) Many of them feel superior because they're convinced we're in the pockets of the gun/ammo/optic companies and, therefore, never have a bad thing to say about anything, while they seem to relish denigrating everything. It reminds me of the "experts" who live on the Internet forums and who revel at telling each other what jerks we gunwriters are.

Some manufacturers take pride in the fact that the guns they send out to writers for evaluation are taken right out of inventory and are not specially selected in any way. It sounds good in theory, but I think it's a false pride and a stupid practice. I've gotten a good number of guns over the years that flat out didn't function properly . . . or at all. To send out a gun to a reviewer without making sure it is at least representative of that particular model is not a smart idea. When I have received a poor sample, I'll return it to the manufacturer, tell him what the problem(s) was, and ask for another. In every such instance that I can recall, the problem was addressed with the second gun, and I was able to review it objectively and with a clear conscience.

If, on the other hand, the same problem exists with the second gun, I would return it and not write about it. I think most of my colleagues feel the same way, and the resulting silence is, in itself, damning. I don't want to waste my or the readers' time putting two thousand words together if the product is a turkey; there's too many good guns out there for that. So if you notice a decided lack of coverage for a particular gun, draw your own conclusions.

I've always questioned the relevance of doing T&E's on a gun that includes accuracy testing using handloads. I feel the reader has a right to expect the writer to critique a gun's design, its history, and how it evolved; he also has a right to expect the writer to comment on the mechanics, functioning, quality of construction, and finish as it relates to the price of the gun. A rifle, however, unlike, say, a camera, is a law unto itself when it comes to accuracy.

The Car Nut

If there are such things as status symbols among gunwriters, they're a Rolex watch and a four-wheel-drive Chevy Suburban. Now I readily admit to being as shallow and superficial as they come, but I covet neither. It just may be the iconoclast in me, but give me a thirty-dollar Timex digital any day. They do so many more things than a Rolex, and they do it better. Moreover, instead of sending your fancy Rolex to the company every five years for cleaning and an expensive "tune up," you throw away the Timex and replace it with a thirty-five-dollar model. Always upward!

As for the Chevy Suburban, I've never had a need for such a leviathan. Even when my two boys, Ian and Sean, were growing up, a station wagon or an SUV was big enough for anything we did as a family. Almost as popular among my colleagues is a Jeep or a pickup outfitted for extreme off-road excursions. The way I see it, that's what my guide is supposed to own. Let him beat the hell out of his vehicle rather than me with mine. Why should I drive something slow, noisy, and uncomfortable for the few times a year I'll actually need its off-road capabilities? This all assumes you have only one vehicle, and most of us don't. Except for the first couple of years when Judith and I were struggling, I've always had a second car.

My daily drivers have always been utilitarian—something that looks good, gets good gas mileage, and is dead reliable. So for most of my life I've driven Hondas and Mazdas. In fact, my current DD is a Mazda6. It's a great car. It's that second car that's important to me—my status symbol, as it were. As a teenager when I could afford only one car, all my friends wanted a 1957 Chevy. I had a 1957 Studebaker Silver Hawk in which I never lost a drag race to a 1957 Chevy. The only reason I owned the Studebaker was that I couldn't afford an MGA. From the time I was old enough to even think about driving, I was a sports car nut.

So, too, was my older brother, Dick. (I never called him Richard.) When I owned the Studebaker, Dick had a Triumph TR3, then an MGA. We competed in hill climbs, and we raced a Porsche 356 Speedster in SCCA, followed by a 911, and finally an Elva-BMW. My brother did pretty well, finishing third two years in a row in the northeast division against two millionaires who had factory backing. We made it to the American Road Race of Champions at Sebring and Riverside.

When I was finally able to afford a second car, around 1975, I bought a new Triumph TR7. Within a year though, Lotus had introduced its Esprit S1, and when I saw the James Bond movie *The Spy Who Loved Me*, I fell in love with that car and had to have it. I read all the road tests and had pictures of it above my desk. Within a year I had one—white with a white leather interior. I think it was one of only three produced in that color combination that made it to the States; the others went to the Middle East. As I recall, I paid around eighteen grand for that car, which was about four times as much as I paid for the Triumph.

As an illustration of how impractical I am—some would say insane—at that time we lived close to the upper Allegheny River just north or Emlenton, Pennsylvania. It was exactly two miles to our mail box, and we had to go through a forest down a steep, dirt logging road no longer used for logging and not maintained by anyone. I had four and a half inches of ground clearance on the Lotus, so I had to crawl my way up and down that road. To get out in the wintertime, our daily driver was a four-wheel-drive International Scout that often needed chains to get up the mountain. We had to make that run twice a day, five days a week, to get our boys to the mailbox where they were picked up by the school bus.

In 1978 we moved about eight miles to the tiny town of Clintonville on Interstate 80. When I say tiny, the population was 435 as I recall, and it was surely the first, and possibly the only Lotus Esprit ever to be seen in that hamlet. I'll never forget the first time I drove into town. There was a small grocery store called Ski's, and it had a small parking lot that could fit about eight cars. It was the only grocery store in town and small enough that the stock boy would carry your groceries out to your car. As the kid grabbed my two bags, he asked: "Which is your car?"

"The Lotus," I replied.

"What color?" he asked.

My next car was a Porsche 944 Turbo, which was almost as out-of-place in Clintonville as the Lotus. I replaced that car in 1991 with another Lotus Esprit. Why? Because it had a new but just as exotic a body style as the S1, and it was featured in another James Bond film, *For Your Eyes Only.* Like my previous Lotus, it was white, just like in the movie.

For all the fifty years I've been an exotic car nut, what I really wanted all along was a Lamborghini. From the Miura, through the Countach, the Diablo, the Murcielago, the Gallardo, the Aventador, and the Huracan, my passion has always been for Lamborghinis. So that's what I've been driving for the past twelve years. I may be a shallow, superficial guy who doesn't spend money wisely, but color me happy. And, yes, the current one is white.

South Africa: Then and Now

Chapter 24

In many ways it was all so familiar. As I boarded a South African Airlines 747 at JFK bound for Johannesburg with my younger son, Sean, I thought back to the time twenty-five years earlier when it was my wife, Judith, who was the one accompanying me. That was 1978. When his mother and I made that memorable trip a quarter century before, Sean was just nine years old. Now, in 2002, I was again traveling to South Africa to hunt but this time with my son.

Our first trip to South Africa long ago was also Judith's first visit to Africa and my second. The previous year I had hunted in Zimbabwe when it was still Rhodesia, and its capital city, Salisbury, was a virtual botanical garden. The time was 1977, and the civil war in Rhodesia was at its height. Just moving about in the hinterlands was a spine-tingling adventure. I mean, when it's a very real possibility that we might drive over or step on a land mine or get into a fire fight, it adds a whole 'nother dimension to the hunt!

Accompanying Judith and me on that first South African hunt were friends of ours, Joyce and Marvel Hornady of Hornady bullet fame. As a small digression, Joyce and I made another safari together the following year in Zambia, but then shortly thereafter Joyce was killed en route to the SHOT Show in New Orleans. Joyce's Piper Aztec crashed in horrendously bad weather into Lake Pontchartrain on its final approach. Judith and I were just checking into our hotel room when we heard the news. The only information available at the time was the type of plane and the fact that it had originated from Grand Island, Nebraska. That was all we needed to know.

Anyway, that first hunt I made in South Africa so long ago was primarily for nyala, and the area best known for these beautiful, spiral-horned antelope is the Zululand region of Natal, situated a couple hundred miles north of Durban just inland from the Indian Ocean. Now I was returning to the exact same area a quarter of a century later to witness my son's virtual retracing of my footsteps—footsteps so vivid in the soil of my memory they could have been made yesterday.

Back in 1978 our professional hunter was Norman Dean, owner of Zululand Safaris and one of the pioneers of ranch hunting in South Africa. Norman had recently taken delivery of two new Toyota Land Cruisers and just prior to our arrival had completed fitting them with the roll bars, high seats, a winch, and all the other accoutrements that define a hunting vehicle. He was quite proud of them.

One evening while hunting on an old, overgrown pineapple plantation where the grass was quite thick and high, Norman drove one of his spanking new vehicles into a six-foot-deep, vertical-walled poacher's pit. I wasn't in the vehicle at the time, but Judith was. She was pitched over the laid-down windscreen onto the hood, and from there into the hole. Fortunately, the Toyota stayed high-centered on the edge of the pit, so it didn't nose over and drop down on top of her.

Nevertheless, she was pretty banged up with a sore stomach, bruised elbows, and a cut on her hand. Safari car-related mishaps are a reality of safari life, for no matter how civilized the hunt, you're still driving over undeveloped land where warthog and antbear holes abound. In fact, I can't think of a single safari among the twenty I've been on that didn't have some issue with the vehicle . . . either mechanically or simply a flat tire or tires.

There were, of course, property/livestock fences in those days, but they were just ordinary strand-type fences about four feet high. They were of no hindrance to wild game. There may have been a few game-proof fences around, but neither of us can remember seeing any. Again, this was the 1970s when ranch hunting was still in its infancy. It was an idea whose time had come, however, and there were a number of reasons why.

For one, recent changes in the game laws not only in South Africa but also in Rhodesia and South-West Africa made game animals the property of the landowner. If, for example, a kudu on my property crossed a fence onto my neighbor's property, it became his kudu . . . and vice-versa. One must keep in mind that the hunting all across Southern Africa had always been fantastic; it's just that it hadn't been developed as a tourism industry as it had in East Africa and Mozambique. Prior to the 1970s, the residents were quite content to keep their excellent hunting to themselves, thank you.

Another reason for the impetus in ranch hunting was the fact that the aforementioned traditional safari areas of the 1950s and 1960s were either closed to hunting or were about to. It was also easier and more economical to travel to Africa than ever before, and no one publicized that fact better than what was then a dynamic young organization known as Safari Club International. SCI popularized the idea that African hunting wasn't all the Big Five; that there was a vast variety of beautiful antelopes that could be hunted for a fraction of the cost of a classic Big Five safari; and that safaris could be arranged in time frames as short as ten, seven, or even five days of actual hunting.

With an ever-growing number of hunters, Americans especially, wanting to hunt on the Dark Continent and realizing they didn't have to shoot a buffalo or a lion or an elephant to truly experience what Africa was about, well, as I said, everything was in place for the ranch-hunting concept to come of age. It didn't take long for the fledgling industry to make landowners realize just how valuable their animals were, and how selling hunting rights to professional hunters or hunting companies could be more profitable than cattle ranching or farming. Of course, when that happened, game-proof fences did go up. Suddenly, wild critters were now too valuable to be left to their own whims to wander wherever they wanted to go.

Another aspect of hunting in South Africa that is markedly different today than it was forty years ago is with the accommodations. Back in Norman Dean's Zululand Safaris camps in the mid-1970s—as with the relatively few other similar operations in existence at the time—tents were the norm. I'm talking nice tents, mind you, with screened windows and sewn-in floor, but tents nonetheless. There was no electricity, running water, flush toilets, cell phones, satellite phones, TVs, VCRs, CD players, GPS units, computers, or email. The hunts may have been rather civilized, but when you were in the bush, you were in it to the extent that there was no instant communication with the outside world. If there was trouble with the vehicle, you had to deal with it or send someone back on foot.

Of course, not all camps had tents. Some consisted of small chalets situated on the ranch where you were hunting, or you stayed in the ranch house proper. The latter offered all the luxuries of home, but it lacked the ambiance most of us want on an African hunt. We want that feeling of being if not *in* the bush, than at least close enough to touch, to hear, and to smell the magic that is Africa. We want to be able to look up and search a star-choked canopy of black for the Southern Cross, and we want to see the orange faces of friends across a flickering fire. We want to "feel" the ambiance of those moonlit evenings where for long periods not a word is spoken across the campfire, as if doing so would be like shouting during a benediction.

Setting the proper atmosphere is what the hunt operators have learned so well. The typical hunting camp in South Africa today is not a "camp" at all, not by any stretch of the imagination. Rather, it is more like a hotel, African style. That's not bad, mind you, unless you're determined to rough it. Today's typical camp ranges from what I'd describe as "deluxe" to "luxurious." Frankly, I've not seen anything but the latter in recent years, and I can assure you I've not been on anything that could be described as a big-bucks hunt.

That hunt I made back in 2002 with my son, for example, had us in two camps because we wanted animals from different areas. One of the camps was called Hannah Lodge in Mpumalanga, and we were there because the area was particularly noted for its large kudu; the other was Tibani Lodge in Zululand, and that area was noted for its nyala. These camps consisted of individual chalets of stucco and thatch, which captured the flavor of native architecture yet were thoroughly modern in all respects. Each chalet was a separate unit with all the amenities you'd expect in a first-class hotel.

The main lodge at Tibani was completely open in the rear, which is something you can do architecturally in that kind of climate. The open back provides an unobstructed view of the bush and a waterhole some four hundred yards distant where from a well-stocked bar and a comfortable stool you could watch animals come to drink in the evening. Just below the main floor of the lodge was a patio with a swimming pool and a few yards beyond that was a *boma* where we enjoyed a traditional South African *braai*, or barbecue, one evening with native Zulu dancing afterward.

That's an overview of the creature comforts offered. What's the hunting like? Actually, that part of it hasn't changed all that much in forty years except for the fact that there's far more huntable game today than there was back then. In fact, according to my friend and colleague, Craig Boddington, he believes there's *ten times* as much game in South Africa and Namibia now than there was when we first hunted there. Prior to 2000, he said the same could be said for Zimbabwe, but after Mugabe's land grab, it's no longer true.

Today it's still up to the client as to how he wants to hunt. You may choose to minimize the use of a vehicle, or not use one at all. Most hunters, however, opt to use the vehicle to get around and spot game. If you see something worth going after, you then pursue it on foot. Generally speaking, within an hour you'll either catch up with what you're after, or you'll know that you've been given the slip.

That hunt with my son was actually a busman's holiday for me. I was testing the then-new 7mm Winchester Short Magnum in a custom Ruger 77 Mk II I had built up using the standard-length action rather than a short one so that I could seat bullets out as far as I wanted. I had a 24-inch stainless, fluted barrel with a long throat fitted by E. R. Shaw, which I glass bedded myself into a Boyds' laminated stock. The scope was a Zeiss fixed 6X42 that has, alas, long since been discontinued.

I was also field-testing the equally new at the time 154-grain Hornady SST, a bullet similar to Nosler's Ballistic Tip, but supposedly tougher. With this bullet seated out to where its base was flush with the base of the neck, I was getting 3,170 fps. I planned on letting my son and others in the party do most of the shooting—I hoped using my rifle. As it turned out, nine critters fell to the 7mm WSM, only two of which I shot myself . . . just to keep my hand in, so to speak. Most of the bullets exited, but the skinners managed to recover four of the SSTs. One had shed its core, and the other three weighed about 60 percent of their original weight. This was good performance for a bullet of that type.

Looking back with a forty-year perspective, there's no question but that today the hunting is much more "civilized" than it was back in the 1970s. But that applies all across Africa, and there's only so much you can do to block out that fact. You can choose to pretend the creature comforts don't exist, but you'll succeed only to a point. Good safari operators and professional hunters understand this and do their best to limit the intrusions of the outside world if they sense that's what you want. They also strive to maintain as much of the safari ambiance and traditions as possible. Given the realities of the electronics age in which we live, I'd have to say they do a pretty good job.

I enjoyed many other safaris to Africa as well. My most recent was for Cape buffalo in the Kigosi concession in northwestern Tanzania in 2008. It was my third safari in that wonderful country; the others were in the Selous in 1999—also a buffalo hunt—and in Masailand for plains game in 1983. If the opportunity comes along, I'd like to hunt in Mozambique. Back in the 1950s Mozambique was the place to hunt in Africa, but it was closed down for decades because of civil war (1977–1992). Only recently has it reopened, and most safaris there are done in the classic tradition using tents in camps far from civilization.

As this is being written, it's July of 2017, and I often reminisce of days long past and of an Africa that I once knew. At this point in my life I don't know if I'll have the chance to go on another safari. I'd like to and I'm in good health, but an old knee injury is starting to assert itself, even though I continue to walk fifteen miles a week. Should the opportunity arise, I just might answer Africa's siren call at least one more time.

One More Buffalo

I t is sad indeed when you find yourself engaged in something you've loved doing all your life and then suddenly realize you may be doing it for the last time. That melancholy thought flashed through my mind as I was catching my breath in the shadow of a termite mound somewhere in the huge Kigosi concession in northwestern Tanzania in October 2008. My PH, Jaco Oosthuizen, and his tracker, Nyoka, were a few feet off to my side glassing a large herd of buffalo we'd been shadowing for more than two hours.

There's something about the Cape buffalo that makes this species different from the other so-called Big Four of Africa. If one is fortunate enough to have hunted the others as I have—lion, leopard, and elephant—one each is enough for most. But when it comes to *nyati, m'bogo*, or whatever else you choose to call him, he's a whole 'nother critter. I think I'm speaking for most experienced African hunters when I say: "When it comes to buffalo, it's tough to pass on the opportunity to take 'just one more.'" It's a good thing there's no shortage of them, and there's not—they roam the savannas and *miombo* forests of East and Southern Africa by the tens of thousands. Charlie Askins, my old friend and colleague, had a goal to shoot one hundred Cape buffaloes, and if he didn't achieve it, he came awfully close.

Normally, a herd of Cape buffaloes wants nothing to do with man. If you're seen or you approach from the wrong direction wind-wise, they're off in a cloud of choking dust, like domestic cattle. But put a bullet in the wrong place on an ol' *dagga* boy, and you may be in for a lot more than you bargained for. Robert Ruark wrote that a wounded Cape buffalo looks at you "like you owe him money," but that's only the half of it.

What you also owe him is respect; he's earned it. If there's a creature anywhere on earth that is more courageous, or clings to life with more tenacity,

I can't imagine what animal it might be. I have seen mortally wounded buffalo do things that if I hadn't seen it for myself, I would never have believed it.

So that's why I was there, hunting *nyati* again. Maybe it had to do with the adage that says if one drinks from the Zambezi, one is destined to return to Africa. All I know is that every time I was on that river, I drank all the water I could. But anyone who knows me knows that couldn't have been much. I'm not big on water.

When I say "hunting nyati again," I've had the good fortune to have hunted them in Rhodesia, Zimbabwe, Zambia, and Tanzania . . . and more than once in three of those four countries. Only two of those several encounters turned out to be a bit dicey. One was on my first buffalo hunt on Namembere Island on the Zambezi River; the other was on a Zambian safari in 1979 when my PH, Gerard Miller, had enough confidence in me to let me help him track down a buff one of the other clients had wounded. In both incidents the bull had circled back and was waiting to ambush us as we followed its trail. Luckily, we spotted the bull before it came at us.

My hunt in the Kigosi concession thus far had been pretty much a typical Cape buffalo encounter. By that I mean, finding the buffalo was easy because the terrain was dead flat and in many places the grass was only a couple of feet high, so we could see the backs of the animals from a long way off. In areas where the grass was too high and you couldn't actually see the animals themselves, the blindingly white egrets that flit above and follow the herd constantly betray their presence. Were I a buffalo, egrets would not make my best-friends list.

Nope, the difficulty in buffalo hunting lies in trying to identify a big bull out of literally hundreds of milling horns and ears and eyes and backs—all amid swirling dust. This was my twentieth African safari and I was no better at judging horns than I had been on my first Cape buffalo hunt in old Rhodesia some thirty-one years before. Seeing an old *dagga* boy by himself or with a couple of other old studs is one thing, but how these professional hunters can tell the difference between a forty-inch and a forty-two-inch buffalo among hundreds of tightly packed bodies never ceases to amaze me.

Looking at the herd of tightly packed Cape buffalo bodies that day on the Tanzanian plain reminded me of a hunt I made in the Bangweulu area of

Zambia back in 1980. We were hunting black lechwe, and before us had to have been at least five thousand lechwes grazing on a shallow floodplain in front of us. I swear every buck I saw was sporting horns of at least twenty-three inches in length, but my PH, Robin Voight, was looking for something over twenty-five inches. I don't know how long we glassed, but it took me only a few minutes to realize that my trying to identify a pair of horns that were maybe 5 percent or so longer than those of a couple thousand others was futile. Besides, that's why you have a professional hunter. Once I came to that conclusion, I just sat there and let him do the glassing. Finally, after a seemingly interminable length of time, Robin said, "I see him," in the hushed voice of a golf commentator—as though the herd three hundred yards away would spook if he spoke any louder.

To make a long story short, it took nearly an hour before the buck worked himself into a position where I had a clear shot. It could easily have gone the other way with the buck moving deeper into the herd and with us losing sight of him entirely. As it turned out, had I entered that buck in the SCI record book, it would have been the new No. 1 back then; today it's rank would be just average.

Anyway, seeing the buffalo you want and getting a shot at it are two entirely different things. The herd we were now shadowing was the sixth we had approached over the past three days, and all of them ended with either not seeing a big bull or not getting a shot at one. Big bulls don't get to be big bulls by being stupid. Any time you have a herd consisting of a couple hundred animals, you can be pretty sure there's going to be at least one or two studs in it.

Getting close to a big bull is an entirely different matter as well. Whenever the herd's disturbed, the animals will cluster together in a tight group with the big bulls always managing to stay near the center. It's difficult to even catch glimpses of these big guys, let alone get a shot. You have to wait patiently until the herd settles down and starts grazing and until there are no others either in between or behind your target. Only when they start stringing out will you momentarily have a clear shot.

This particular hunt was one of those ten-day "buffalo only" hunts that were (and still are), being offered by some outfitters in Tanzania. I believe these deals offer the best chance at a really good bull—say over forty-two inches. The license I had allowed me to hunt a member of the Big Four in what is probably the best buffalo country in Africa, and do it for considerably less than the cost of a multispecies fourteen- or twenty-one-day license. Hell, in three days I'll bet Dick Metcalf, my friend and colleague, and I saw more than fifteen hundred buffaloes, as did the other client who was hunting out of the same camp but in a different area.

The Kigosi concession is an area some seventy miles north to south, and thirty-five miles east to west. If memory serves, Jaco said it was around 1.6 million acres. The area we were hunting was dead flat, and though bone dry while I was there in October, it is flooded during the rainy season.

One feature that I found unusual was that most termite mounds in this area were covered with long grass and pinchy, palmetto-like plants that made lying down impossible. In all other areas in Africa where I've hunted, there always seemed to be a termite mound within sight that was either bare earth or had only sparse grass growing on it. These handy termite mounds not only furnish cover for a stalk but they also provide height for a commanding view. Finally, the sides or top of the mound itself provide the hunter with a stable rifle rest that allows for a steady prone-shooting position. Without the advantages a termite mound can provide, my only recourse for a rifle-steadying rest was the stick tripod that Nyoka always carried. Because the grass was too high for sitting, much less lying prone, I had to use the tripod from a standing position.

There were at least three hundred buffaloes in the herd that Jaco was now evaluating. We were at the edge of a palm-covered termite mound that had provided the cover for us to get this close, which was about a hundred and fifty yards. It was, however, the last bit of cover between us and them, so this was as close as we were going to get.

It's funny how things suddenly pop into and out of your head, and at the strangest times. It was when I sat there quite detached from what was going on that the thought this possibly might be my last safari flashed through my consciousness. A moment later that, too, evaporated. Suddenly, I began to think about why I had chosen the rifle that was now leaning against my shoulder.

For all my previous buffalo hunts in Africa and Australia I had used a .375, either the H&H or my wildcat version thereof, the .375 JRS, which is simply the H&H case "improved." In either case, I never had cause to question whether or not I was using enough gun. Nevertheless, this time I wanted to use a .416, for it delivers a bullet of larger diameter that's also 25 percent heavier and arrives with substantially more energy. As good and as versatile as the various .375s are, it's not generally considered a "stopping" caliber; the .416 is.

In commercial chamberings there's not a lot to choose from. There's the .416 Rigby, the .416 Remington Magnum, and the .416 Ruger. There's also the proprietary Dakota and Weatherby versions, which are excellent, but I wanted to stick to a more mainstream cartridge. The Rigby version requires a true magnum action and guns so chambered are generally expensive. As for the .416 Ruger version, it had just been announced a couple of weeks before I left for Africa, and they could not get a gun to me in time. I decided to go with a Remington 700 Safari Grade in .416 Remington Magnum, a cartridge that ballistically duplicates the legendary Rigby version. At the time Remington offered only one load for its .416: a 400-grain Swift A-Frame bonded core. In the event Jaco wanted me to have solids available, I brought a handload topped with Barnes's 400-grain slug.

Peering through his binocular, Jaco said, "There's one, Jon." Shocking me out of my reverie, I turned to Jaco and saw Nyoka already setting up the tripod behind him. To clear the termite mound, the tripod had to be placed off to the side where I was exposed to a few hundred eyes, albeit myopic ones. Thus began another of the same ritual we had gone through a couple of times already that day—of Jaco trying to describe to me the one specific animal he was observing through his binocular at 10X while I was looking through a riflescope set at 2X.

"He's got his head down . . . no, now it's up and he's turned to his left and touching noses with a . . . no, now he's gone back to grazing." If you've never been in such a situation, it's hard to visualize how difficult and frustrating it can be. Suddenly, like a gift from Diana herself, one of those lovely white egrets chose to land on the exact bull that Jaco had singled out as the one we wanted. Now there was no question as to which one I was supposed to shoot. He was 160 laser-measured yards away.

As my breathing and pulse accelerated—normal when game is in one's sights—I took stock of the situation. I knew that to shoot from a standing position with a one-point rifle rest is problematical. It's just not steady enough for distances of more than a hundred yards or so—at least not for me. So, as I waited for the opportunity for a clear shot to present itself, I was not as confident as I would have liked. My hold was simply not steady enough for me to want to pull the trigger, but I did anyway.

The 400-grain A-Frame broke the bull's front shoulder, but it was too low and too far forward to catch any of the heart or lungs. In other words, it was a lousy shot. The bull tried to stay with the herd as it thundered off in a choking cloud of dust, but he soon started to lag behind. It was only after about fifteen minutes of tracking and a couple more shots before I was able to catch up with that courageous animal and bring him down with a brain shot. At 44¼ inches and a 14-inch boss, it was the best buffalo I've ever taken, but it was also the least satisfying.

After the boys skinned my bull the following day, they found a crude lead ball just inches from where one of my Swift A-Frames had lodged, undoubtedly put there by a poacher using a primitive muzzleloader. Believe it or not, this was not the first buffalo I've shot that was carrying poacher's lead. My very first buffalo shot in Rhodesia so many years before had also carried poacher's lead, as did another old *dagga* boy I shot in Zambia a couple years later. What are the chances of that?

Guns I Wish I Still Had...and Those I'll Never Part With

Chapter 26

I t's a good thing I don't have a pack-rat mentality and that I'm not sentimental about guns. I couldn't afford to hoard because in all the years I've been writing about guns, literally thousands have passed through my hands. The vast majority of them I parted with having no regrets. However, there have been a few that, in retrospect, I dearly wished I had kept. It's what real estate people refer to as "seller's remorse."

Not that I've actually sold a lot of guns mind you; in fact, I've sold relatively few. The same can be said for the number I've traded or given away. Among those, and the hundreds and hundreds of guns I've returned, there are several that come to mind that I do regret not keeping. As a result of those ill-advised divestitures, there are also a few guns that I can't see myself ever parting with under any circumstance.

In the former category there was the Browning T-Bolt, a neat little .22 rimfire rifle made in Belgium by FN and marketed here by Browning from 1965 to 1974. The T-Bolt was based on a unique straight-pull action that required nothing more than a rearward pull and forward push of the bolt handle. The locking lug was a round, dime-size chunk of the right-side receiver wall that fit flush when the action was closed. It was the slickest thing I ever saw and I just had to have one.

Now, I had owned several .22 rifles before that T-Bolt, so I had a pretty good idea of what kind of accuracy one could expect from a sporter-weight rifle. I often wonder if that T-Bolt was as accurate as I remember it, or was I just less critical back then? All I know is that I've tested very few sporter-weight .22s that I thought were more accurate than what I remember that little Browning to be. A lot of dead fox squirrels would attest to that if they could.

Unfortunately, the T-Bolt came into my life at a time when I could at long last start pursuing my passions—centerfire rifles and big-game hunting. As a result, the T-Bolt had my attention but for a brief time before being relegated to a back shelf of my gun cabinet. One day while casually inspecting my guns, I noticed some rust appearing just above the seam line along the barrel channel. Upon removing the barreled action from the stock, I was appalled to find that every square centimeter of the barrel and receiver that was in contact with wood was badly pitted. I couldn't understand it because that rifle was never subjected to rain or snow without being thoroughly cleaned, dried, and oiled.

I later learned that in the mid-1960s Browning had purchased a bunch of walnut for which, believe it or not, salt had been used in the drying process. Literally every Browning firearm stocked with that wood had rusted wherever metal came in contact with it, just like on my T-Bolt. As I recall, Browning made good on all those guns, but by then I had long since traded off my T-Bolt in disgust. It's one gun I wish I still had, rust and all, if for no other reason than to see if the passage of time tightens groups.

Another gun I wished I still had is a custom Ruger No. 1 with which I took my first Cape buffalo in Rhodesia, my first elephant in Namibia, and a 46½-inch sable in Zambia. It was originally a No. 1-H Tropical model in .375 H&H that I had rechambered for my wildcat .375 JRS. This is simply an "improved" version of that grand old cartridge based on what was then the brand-new 8mm Remington Magnum that had simply been necked up to .375. It's a very practical wildcat in that you can safely fire factory .375 H&H ammunition in it in a pinch. Doing so simply fire forms the cases to the JRS chamber. You can also neck up 8mm Remington Magnum brass or neck down .416 Remington cases. Either way, my version squeezes nearly 2,700 fps from a 300-grain bullet that generates about 150 fps more velocity and 750 ft-lbs more energy than the standard .375 H&H. Finally, lending a distinctive appearance to the gun was the fact I had switched the original Alexander Henry-style forearm that comes standard on the model 1-H, which I've never liked, for the one that's furnished on the No. 1-B Standard Sporter.

Anyway, one evening while I and some friends were dining at a restaurant in Chicago, the owner, who was a gun aficionado and an avid *Shooting Times* reader, caught me at a weak moment and offered to comp the entire meal for the eight of us, for the Ruger. (It was a pretty serious tab!) As a bonus, he'd throw in a bottle of 1955 Chateau Margaux for me to take home. When I said no, he upped his offer to two bottles. Maybe it was because by then I had stopped using that rifle for dangerous game, or maybe it was the wine I already had in me, but whatever the reason, I agreed.

Yes, the dinner was memorable, and I had gained two bottles of Chateau Margaux. On the first occasion I opened a bottle, I found it had turned. With tears in my eyes, I emptied it into the kitchen sink. The other bottle had kept, and it was celestial. If I had to do it all over again, I would have kept the Ruger.

Another Ruger No. 1 for which I have seller's remorse is a 1-B in 6.5 Remington Magnum. It was forty-some years ago that I ordered the gun as a barreled action through the company's press relations department. I had a spare buttstock and 1-B forearm on hand, so when the BA finally arrived, I stuck the wood on it and proceeded with whatever editorial project for which I had ordered it. What I didn't realize was that Ruger never chambered any of its No. 1s for the 6.5 Remington Magnum, at least not as a cataloged item.

To make a long story short, a prominent Ruger collector who had read the article contacted me to ask if I would be willing to sell it. He was quite persistent, and I, not thinking there was anything really special about the gun, relented. Now, there may be other No. 1s out there in 6.5 Remington Magnum that made it out of the factory, but all I know is that there was one for sure!

Two other guns I regret having parted with were the Remington 591 and 592, the first and only production rifles ever chambered for the 5mm Remington Rimfire Magnum. I particularly regret having returned those guns to Remington now that we have the .17 Mach 2, .17 HMR, and .17 WMR. Announced in 1969, the 5mm Remington was truly revolutionary at the time; it was based on a unique bottlenecked case that launched a 38-grain jacketed bullet of .204-inch diameter at 2,100 fps. Essentially, it did nearly 50 years ago what the .17 Hornady Magnum Rimfire does today.

The only difference between the guns themselves was that the 591 was the "clip"-fed version, while the 592 had a tubular magazine. The rifles (as well as the cartridge itself), were so much more accurate than any .22 Winchester Magnum Rimfire I had tested up to that time. Moreover, the 5mm's 38-grain jacketed bullet was more streamlined than those of the .22 WMR. The 5mm was faster, hit harder, and had a flatter trajectory, which made it an effective groundhog cartridge out to 125 yards or more.

Little did I know when I returned those guns to Remington that within a few short years both they and the great little cartridge for which they were exclusively designed, would be out of production. Today, the guns are real collectors' items, as is the cartridge itself; an unbroken box of fifty is worth quite a bit I'm told.

Another "seller's remorse" episode concerns a highly customized Ruger No. 1-B barreled in John Lazzeroni's 7mm Tomahawk by Broad Creek Rifle Works. This rifle has a custom quarter rib that, unlike the original, contacts the barrel its entire length and is machined to accept Talley rather than Ruger scope rings. I've always considered the No. 1's ring spacing as being much too narrow, so I had new saddles cut so the rings would span the entire body tube of the 6X42 Leupold scope I planned to mount.

The hammer had been Swiss-cheesed to lighten it for a faster lock time, and a Moyers replacement trigger was installed. The safety's thumbpiece that normally sits *on* the receiver tang and often interferes with ejecting cases had been recessed into a milled slot. The forearm hanger had been extended and threaded to accommodate an externally accessible nylon-tipped screw that applied dampening pressure to the otherwise free-floated barrel. Through a small access hole in the forearm, a hex key was used to increase or decrease dampening pressure to tune the barrel for best accuracy.

That Ruger saw action on a Cape buffalo hunt in the Selous Reserve of Tanzania as my "light" rifle, but I used it only to pot plains game for camp meat. The reason I no longer have it is due to another collector who wouldn't take no for an answer and made me the proverbial offer I couldn't refuse.

So much for guns I regretted selling. Under the "Guns I'll Never Sell" heading is a Winchester Model 70 chambered in my .375 JRS. Around the mid-1980s the Winchester people asked me if they could start offering my wildcat as an option through their custom shop. Not that they actually needed my permission; it was really a courtesy call that I greatly appreciated.

Anyway, about a year later a package arrives unexpectedly from U.S. Repeating Arms and in it was a Model 70 Custom Express grade in .375 JRS. It has the standard Winchester barrel stampings, but the receiver carries no serial number; just a simple "JRS" on the right side. That makes for one very cool gun! I have yet to use it on a hunt.

Another gun I'll never part with is the Remington 700 on which I built my original 7mm JRS, a .280 Remington-based wildcat that maximizes the powder capacity of that slightly lengthened .30-06 basic case. The rifle is unique in several other ways. For one, the stock is an all-walnut laminate, but the layers are stacked horizontally rather than vertically. I built the rifle in the late 1970s when that was the only wood laminate that Fajen could get at the time. It's a terrible-looking thing because it's simply a stack of 5/16-inch-thick strips of wood. Luckily, with nothing but end grain visible on either side, it soaked up the stock finish to where it turned very dark and you can hardly see the various layers.

Another unique aspect of the rifle is its barrel—it has a step in it like on a military Mauser. The barrel had been fitted by E. R. Shaw, but when they returned the barreled action to me, it was of a heavier contour than I wanted. Not wanting to wait for them to make another barrel, I had them stick that one on a lathe and turn it down to a smaller diameter, starting about five inches from the receiver. It looks neat!

I lapped the action on that rifle to where it was so smooth that elevating the muzzle just fifteen degrees would have the unlocked bolt slide open. Contributing to that smoothness and lack of bolt friction was a two-inch piece of coat hanger wire that I had brazed to the upper left edge of the magazine follower so that it didn't intrude into the bolt raceway. It was purely an aesthetic thing that eliminated the *click-clack* you get when you cycle the bolt of an empty rifle, yet it still fed perfectly. I brought that follower with me to the Remington Writers' Seminar that year and showed it to their design team. It took a while, but two or three years later the follower on the Model 700 was changed accordingly.

This brings to mind another product that I was responsible for—the 140-grain .270 caliber bullet. Back when I was with *Shooting Times*, I had a regular column called "Bullshots" and in one installment I pointed out that the 20-grain gap in .270 bullet weight line-up was too great, yet no ammunition or bullet manufacturer up to that time had seen fit to split the difference. The only choice was 130 or 150—period. I thought it was high time to rectify that oversight and gave my rationale for doing so. I then ended the column by asking those readers who agreed with me to write to Joyce Hornady. Within eight months Hornady introduced a 140-grain .270 (.277 inch actually) Spire Point bullet. Soon thereafter every bullet maker and ammunition manufacturer offered component bullets and loaded ammunition in 140-grain weight.

I digress. I hunted with that original 7mm JRS rifle almost exclusively for several years and with it took more game in more places than any other rifle I've ever owned. It's long since been retired; in fact, it still has a strain gauge epoxied to the barrel from the time when I brought the gun to Bill Davis's ballistic lab for pressure testing. Over the period of time that I was using my original 7mm JRS, I built three others, one based on a Winchester Model 70 action, one on a Sako L61, and the third on a Ruger 77 Mk II. All shot as well or better than the original, but together they saw very little time afield.

As I said, it's good that I'm not sentimental about guns, but I do have regrets about having parted with a few of them. With the passage of time, some have taken on a sentimental or monetary value they simply didn't have back then, and I'm sorry now that I let them go.

Fortunate Hits and Mysterious Misses

Chapter 27

L
ives there the hunter who hasn't experienced at least one mysterious miss in the field? I think not, especially if you've done a reasonable amount of hunting in your lifetime. I'm not talking about missing a challenging shot—like offhand at a running antelope or bounding buck. Nope, I'm talking about when you've got an animal standing well within range, you've got a rock-steady hold, and still you miss.

It's happened to me more than once, though I must say, considering the number of animals I've taken in fifty-five years of hunting, they've been mercifully few. It's not that I'm such a great shot, mind you; any good competitive shooter could clean my clock when it comes to standing on one's hind legs and shooting off-hand. The fact that 99 percent of the shooting I've done has been off sandbags might have something to do with it. In other words, most of the centerfire rounds I've fired have been in the testing of guns and ammunition, which does not reflect my shooting ability. In fact, when testing guns, the point is to take the human factor out of the equation as much as possible.

I do, however, practice field shooting on a regular basis and consider myself fairly adept at quickly assessing whatever may be available to help steady my rifle. By that, I mean getting into the steadiest shooting position possible under the circumstance, and taking advantage of whatever rifle-steadying aid is handy, whether it be a rock, log, the side of a tree, or a sapling, a rucksack, even a binocular turned on end.

Another . . . *skill*, if you want to call it that, which all experienced shooters develop, is *knowing* when you've made a good shot. Not that a perfect hold can't result in a miss because one can always misjudge distance, drop, or wind. I mean knowing that when you pulled the trigger, the reticle was exactly where you wanted it. Conversely, you know when you've pulled a shot, even if it's as little as a quarter inch. The point I'm trying to make here is that you know when you've made a good shot.

Still another contributing factor to my not having missed or lost game very often is that I rarely pull the trigger unless I'm reasonably certain I can make the shot. I'm sure there are guides and professional hunters I've hunted with who wished I hadn't been so cautious, but I won't be rushed or talked into taking a shot I'm not confident I can make. Misses and mistakes haunt me too much.

Take the time in Montana when I was hunting pronghorn and had worked my way to within a couple of hundred yards of a small band among which there was one good buck. I was able to get that close because there were a lot of small boulders strewn around, making my silhouette just one of dozens the antelope saw when they looked in my direction.

I slowly eased my rifle into position and found a small rock within reach that I was able to place beneath the fore-end. With the toe of the butt resting on the ground, I had a hold that was virtually benchrest steady. I placed the reticle one-third of the way up the buck's shoulder and squeezed the trigger.

At the shot, the entire band, my buck included, took off at a dead run. I was able to watch them for more than a mile before they went out of sight. The buck never missed a step. I'm sure it was a clean miss, yet at the moment I pulled the trigger I hadn't the slightest doubt that it had been anything but a perfect shot.

As I lay there trying to figure what went wrong, all I could think of is that somehow my scope had gotten whacked, which, of course, is the most common excuse for missing there is in the hunting world. I was still lying there feeling sorry for myself when I heard a distant shot off to my left. Moments later here comes this band of goats into view, running full tilt. As good luck would have it, they were headed right toward me. As even better luck would have it, they came to a stop in virtually the same place the buck I just shot at had been standing a few minutes before!

Having no idea where my errant shot had gone, I had no choice but to take the same hold as before, i.e., a third of the way up the chest. At the report, the buck dropped stone dead, not more than twenty-five feet from where the other buck had been standing. The bullet hole was precisely where it should have been. Go figure!

Another episode concerns a nice 6x6 bull elk I was hunting in New Mexico many years ago. We've all heard stories of how a miss was caused by the animal bolting at the exact moment the trigger is pulled, but up to that time I had had no reason to believe it had happened to me. I could understand how it's possible, mind you, given the speed and reflexes of wild animals and the several hundredths of a second that transpire between the decision to pull the trigger and the bullet's arrival.

Anyway, if ever I was the victim of such unfortunate timing, it was during this elk hunt. My guide, L. J. Armstrong, and I had spotted this nice bull crossing in front of us along the far edge of a draw. We caught only glimpses of him as he moved among the fir trees, but if he stayed his course he'd come into a small clearing less than one hundred fifty yards away. Between us and the bull the ground dropped away slightly, so I had a clear shot. I also was in a steady prone position.

The bull was moving at a right angle to us at a steady walk. Though I didn't want to shoot while he was moving, I figured I had no choice because he'd be in the clearing for just a few steps. The moment he cleared the trees, I found him in the 6X Leupold and was about to pull the trigger when he suddenly changed direction. He was now angling toward us. *Less lead*, I told myself, and was again about to pull the trigger when he stopped. *Perfect*, I thought, *now I could just hold dead-on*. With the bull facing at seven o'clock, I put the cross hair just a little to the right of center on his chest and fired.

"Ya' hit 'em," said, L. J. "I saw him lurch forward as he ran into those trees."

I was sure it had been a perfect shot and that we'd find him close-by. What we couldn't see from where we were, but discovered on reaching the spot where the bull had been standing, was that the reason he stopped was a deep, steep-sided erosion ditch about five feet wide and about three feet deep.

L. J. was sure I had hit him, but we could not find a single drop of blood. To make a long story short, as we scoured the area looking for some sign that the bull was hit, I spotted movement up ahead. It was the bull, bedded down behind a small bush. *He had to be hit*, I figured, *'cause no healthy bull elk would bed down seventy-five yards from where he had been shot at!* All I could see clearly was his neck and head, but he was only about sixty yards away, so I didn't hesitate to take the neck shot.

A quick autopsy showed that I had indeed hit him, but it had been a horrible shot. The 7mm 150-grain Nosler Partition had entered behind the last rib on his left side and came to rest in his right ham. The bullet had impacted nearly two feet to the right of where I held! The best explanation I can come up with is that I fired at the precise moment the bull jumped the ditch. I couldn't see it because his jump coincided with my gun's recoil, and L. J. thought his jump was a reaction to being hit. It was a miracle we got that bull because I've seen elk go for miles with more serious wounds. The fact this one was sick enough to bed down as close as he did, well, it was fortunate, indeed.

Another incident involving very similar bullet placement and results occurred many years ago on a whitetail hunt in the Texas Hill Country. My guide and I were returning to the ranch house for the midday break when we spotted a deer high up on a hill. We got our binoculars on it just in time to see a nice ten-point buck walk beneath a small tree. His body was visible, but his head and antlers were now obscured by low-hanging foliage. I decided to try for him.

The ranch road had recently been graded so there was a mound of soft earth lining the road that made a good, steady rest for my Ruger No. 1 .25-06. Getting out of the truck and into shooting position took maybe thirty seconds. When I found the buck in my scope, he appeared to have not moved, which is to say facing away toward two o'clock. His neck, head, and antlers were still obscured by branches.

Figuring he was some three hundred yards up the hill—this was long before laser rangefinders —I placed the reticle about five inches high and about twelve inches behind the shoulder to allow for the angle of entry. I then sent a 120-grain Hornady HP on its way. The buck simply collapsed in his tracks. Something wasn't right, however. As he fell, he appeared to be facing in the opposite direction I thought he should be.

Sure enough, during the time I was getting out of the truck and into position, the buck had swapped ends. I couldn't see it because his head was still obscured, but when I fired, the buck had been facing eight o'clock rather than two o'clock. The bullet had entered midway on his body and lodged beneath the skin on his right rump. Another case of terrible bullet placement, yet I couldn't have asked for a better result. I still can't figure out what caused that deer to die so instantly when no vital organ had been hit.

Then there was the time I was hunting black bear in Quebec. I was in a ground blind overlooking a bait that had been hit hard the night before. Although I didn't need it for a shot that close, the outfitter had even rigged a rifle rest for me! My rifle was a 6mm Remington in a Ruger No. 1 pushing a 100-grain Hornady Spire Point. Not the best bear caliber, I'll grant you, but I had killed a bear in its tracks the year before, and would kill two more with that same rifle.

Anyway, the bear materialized about ten minutes before dark. I waited until he was busily rummaging before raising the Ruger into position. As I said, I had a perfect rest, the bear was no more than forty yards away, and when I pulled the trigger, I would have bet my house on the outcome. At the shot, I heard this god-awful bawl and then saw the bear vaulting into the thick brush behind the bait. There was a loud thrashing of underbrush, then silence. I figured it had been death throes I had heard, so I fully expected to find a dead bear within a few yards.

No such luck. When my guide arrived a few minutes later—he had been parked within earshot—not only did we not find a bear, there was no sign of it being hit. Darkness prevented us from looking for more than a few minutes, but four of us returned the following morning and scoured the area for more than an hour. The underbrush was incredibly dense, but we felt that if there was a dead bear anywhere within a hundred and fifty yards of that bait, we would have found it.

I've taken quite a few bears over the years and have been in camps where I've seen another fifty brought in by other hunters . . . along with their stories. I know a bear with winter fat can bleed precious little and go a long way, even if mortally wounded, but to not bleed at all and go more than a hundred and fifty yards, well. . . . As you can tell, I still can't accept that I could have missed clean at that range.

Such is hunting.

Bucket List Check-Offs

Chapter 28

Every hunter has a bucket list, no matter how unrealistic it may be. On the other hand, one's candidates for the list can also be quite modest and attainable. For those who've hunted whitetails in the East all their lives, a bucket list hunt could be nothing more expensive or exotic than a trip out West for mule deer or antelope. As a young boy growing up in Ohio not yet old enough to get a hunting license, for me a hunt in neighboring Pennsylvania, where unlike Ohio, centerfire rifles were allowed for deer and bear, seemed pretty damn exotic!

Just how and why the desire to hunt certain animals over others develops, I can only speak for myself. For me my bucket list started with the jaguar. I couldn't have been more than twelve or thirteen years old at the time when I read about a guy whose name, if memory serves, was Sasha Siemel and he killed jaguars in the Mato Grosso jungles of Brazil using nothing but a spear! This guy would force a jaguar to attack him, and when it did, he'd stick the butt of his spear in the ground and the leaping cat would impale himself on the business end. At least that's how the stories went, but even with the naiveté of youth, I questioned how you could get a jaguar to charge unless it was wounded and somehow felt cornered. Just how do you arrange such a scenario, not just once, but multiple times?

Now, I had no desire to adopt ol' Sasha's questionable method of feline dispatchment, but for some inexplicable reason I became obsessed with collecting a jaguar. Of course this was back in the 1950s when it was still possible to hunt jaguar in Mexico and other Central and South American countries and import the trophy legally. That all ended when it fell under the Endangered Species Act of 1973.

It may have become latent, but my passion to hunt jaguar never wavered, even after my having taken three leopards in Africa in the late 1970s and early

1980s. Back then leopards were also listed as endangered, but I decided to hunt them because a department of Interior guy told me that by the time I returned from my first leopard hunt, it would be off the endangered species list and I'd be able to get mine into the country. He was wrong. It took several years, but eventually I was able to import one leopard rug into the States. There was, however, no chance that the jaguar would ever be taken off the endangered species list. That meant I could not legally import one into the States, so I felt there was little point in my trying to collect one.

My attitude changed when I became friends with Ernesto Zaragoza, a well-to-do Mexican who lived in Guaymas, in the state of Sonora. My outfitting friend in Chicago, George Daniels, had arranged a dove hunt with Ernesto's Solimar Safaris. At that time I was hunting editor at *Guns & Ammo* and while down there Ernesto told me how he wanted to expand his outfitting business to include desert mule deer, Coues deer, and duck hunts. He invited me back to his operation for these animals, and, long story short, we became good friends during the several hunts I made with him.

We even hunted elephant in Malawi together in 1987 after that country reopened to hunting for the first time since the early 1950s. But alas, within a few weeks of reopening, the antihunting people managed to close it, and it remains closed to this day. We, therefore, became members of a small group of maybe twenty people who have hunted Malawi in the last seventy years. By the way, Ernesto got his elephant, but after years of haggling with that government, never got his ivory.

Anyway, one evening while we were sitting around the fire in Solimar's desert mule deer camp, Ernesto turns to me and out of the blue says: "I've arranged a jaguar hunt for next March. Are you interested?"

The fact I could never bring a jaguar into the States suddenly became moot. I now had a friend in Mexico whose magnificent trophy room in Guaymas would be a worthy domicile for my jaguar, were I fortunate enough to get one. Yes, I wanted a jaguar bad enough to be satisfied with it permanently residing in another country!

In late February of 1987 Ernesto and I headed to Campeche, a Mexican state on the Yucatan Peninsula. Sharing camp with us was another hunter, a very wealthy industrialist from Milan—Mario I think his name was. With him was his clothes-designer girlfriend whose pendulous mammaries had to have made standing up straight rather difficult for her.

In the dining tent that evening this fellow told us that he "limited" himself to spending a half-million dollars a year on hunting. He then related how he and his girlfriend—she was not a hunter—hadn't been home since early January. They had spent the first three weeks of the year in Ethiopia trying to track down a hundred-pounder that a professional hunter had seen while on safari with another client. Mario had hunted with this PH before and the two of them had an understanding that if the PH spotted a really big bull, he was to call this guy immediately, in which case he'd be on a plane within twenty-four hours. As it turned out, they hunted for three weeks without seeing anything approaching a hundred-pounder. I've often wondered whether that PH actually saw such a bull, but I have to admit it was a way to get another seventy or eighty grand out of that guy.

In any case, if memory serves the two flew from Ethiopia to Sydney and then on to Darwin, the jumping off place for Asiatic buffalo and banteng hunts in the Northern Territories. At least that had been the drill when I did the same hunt a couple years before. After spending three weeks there, it was on to Argentina for some dove shooting before joining us in Campeche.

On arrival at our tented camp, which was about sixty miles west of Cancun, I was amazed how different the place was from what I had imagined. I was expecting . . . well, *jungle*, but this place was a virtual hardwood forest, with very little brush or foliage of any kind at ground level and with dry leaves covering the forest floor.

The modus operandi for jaguar hunting—at least for this particular outfitter friend of Ernesto's whose clients had taken more than a hundred cats over the years—was different from how it's done in Africa. In my many hunts for leopards, the blinds I've used were all ground blinds. Here they used tree stands, but these were not like the machans or a *hochsitzs* that have you seated on a platform made of boards. Here my blind consisted of a hammock strung about thirty feet above the forest floor almost directly over the bait. Now a free-swinging hammock is hardly the steadiest of shooting platforms, so to provide some stability, my guide Nacho lashed two thick saplings horizontally about two feet below on either side of my hammock. As in Africa, blinds are constructed only after a bait is taken, and mine was literally built around me as I laid there. Several times I rehearsed swinging my feet out of the hammock while Nacho determined the correct placement of the saplings for me to get the best footing for a shot toward the bait below.

Speaking of bait, our PH Chico used horse meat that was brought into camp by the horses themselves. Instead of having to haul dead critters some twenty miles into the bush, Chico would buy old swaybacks that were scheduled to become soap, then had his guides ride them into camp where they were put up in a small corral to be dispatched as needed. What I found bizarre was that Mario, the Italian zillionaire client, who had shot almost every big-game critter on earth, got incredibly excited over the prospect of Chico letting him shoot a bait horse in a corral!

As for his well-endowed girlfriend, she would sun herself in front of the mess tent dressed in the most revealing thong I have ever seen. The two pieces combined—top and bottom—couldn't have covered nine square inches. I'm sure she got her jellies off knowing that the camp staff boys were probably drooling in their tents.

No bait had been touched the night before our arrival, and it wasn't until our second day in camp that we found two of the baits had been taken the night before. We then commenced building my tree stand. Nacho and I were settled into our perch about an hour before dark, he armed with a powerful spotlight, and me with a 12-gauge Browning Citori over/under loaded with Federal Premium 3-inch 00 buckshot.

As night fell, I couldn't get over how quiet the forest was. Not the chirp of a bird or the bark of a squirrel could be heard. It was so deathly silent I could hear myself breathing. Suddenly the stillness was broken by the faint rhythmic crunching of leaves off in the distance. It got louder and louder, and whatever it was, it was obviously heading my way. What I found so amazing was that there was no hesitation in the gait, no stopping to check visually or scent-wise as to whether there might be danger ahead. It was a steady *crunch, crunch, crunch, crunch* until it stopped in the blackness below my precarious perch.

What followed happened in a blink of an eye. Nacho nudged me out of the hammock and my feet quickly found the saplings that would steady me. As rehearsed, Nacho was strategically positioned behind me where he could shine the light down the barrel so that I could see the sights and whatever was below. When I nodded I was ready, the light went on and the Citori went off.

Being almost directly above, I aimed between the cat's shoulder blades. He went down with a growl, but a second later he was up and struggling to get his feet under him.

"Shoot again," Nacho urged.

I did and all feline movement stopped. Talk about adrenaline! I was literally shaking with excitement for I had just fulfilled the most unlikely quest on my bucket list. By the time we got back to camp and did the compulsory photos, all with flash, it was pretty late, so I postponed my celebrating until the next morning.

Around nine o'clock the next morning I sat down at a picnic table that was about twenty feet from the mess tent, and maybe twice that distance from the two tents of the camp staff. I was the only one in camp; everyone else was checking baits, even Miss Mammary. With me was a full bottle of Patron, which over the course of the next three hours I dutifully emptied. Ernesto told me later that day that the camp staff had had a bet that I wouldn't be able to get back to my tent without help. They lost.

As it turned out, I killed the last jaguar to be legally hunted in Mexico; the season was closed after my hunt and will surely never again reopen. Ernesto had a full body mount done of my cat, and it has resided in his magnificent trophy room overlooking the Bay of California lo these many years.

I think of that jaguar hunt often, and the one thing that has always struck me was how boldly that cat came to the bait. From the moment I could hear the faint rustling of leaves to the moment he arrived at the bait below me, there was no hesitation in his gait. I've long since realized that the jaguar has no natural enemies and nothing to fear. After dark, he is truly the king of the jungle. Oh how I wish my jaguar could be in my trophy room instead of Ernesto's!

******

The next animal to go on my bucket list was the Javan rusa stag. Again, the how and the why we desire to hunt certain animals over others are different for everyone. For me it was as capricious as simply seeing a picture of a rusa sometime back in my early twenties. I thought it was the most beautiful deer I had ever seen. Whether I was aware of it at the time or not, it went on my bucket list.

Fast forward to 1994 and the annual Safari Club convention in Reno. By that time I had been attending this event every year since the mid-1970s, so I had yearly reminders of the vow that I had made years before to someday hunt a rusa deer. These reminders came in the form of the photos and mounted specimens that were always on display there. It had been some two decades by then, and still the planets just hadn't lined up right for me to scratch the rusa off my bucket list. It was seldom out of my thoughts, but it had certainly been occupying a back burner.

As I was sauntering down the aisles at that 1994 SCI bash, I passed the exhibit booth of outfitter Bob Penfold, a guy who specialized in hunting in Australia, New Zealand, and New Caledonia in the South Pacific. In fact, his operation was called "Hunt Australia." Anyway, in his booth was a shoulder mount of a rusa stag Bob himself had taken in New Caledonia the year before. That really caught my eye . . . and well it should have, for at the time it ranked No. 1 in the SCI record book.

As I gazed at it, I realized that I had not changed my opinion—to me it was still the most beautiful deer in the world. The rusa's lyre-shaped horns are so perfectly symmetrical they are literally mirror images of one another. All rusas belong to the deer family whose antlers always consist of a soaring main beam that can be thirty-six or more inches in length (Penfold's buck had forty-one-inch main beams), on which there is a pronounced brow tine and one G2 about half-way up. If a mature rusa doesn't have this specific antler conformation, it's an anomaly. The axis deer or chital that has adapted so well here on exotic game ranches in the southwest belong to the same deer family and sport the same antler conformation.

Anyway, after a brief conversation with Bob about hunting rusa in New Caledonia, I was hooked. I had been putting it off for so too long that I absolutely had to hunt rusa. Now it so happened that Bob had two openings for that year's two-month season, one in August, and one in September. When I learned the August slot was the opening week of the season, I booked it then and there.

For this hunt I took an all-stainless Ruger 77 Mk. II in .280 Remington rechambered to my 7mm JRS wildcat, which I glass bedded into a Fajen black/gray laminated stock. I topped it with a Leupold 6X42 fixed-power scope.

Before talking to Bob, all I knew about New Caledonia was that it was a large island to the northeast of Australia, a French protectorate, and that in World War II it was a base for our PT boats. It was also the backdrop for the TV show *McHale's Navy* that was popular in the early 1960s.

I thought sixteen hours in an airplane—the time it usually took for me to get from Pittsburgh to Johannesburg—was long, but to get to Nouméa, the island's capital, took twenty-one. I arrived frazzled. John Berry, Penfold's camp manager, met me at the airport and then drove us for two hours to the camp. It was the middle of the night as we were driving, so I wasn't able to see what the country looked like. Totally drained, I slept in the next morning, and when I did awaken I saw we were in a valley surrounded by rather steep hills rising about twelve hundred feet in every direction. That was from a base elevation that was only fifty feet or so above sea level. I also discovered camp was a modest but comfortable cabin that had once served as the office of a cattle ranch.

The guide assigned to me was a young Kiwi named Tom Condon, who pitched up around four o'clock that afternoon and introduced himself. Even before we got into Tom's truck, he had spotted three bucks on the hillsides surrounding camp. Talk about an optimistic start of a hunt!

I had no idea how representative our hunting area was compared to other areas on this two-hundred-and-forty-mile-long island, but the terrain surrounding camp were absolutely ideal for deer. All the dirt roads were at base level and there was an eclectic mixture of large tracts of semitropical jungle and scrub oak interspersed with open meadows. It many ways it looked like elk country back in the States. That kind of terrain continued about halfway up the hills, then thinned toward the summits to where it was just grass and bare rock. Between the meadows that skirted the roads and the bare hilltops, it was easy to spot game two and three miles away. Of course, the most advantageous place for spotting game is from the high ground, so that became our objective—to get up top and glass. With four days to hunt, I wanted to be highly selective as to what I would shoot, and with the option of taking a second animal for another five hundred dollars, I could be doubly so.

In all my years of hunting, I have never experienced a more enjoyable hunt. Everything was perfect. The weather was 75 degrees by day, plummeting to a bone-chilling 70 degrees at night. There were no bugs, no wind to speak of, no rain, and the rut had begun, so the bucks were moving with less caution. We took breakfast and lunch at the ranch house, and dined at a nearby French restaurant every evening . . . and then there was the view. I discovered upon reaching my first hilltop that we were less than two miles from the ocean, from where I could see the waves crashing against the breakers, sending huge clouds of mist that kept feeding a perpetual rainbow. It was a breathtaking sight and it was like that from most of the hills we topped.

"Why didn't you tell me we'd be this close to the beautiful blue South Pacific," I chided Tom.

He retorted, "You didn't ask."

Once we reached a vantage point, I don't think there was ever a time that there wasn't at least one rusa stag in sight, and more often than not we were glassing several at a time. Most of them were too far away—to where getting to them would take so long that the chances they would still be in the same open place was unlikely. We saw at least thirty bucks over the next three days that were of trophy class, thirty inches or better, within shooting range or close enough to stalk successfully. I was holding out for a stag of thirty-four inches or better, but we saw nothing that Tom thought was that good.

On the morning of the third day I relented and took my "insurance" buck; it went 32 ⅞ inches and fell to a very satisfying 400-yard shot. It was a fine buck, quite a bit better than average, but at that point I had one more day to spend that five hundred dollars I still had in my pocket should we stumble on a better critter.

Long story short, we really worked hard that last day but saw nothing better than the buck I already had. We had about twenty minutes of shooting light left when we reached the truck.

"Who knows, Jon, maybe we'll see Mr. Big on the way back to camp."

"Well, it wouldn't be the first time I've scored with minutes left on the last day of a hunt," I replied.

Sure enough, not ten minutes into our ride back Tom hit the brakes and grabbed his binocular. After a quick look, he turned to me and with urgency in his voice said, "Jon, that one on the left is a helluva buck."

In a clearing at the base of a hill about 250 yards away were two bucks jousting, and one was markedly bigger than the other. I was on the far side of the truck, so I was able to get out with my rifle and shooting sticks without being seen. Tom then immediately drove off, a diversionary tactic that often works. By drawing the attention of an alerted animal to a threat it believes is going away, the hunter has a better chance at getting his prey. This was one of those times. Luckily, a few yards from the road there were some small bushes between the sparring bucks and me that I was able to use for cover. With shooting light waning fast, I sat down, got my shooting sticks set up, and put the Leupold's Duplex reticle where it had to be. I heard the *thwop* of the handloaded 140-grain Barnes X-Bullet and was pretty sure it went where I thought it did, even though both bucks bolted into the trees a few yards away.

I waited for Tom to come back with the truck and a flashlight because by then it was quite dark. We found the buck stone dead about forty yards from where it had stood. And what a buck he was! He had two perfectly matched 34½-inch beams with huge brow and G2 tines that pearled all the way up to the ivory tips, and he measured 9¾ inches around at the bases. When I compare my buck with the picture I took of Bob Penfold's buck at the convention that year, mine could pass as its offspring, so similar are they.

Scratch another thing to do or hunt from my bucket list!

******

Another item to be scratched off my bucket list was the mid-Asian or Siberian ibex, which supposedly is the largest of several subspecies inhabiting the Eurasian continent. Here again it was simply a matter of my seeing a photograph as a young man of some lucky hunter posing with his trophy. I was struck by the impossible length and weight of the horns in relation to the size of the animal. I thought, *How could a critter the size of a Great Dane support horns of such sweeping arc?* They looked like huge scythes glued to its head. When I discovered this particular ibex often attains lengths of fifty inches or more and measures ten inches at the base, there was no question about it: I had to get me one of them!

As with my two other check-offs, some years would pass before I was able to actually hunt one, and I wasn't an ibex virgin when I did. In 1982 I took a Gold Medal ibex in the Gredos Mountains of Spain. The lyre-shaped horns were impressive, but they weren't as spectacular as the sweeping arc sported by its Asian cousin. My first opportunity at the "real thing" came in 1993 when my hunt-booking buddy, Paul Merzig, put a hunt together with Sergei Shushunov's Russian Hunting Agency. Sergei was an expatriate Russian doctor practicing in the Chicago area who also owned his own outfitting company that specialized in conducting hunts in Russia and Asia. We booked this hunt for late October of 1993, and I can honestly say that I've never looked forward to making a hunt more than I did this one. We'd be hunting at altitudes above ten thousand feet in the Tien Shan Mountains of Kyrgyzstan.

Anyway, my visa arrived in good time, but for some reason that I can't recall now, Paul's was delayed. Perhaps he applied late or it was a matter of his passport's expiration date. All I know is that when it came down to just a couple of days before we were supposed to go, Paul was frantically trying to get someone in the Kyrgyz Consulate on the phone or telex. Then it was D-day morning, and Paul's passport still hadn't arrived, so now I had to make a decision. Should I drive to the Pittsburgh airport and board my plane for Chicago or wait for him? We were supposed to meet in Chicago before catching our flight later that day for Bishkek. Paul said he always got his mail by 10 A.M., and my flight didn't board until 11, so in the hopes his passport would arrive that morning, I decided, *What the hell, I've got to run out the string. It could still work.* I decided to catch my flight and call him from the airport.

The problem was that I had no idea who our outfitter was because Paul had taken care of all communication pertaining to the hunt via telex. I wasn't about to make this hunt alone, so with fingers crossed I called Paul as my Chicago-bound flight was boarding. His mail had arrived. No passport. It was one long and galactically disappointing drive back home that morning.

Even though this hunt didn't work out, we would enlist Sergei's company the next year, in 1994, for a European brown bear hunt in Russia. The following year we also went with Sergei for a maral stag hunt in Siberia. By this time, we knew Sergei well. Twelve years would pass before the planets aligned and once again through Paul I booked a Siberian ibex hunt in Kyrgyzstan with Sergei, with the caveat that Sergei had to accompany me on the hunt. It's always good to have the booking agent with you on a hunt in case problems arise, and my past experiences of hunting in Russia had led me to believe that I had every right to expect snags to occur.

The big day finally arrived. My flight from Charlotte to JFK to Istanbul to Bishkek in Kyrgyzstan took eighteen hours, and then it was thirteen more hours by SUV on remote roads to camp. At one point I was pretty sure we were in China, we were that close to the border. As we pulled into camp, I suddenly realized just how badly I must have wanted to do this!

It's a good thing, too, that I was so committed to this hunt because the altitude proved punishing. Base camp was at 9,600 feet, and I found at first that any sudden movement left my lungs gasping for air. After walking about fifty yards to where I checked out my rifle on a two-hundred-yard target, I was panting like *The Little Train That Couldn't*. If I thought the air at base camp was bad, I realized it was like Jell-O compared to what I experienced the next day. After nine hours in the saddle we reached an altitude of over 12,000 feet, and I swear, just getting off the damn horse was exhausting. It was nothing short of grueling just walking around, and as for climbing, forget about it!

Constantly on my mind was HAPE, high altitude pulmonary edema, a potentially fatal malady. According to the research I did, at 8,500 feet about 1 percent are affected; at 13,000 feet the percentage is much higher. The lack of oxygen affects the heart, and the symptom is the inability to catch one's breath. The only "cure" is to get down to a lower altitude . . . and fast!

Though it took a while after any exertion whatsoever, I was always able to catch my breath. Danier, my one guide who spoke a little English, said I'd be OK; I don't know what my other guide, Assan Ali, thought on the matter because he spoke no English. The terrain was so rugged, so remote, and so vast that it made me think how utterly dependent I was on these two men and our three horses. My horse, incidentally, had been attacked by wolves the year before while he was hobbled for the night at a fly camp. He carried some serious scars on this right flank as a memento.

To make a long story short, we saw about thirty ibexes that first day, but only two were shootable males, and none was positioned where we could approach within a thousand yards without being seen. This is typical of sheep and goat hunting. I should add that we saw more Marco Polo sheep that day than ibexes.

Anyway, with less than three hours of daylight left, Assan spotted two males bedded down on our side of the valley. He gestured that one of them was a good trophy, but try as I did, I couldn't see through my binocular what he saw through his. I trusted Assan's experience, so off we went. After nearly two hours on horseback we got within, maybe, a thousand yards of what we hoped were the still-bedded critters. To save me unnecessary exertion, Assan and Danier went on ahead. Danier told me that if on reaching the next vantage point and confirming that our quarry was still there, only then would they motion me to catch up. Let me tell you, 12,000-plus feet is no place for a sixty-seven-year-old man, even one in pretty good shape. I needed at least four or five days to acclimate to the altitude, and that was a luxury I just didn't have.

The ibex was still there, and I now began the most agonizing eight hundred linear yards I've ever traversed. Every step was either climbing or descending. Getting from A to B required getting across three shallow but steep ravines of loose, snow-covered rocks with sheer drop-offs a few yards on each side. If you started to slide and couldn't stop, you would be completely out of luck. I had to rest and catch my breath every few yards.

Each time I got close to the guys, they signaled me to come closer. I thought I was going to croak. Then I realized from their gestures and excitement that we must have reached a point where a shot was possible. I laid there just beneath the crest of the ridge for five minutes before easing up and peering over the top. I couldn't believe it: My guys had gotten me within 185 laser-measured yards of the still-bedded billy! Even better, his horns looked like two huge scythes. With the aid of a short Harris Bipod and a steady prone position, it was an easy shot. The billy simply rolled over twice, then slid like a rocket five hundred yards down yet another steep ravine, breaking the tip of his left horn en route. It took a half-hour to reach him, but somehow that half-hour wasn't nearly as exhausting as the previous ones!

******

The fourth and last resident of my bucket list was the sitatunga, and it was actually the first to be scratched off. Why a sitatunga you may ask? Well you might, because many people—including those in the hunting community—have never even heard the word, let alone know what it is. To be perfectly honest, it went on my bucket list simply because it sounded so exotic, so . . . *elitist* if you will. The fact that it was an absolutely gorgeous animal also had something to do with it.

The sitatunga belongs to the spiral-horned-antelope family as opposed to the much larger ring-horned family. To my mind, members of the spiral-horned family include the most beautiful animals in all of Africa. In addition to the sitatunga, I'm talking greater and lesser kudu, bongo, common and mountain nyala, bushbuck, and common and giant eland. The sitatunga's primary habitat is papyrus swamps where it spends the daylight hours well hidden, coming out in the open only in early morning and late evening. Its hoofs are unusually long and splayed to prevent them from sinking into the ooze and matted reeds of the swamps.

My first attempt to eliminate the sitatunga from my bucket list was unsuccessful. It occurred on my first safari to Zambia in 1979. Our hunting area was the Tondwa concession in the Lake Mweru Wantipa area in extreme northeastern Zambia, a region that had only recently been opened to hunting. My wife, Judith, was with me, and my PH was a very famous guy by the name of Bryan Smith.

It was probably the most primitive of the twenty hunts I've made in Africa, which made it all the more memorable because everything about our camp and concession area was like I had always pictured what the classic East African safaris of yesteryear must have been like. Our accommodations consisted of huts of thatch, and the camp area enclosed by a *boma*—a fence of sticks and thatch to keep the lions, which we heard roaring every night, from wandering into camp. It was Bryan Smith who had bulldozed the roads into the area and set up the first hunting camp.

The reality of a hunting safari is that every hunter must set priorities on what is realistic to accomplish given the time allotted. With this being my first visit to Zambia and my first crack at lion and leopard, I decided that the sitatunga would have to go on the back burner. As it turned out, I was able to devote only my last evening to hunting this elusive ungulate.

Bryan had no experience hunting sitatunga in this area, so we spent the late afternoon visiting villages on or near the water asking if anyone had seen sitatungas recently. Bryan knew there were large areas of papyrus reeds in the lake's shallows and he had been told that they held a goodly number of the critters.

With Bryan not having had time to explore the area or build a blind, we simply set up about a hundred yards from the shoreline near a stand of papyrus and hoped for the best that something would venture out in the waning light. We were in an open area far enough from the water that while the mosquitoes were bad, a welcomed breeze and Cutter's [bug repellent] made them bearable.

We had about thirty minutes of light left when one of the villagers came running up to tell us—to tell Bryan, that is, because I didn't speak any of the several dialects used in Zambia—that he had seen a big sitatunga not more than a half-mile from where we were. Of course, to the typical native everything is big, but at that point Bryan decided to take a chance and give this guy the benefit of the doubt. Trouble was, even though this place was only a half-mile away, our vehicle was some twenty or more minutes away.

After a short confab with the local, Bryan turns to us. "He says we can take a shortcut across water that's about knee-deep."

"You up for that, sweetie," I asked Judith. "If not, stay here and we'll pick you up after dark."

Ever game, Judith replied, "No, I'll go with you."

As we approached the marsh, the mosquitoes got worse. Once we were in the water, it was worse, and the farther from shore we got, the worse they got. So thick were these accursed insects that we had to pinch our noses closed and breathe through our hand-covered mouths. When I waved my hand in front of my face then closed it into a tight fist, crushed mosquitoes oozed out from beneath my fingertips. Worse, the water was crotch deep in places. With every step, we sank into the muck, drastically slowing our progress.

By the time we reached the far side of the lagoon, it was almost dark, but not dark enough for me not to see a mixture of water and blood streaming down Judith's legs as she stepped out of the water. Leeches! We were all wearing shorts and we were all bleeding. If there's anything more disgusting than a leech, I don't know what it could be . . . other than maybe a tick? Anyway, the leeches were very democratic, grabbing onto us all equally. I bet each of us ripped off about a dozen of those repulsive things.

Turning to Judith, I said, "Right out of *African Queen,* eh Jude?"

It took only a second for her to reference the scene where Charlie and Rosie get caught up in a cloud of mosquitoes just after tying up at what otherwise was an idyllic spot on the Ulanga.

So, after all that, bloody legs, welts, and a whole lot of scratching was all that came of my first sitatunga quest.

My next opportunity came three years later in 1982 and it was again in Zambia. This time we were in the Bangweulu area where vast floodplains and marshes are home to not only the sitatunga but also to black lechwe and tsessebe, two animals I also wanted very much to collect. My guide was a young South African by the name of Robin Voigt who had not yet gotten his dangerous game certification. Like all my several safaris to Zambia in the 1970s and 1980s, my hunts had been booked with Zambia Safaris, which was one of only two such government-licensed hunting organizations in the country at the time.

Once priorities are set, game-wise, the usual modus operandi is to concentrate on hunting that animal and relegate the others to whatever opportunities present themselves. However, in this case Robin suggested we get the lechwe and tsessebe out of the way first so we could then concentrate solely on sitatunga. Judith and I had come to Bangweulu directly from another safari, and I had allotted only four days of hunting to collect all three.

"I'm pretty sure I can put you onto both animals tomorrow," our young PH explained on the long ride to camp. "I know exactly where they are, and they're both in the same general area. Let's do that, and then we can concentrate on getting you your sitatunga because that's not going to be so easy."

Well, he was right about the other two. After a two-hour drive from camp that first morning, we came upon a herd of black lechwes on this bone-dry floodplain, and I mean a herd. There had to be about five thousand of them if there was one! They were everywhere and they were not too concerned by our presence. With that many animals I figured I could afford to be highly selective as to what sort of buck I'd shoot, but it proved not as easy as I thought. I realized I had to rely entirely on Robin's expertise to pick out an outstanding trophy because to me there were literally hundreds and hundreds of good representative specimens. To me they all looked like the length of their horns didn't vary by more than a couple of inches.

Of course picking out an outstanding buck from among hundreds of good ones is only half the battle. Trying to keep track of that one animal when it's constantly moving and intermingling within a herd is both difficult and frustrating. Then getting a clear shot at it adds yet another dimension of difficulty. I'm not sure how long we chased and glassed that herd, but I think Robin just tired of it, as did I. I think he figured that if he put me onto a buck that was just a little better than average, I'd be happy, and I'd probably not know the difference anyway. As luck would have it, Robin spotted a good buck at the fringes of the herd where there were no others in front or behind it, thus offering a clear shot.

"Take that one, Jon!"

I did.

As it turned out, had I entered it in the Safari Club record book, it would have ranked No. 1 at the time because there were not many black lechwes entered back then. That is no longer true; there are now many entries that are much better than mine.

I should perhaps interject here that I have taken many animals that would have made the Roland Ward and Safari Club record books, but I have never entered any of them. Though I am a trophy hunter of the highest water, I compete only with myself. Knowing how a given trophy scores is enough for me. The only animal I have in a record book is an elephant. It's listed in the nineteenth edition of Roland Ward's record book for Africa under the category of elephant body size. I took my first elephant in the Damaraland region of South-West Africa in 1978; it measured 11 feet, 1 inch at the shoulder and 27.2 feet from the tip of the trunk to the tip of the tail. It ranked No. 28 at the time. It was entered by my PH, the late Volker Grellmann.

With the tsessebe and black lechwe out of the way, we were free to concentrate on getting my sitatunga. The next day Judith and I stayed in camp while Robin and his tracker—Joseph as I recall—spent the day building two tree stands, with each of them manning one of them that evening until dark to see what they could see. Joseph saw a tsessebe, but he said it was too far away and visible for only a few minutes. Robin saw two, and one was within range, so that's where we ended up that evening.

I'm sure boards were in short supply in such a remote area of Africa because our tree blind—*machan* to be more correct—was barely a floor. No two boards were parallel or at the same level, and there were gaps between them almost large enough for Judith to fall through. Trees large enough to host a machan and strategically located near the shoreline were also scarce. I was just grateful we had an elevated stand, period.

It was a perfect set-up. Though we were only about twelve feet off the ground, we were high enough to have a commanding view of papyrus as far as the eye could see, interspersed with open areas of matted reeds similar to cattails. The papyrus grew to a height of eight to ten feet and was so thick that, like in the movie *Field of Dreams*, if an animal took three steps into the vegetation, it would disappear.

With about twenty minutes of daylight left, Robin spotted a buck just emerging from the thick stuff. It didn't take long. "He looks good, Jon. I'd take him."

I never questioned Robin or even checked the buck out with my binocular. I had already gotten into a makeshift prone position that enabled me to get a two-point rest for my Remington 700 chambered in my 7mm JRS wildcat. It was a steady-enough hold and I easily made the 200-yard shot.

Judith stayed in the machan to take a few photos of Robin and me wading out to my prize. Remembering my experience at Lake Mweru three years before, I was wearing long pants, so if there were any leeches around, I'd be OK. It took an awfully long time to cross those two hundred yards through the matted reeds covering the surface of the open areas. As we approached the downed "swamp thing," Robin cupped his hands over his ears and almost crying, said: "Oh Jon, oh Jon, I'm so sorry."

Before I could say anything. . . .

Robin explained his distress by saying, "He's not even an adult. I really messed up." He then said that he had hunted sitatunga only twice before and was not that experienced at evaluating horn size.

"I'm going to eat this one, Jon," Robin said.

What he meant was that he would put this sitatunga on his own license. "We're going to continue hunting tomorrow. I'm going to get you a good one," he promised.

The next evening he did, and from the same machan we were in the night before. In fact, the one I shot that night wasn't fifty yards from where the other one had stood the previous night. It was a much better-than-average sitatunga, but it was missing his left eye and the left side of his face was badly damaged and infected, making the cape unusable for a shoulder mount. So . . . you guessed it: I used the cape from the youngster and the horns of the big one. To see it hanging on the wall of my trophy room . . . well, let's just say it looks a little strange seeing such large horns on such a little head!

The Ever-Changing
Perfect Rifle

Chapter 29

I think it's safe to say that among all gunwriters past and present, I'm surely among the least catholic. By that I mean, whatever my level of expertise may be, it's limited to modern rifles and cartridges. I don't write about shotguns, handguns, black-powder guns, antiques, or until recently, ARs. I'm better than average when it comes to shooting shotguns and handguns, but my interest in them, and my knowledge of them, is not enough for me to presume to write about them as if I were an authority. As I've stated elsewhere in this book, I have nothing but respect for those of my colleagues who seem to be so knowledgeable and expert at so many areas.

Being a narrowly focused rifle wonk isn't easy. It takes years to develop a passion that embarks us on a lifelong odyssey. At first we're easy enough to please. That's because for most of us our involvement begins when we're relatively young, when we're just glad to own *any* gun, much less give thought to its design, its features, and the way it functions.

At first, factory production rifles are more than adequate to keep us happy. I mean, with so many makes and models to choose from, how could you not find exactly what you want? Indeed. But sooner or later, as we accumulate both guns and knowledge, we find ourselves favoring certain design and cosmetic features over others. At that point, every time we pick up a new rifle, thoughts like these arise: *For the most part I like this action . . . but I don't like the bolt shroud or the safety. I also wish it had a hinged floorplate instead of a detachable box. And I wish. . . .*

Sound familiar? When we do that—whether we realize it or not—we're actually designing a gun of our own. We take a feature from this gun, another from that one, and soon we have an imaginary composite of our ultimate rifle. The problem is that some features we deem desirable may be incompatible with others, so compromises are inevitable. That's the way it always is.

When I first started out in this business, I used to think that if we couldn't improve on the then seventy-plus-year-old 1898 Mauser, something was wrong. Since that time, my ideas as to what makes the perfect rifle have evolved, just as has my idea of the perfect cartridge. After all, technology advances and new products are constantly surfacing, and to not at least consider them would be stupid.

Until about a decade ago I had always favored the basic design features of the '98 Mauser, but I've since changed my mind to some extent. It is still my choice for a dangerous-game rifle, but I have come to appreciate other action types equally well for general hunting applications. When I say the "basic Mauser system," I mean twin-opposed locking lugs at the head of the bolt that engage abutments within the receiver ring. Other features that characterize the Mauser are a nonrotating extractor, a controlled-round feeding, an inertia ejection, a fixed staggered-column internal box magazine, and a fire-control system where the safety and trigger are independent of one another. These distinguish the original '98 Mauser, but every one of these features has been improved in one way or another in the variety of bolt-action rifles that have come along since.

To my mind two of the best current examples reflecting the evolution of the Mauser are found in the Winchester Model 70 and the Ruger 77 Hawkeye. I'd also include the Montana Model 1999, which is a virtual clone of the Model 70 but with some added unique design details that I believe make it even better. All three, along with the Czech-made CZ 550, are modified Mauser-type actions.

I prefer the system known as controlled-round feeding (CRF) for a dangerous-game rifle because it's almost impossible to jam the action by double loading. The reason for this is that the extractor takes possession of the feeding cartridge as soon as it rises from the magazine and clears the feed rails. With non-CRF actions, the cartridge is simply pushed ahead of the bolt, but the extractor doesn't engage the case rim until the round is fully chambered and the bolt handle is partially lowered. Therefore, between the moment when the cartridge clears the feed rails and the time when the nose of the bullet is well into the chamber, the round is just lying there in a no-man's land, as it were.

If for any reason—like in a panicky situation with dangerous game or just out of sheer excitement—the bolt is withdrawn before the extractor engages the rim of the cartridge, that round is stranded in the chamber. Pushing the bolt forward strips another round from the box, but with the chamber already occupied, it's jamsville. With CRF, however, the cartridge always moves with the bolt, so in the aforementioned scenario it would be ejected, not stranded in the chamber. Also, a CRF action will reliably cycle regardless of the rifle's orientation, even if turned on its side with the ejection port facing the ground. With a non-CRF action, doing so would have that cartridge falling out of the rifle. It is this added dimension of reliability under all circumstances that makes the Mauser system my choice for a dangerous-game rifle.

There's another feature of a dangerous-game rifle that I've never changed my mind about, and that is a hinged floorplate, though I have to admit there are some excellent detachable magazines out there. The perfect solution as I see it is to have the trigger guard bow, floorplate frame, and the magazine box itself all one piece, as it is on the '98 Mauser. It is an expensive solution, however, and that's why most production, semiproduction, and custom rifles have separate sheet-metal magazines. Since this is a wish list, my perfect rifle would have a bottom metal unit like the one made by Sunny Hill, which in addition to being all one piece as found on the '98 Mauser, has a straddle-type floorplate.

When earlier I described the Ruger, Montana, and Winchester actions as being *modified* Mausers, I meant that one of the design departures from the '98 on these three actions is that the left locking lugs do not have a split to accommodate the ejector. Obviously, having two *solid* locking lugs is more desirable. By moving the ejector from the nine o'clock position to seven-thirty, the slot in the bolt head through which it contacts the spent case is *beneath* the left locking lug, not through it.

Another feature I want is to have the bolt stop/release and the ejector be separate components; on the Mauser they are combined in the same subassembly on the left side of the receiver bridge. I prefer the Model 70 solution whereby both components consist of simple blades of hardened sheet stock. Each requires nothing but a pivot pin and a spring. An upward extension of the bolt stop juts up unobtrusively behind the left side of the receiver bridge, and by pushing it forward, the front section is pivoted downward out of the bolt raceway—no linkage, no multiple components. Simple. In a hunting rifle—especially a dangerous-game rifle—I like simple.

Simple also, like on the '98 Mauser, is the trigger of the Model 70 and Montana 1999; they are independent of the safety mechanism. The trigger is one component, the safety is another. To my mind this simplifies both. The safety withdraws and locks the firing pin from contact with the sear. The trigger is just the trigger; it's simple, and everything is exposed where it can be seen. Nothing is hidden in a housing because there is no housing.

On the other hand, what happens if the trigger is not independent of the safety? If for some reason the trigger is pulled and the trigger does not return to where it's supporting the sear, it will release the safety and cause the gun to fire. How can that happen? It can be the result of ice forming in the trigger mechanism, or it can also be from lubricant freezing, or from dust or a foreign object. It can be the result of the wood stock swelling to where the trigger drags against the side of the cutout in the ceiling of the guard bow. All of these factors can prevent the trigger from returning to its rest position. I've had most of the aforementioned happen to me.

So much for features I would want in a dangerous-game rifle. For all other types of big game—nondangerous critters—I've come to appreciate other action types and features as well as or better than those of the Mauser.

One fire-control system I like just as well as the Model 70s is that found on the Ruger 77 Hawkeye. No mechanism is absolutely foolproof or idiot-proof, but the Ruger's is as close as anybody has come. In the safety lever's intermediate position, a robust steel shaft rotates to where it positively blocks trigger movement. When the safety lever is pivoted fully rearward, the trigger remains blocked, the firing pin is locked, and the bolt is locked.

Equally good yet completely different from the fire-control systems just described are the manual cocking safeties found on the German Blaser R8, Merkel RX Helix, and Sauer 404, to name three. Now a manual cocking system sounds like something that belongs on an entry-level .22, but this type of safety is quite different and highly functional. On these rifles a sliding thumb piece is located on the rear receiver tang right under the thumb that must be moved both forward and upward under mainspring pressure. In so doing the striker spring is compressed and the action cocked. It works silently and can just as easily be de-cocked by pushing down and allowing the thumb piece—using dynamic tension—to return to its relaxed position. One can also work the bolt, in which case the gun is automatically de-cocked.

The beauty of this type of fire-control system is that the gun can be carried with a loaded round in the chamber in perfect safety. Only for the first shot must the action be manually cocked. It's an excellent system, but unfortunately, it's impossible to incorporate into any existing American rifle.

While I prefer a fixed magazine with a hinged, straddle-type floorplate for a dangerous-game rifle, for all other applications I've come to like detachable magazines, so long as they are of unified polycarbonate and fit flush with the belly of the stock. There are many excellent examples of this type, some of the best being found on the Sako, Tikka, Ruger American, T-C Venture, and Winchester XPR. All are feather light, indestructible, and their integral feed rails have a natural lubricity that makes for a smoother, quieter cartridge feed.

I've also warmed up to the "fat-bolt" genre of trilug bolt-action rifles like the Ruger American, Winchester XPR, and Thompson-Center's Venture. All have the shorter, sixty-degree handle lift that makes for extra clearance between the hand and the scope's ocular bell. The only downside is that the shorter bolt throw increases the cocking effort required to where it makes cycling the action from the shoulder difficult. In fact, I recently tested one such rifle that required sixteen pounds of handle lift to cock the action, a feat I could not accomplish without lowering the gun to the port-arms position. In sharp contrast, I have slicked up twin-lug actions to where only three pounds of handle lift was required to cycle the action and where elevating the muzzle just fifteen degrees would have the unlocked bolt slide open.

Also, with a three- or multilug design, you could have the locking abutments within the barrel itself rather than in the receiver ring. This eliminates the stressed components from three to two. In other words, only the bolt and barrel are subjected to firing stresses; the receiver is relegated to being a mere housing for a bolt, a magazine, and a fire-control system. As such, it can be made of an aluminum alloy instead of steel, which makes for a lighter rifle. Also, in theory at least, a direct lock-up with the barrel should provide the potential for greater accuracy because there's only two rather than three components involved in the locking system.

Fat bolt tri- and multilug actions that lock up within a barrel extension also make possible barrel/caliber interchangeability, a feature most European-made rifles offer but are not found on the three American-made guns mentioned earlier. I'm not a fan of barrel interchangeability, but I do like the idea of the bolt locking with the barrel rather than with the receiver.

Continuing on the simple theme, I have always preferred integral scope mount rails. It just makes the most sense to me for rings to attach directly to the receiver without the need for six other components—two separate bases and the four screws to hold them on. Ruger, Sako, CZ, Tikka, T-C's Venture, and E. R. Shaw's Mark X all offer this decided advantage. While the first four of the forgoing are proprietary systems, the Venture and the Mark X employ the Weaver-compatible Picatinny rail as popularized by ARs. The advantage of a Picatinny rail is that it gives you the potential for placing both the front and rear ring in multiple positions along the rail for greater scope mounting latitude.

In the case of a parallel dovetails like on the Ruger, Tikka, and CZ, a recoil surface on one or both rings is necessary to prevent the scope from inching forward under recoil. The Sako dovetails are wider at the front than at the rear so that any forward movement of the scope just tightens the rings all the more. Apparently, though, Sako doesn't feel the taper alone is sufficient because there's a projecting tit on the rear ring than engages a slot behind the dovetail, thus fixing its position.

Another safety consideration is how the bolt is designed, and here the Montana, Ruger, and Howa actions excel. On any action where the root of the bolt handle turns down into a slot in the floor of the receiver to serve as a nonbearing safety lug, I want the bolt handle to be integral with the bolt body, i.e.; not brazed on and not collared on. I want it to be *one piece*. All three also have huge vent holes in the bolt body, but the Montana has vent holes on both sides of the receiver ring as well, a gas baffle behind the left locking lug that blocks that raceway, and a second baffle on the bolt sleeve that deflects any gases from a ruptured case or pierced primer away from the shooter's eyes.

Lastly, I don't care if the receiver is a casting or a forging, but I'd want a flat bedding surface and a beefy, integral recoil lug with lots of surface area.

Not that there's anything wrong with tubular receivers having separate recoil lugs. After all, that's how the Savage 110, Remington 700, and a host of other rifles both domestic and foreign are made. It's easier and less expensive to produce a tubular receiver, and there's no question as to its accuracy, strength, or reliability. It's just that, if I had my druthers, I'd want a flat bedding surface like those found on the Winchester, Montana, Howa, et al.

Picking the features I like best on the relatively conventional American bolt-action rifle is a study in frustration. Compounding that frustration is the fact that I'm also fascinated by straight-pull rifles like the Merkel RX Helix and Blaser R8, which I feel best exemplify the genre. So totally different are these rifles from our American concept as to what constitutes a bolt gun that it's like night and day, black and white. By reducing the four motions needed to cycle the typical turn-bolt rifle to a simple back-and forth movement of the bolt handle is in itself a game changer.

Bottom line is: Nobody makes the perfect rifle!

My Buffalo Baptismal

Chapter 30

With this chapter, I take up where I left off in the Introduction—recalling my first safari. For a hunter to be in Africa on the first day of his very first safari is a day like no other. No other day will ever compare. That's how I felt on my introduction to the Dark Continent some forty years ago. I have since been back many times, but you know what Thomas Wolfe said about going back home: You can't.

Oh, you can return, of course, but your first safari is so indelibly and unalterably seared into your being that it defies recapturing. One's first safari always transcends expectations, and all previous hunts pale by comparison. The fact that a Cape buffalo was my baptismal rite to hunting in Africa made that day so long ago even more extraordinary yet.

I never planned for my first animal to be a Cape buffalo. I had, of course, planned to hunt *m'bogo*, but not right out of the chute. In all immodesty, I had by 1976 already done my share of hunting in North and South America, and Europe, too, but none of it was for critters that could maul, impale, dismember, disembowel, eat, or just plain stomp you into toe jam. To hunt buffalo before getting my feet wet on some of the more common first-hunt animals like impala, warthog, duiker, kudu, etc., seemed somehow . . . well, *disrespectful* and presumptuous in the extreme.

I had little choice in the matter, however. To tell the truth, I forget the details now, but it had something to do with the schedule of the game guard. By law, a game guard had to accompany my professional hunter, John Tolmay, and me if we were to hunt buffalo. As it turned out, the game guard was none other than Clem Coetzee of the Matusadona Game Reserve, a hunter and conservationist who would become known throughout Africa and the world for his work with elephants and black rhinos. Anyway, Clem was available to hunt buffalo only one day—and that just happened to be my first day in Kariba. So it came down to hunting buffalo first or not at all—not a tough choice.

As if being in Africa on my first safari weren't enough excitement for me, the Rhodesian civil war was at its height. Two days before we arrived in Kariba, the town had been shelled from the Zambian side of the Zambezi. Gun boats patrolled Lake Kariba, and we could see Rhodesian troops guarding the runway as we landed, for it was not unheard of for "terrors" to shoot at incoming flights with their AKs. A couple months later that very same flight from Salisbury to Kariba made world news when it was brought down by antiaircraft fire. About half the passengers survived the crash, only to be butchered by the "freedom fighters" who arrived on the scene soon thereafter.

Lake Kariba had been formed some eighteen years earlier, in 1958, with the completion of a huge dam on the mighty Zambezi River at Kariba Gorge. It would be on Namembere, the largest island on the 185-mile-long lake that I would be hunting with John and Clem.

To cap off the assault of imagery and emotion I felt upon my arrival at Kariba, we proceeded to the dock where we boarded *The African Queen II*. It was a boat that had obviously led a long and hard life, but she sure looked lovely to my impressionable eyes, and similar enough to the one in the movie that if Bogie and Hepburn had come out to greet us, it wouldn't have surprised me in the least.

How can it get any better than this, I thought, as we steamed into Lake Kariba. By then it was late afternoon as we headed first for Tashinga, where we'd pick up Clem at his headquarters, then onto Namembere Island where we'd spend the night on *The Queen* before hunting the next morning.

Traveling with me were two friends, George Daniels and Howard Wells. Howard was from Pittsburgh and worked as a manufacturers' representative in the guns/hunting industry. Howard was the only other hunter besides me. George, along with his partner, Paul Merzig, headed up International Sportsman Adventures, a Chicago-based travel and hunt-booking agency. George and Paul were quite literally the pioneers of affordable African ranch hunting back in the early 1970s. Thousands of Americans, who otherwise could never have afforded it, were able to hunt in South Africa,

Rhodesia, and South-West Africa thanks to the packaged hunts first put together by ISA.

At Tashinga Clem was waiting for us in his office. After checking in with his headquarters by radiotelephone, we enjoyed a sundowner before boarding *The Queen*. While sipping on what I had discovered to be truly excellent South African cabernet, Clem began filling us in on the area and the animals on Namembere Island.

About twenty-five square miles in area, Namembere is the largest of the Sibilobilo Islands, which were created by the rising waters of the Zambezi when the dam was completed. Isolated there on the island were a few elephants, rhinos, some sable, impala, warthogs, and a herd of about eighty buffaloes. The island was hunted only to cull, and then only by special arrangement with the game department. How George arranged for Howard and me to hunt there remains a mystery I shall forever savor.

Clem informed us that we could take two buffs off the island, two sables, and whatever impalas we wanted. Clem told us that the past couple of days had been unseasonably hot for that time of year, and the buffalo had been staying on one side of the island. The bad news, he said, was that the buffaloes were hiding from the heat in dense, shrublike trees called *jesse*. The vegetation made seeing the animals, let alone hunting them, very difficult.

"Maybe we'll luck out," said Clem, and they will have left the thick stuff. If not, it'll be sticky going."

Sticky going indeed! To make things even stickier, I was using a Ruger No. 1 single-shot rifle chambered for my brand-new wildcat .375 JRS. So, on my first day of my first safari in Africa, I would be taking a single-shot rifle into thick *jesse* to hunt a buffalo. If Clem and John were questioning the prudence of going into the bush with some greenhorn presumptuous enough to figure one shot was all he'd need, they didn't show it . . . much.

Just months before I had taken the then-new 8mm Remington Magnum case and simply necked it up to .375 with no other changes. Not having the sloping body and shoulder of the original .375 H&H, the 8mm magnum case was, in effect, already "improved" and had nearly a 10 percent greater powder capacity. My rechambered No. 1 with its 24-inch barrel using 85.0 grains of 1MR-4350 gave me just shy of 2,700 fps with a 300-grain bullet.

Muzzle energy was right at 4,800 foot-pounds. No sir, it wasn't that I was having doubts about the cartridge itself—I was having second thoughts about going into dense thickets after buffalo with a single-shot rifle. That's what I meant by "sticky."

On our way over to the island that evening we were flagged by one of those gun boats I mentioned. It was a little disconcerting to be under the cold stare of a turret-mounted .50 caliber Browning as the Rhodesians checked us out up close. Satisfied we were who we appeared to be, they cheerfully wished us luck and sent us on our way.

As we approached Namembere, Clem hoisted his binocular for a moment, then dropped it to his chest and began nervously tugging at the neck strap. "They're still in the bloody *jesse*," he reported.

By now John and I were also glassing the same area. I expected to see something that looked like a herd of buffaloes—or at least something black—but I saw nothing but thick bushes growing right down to the water's edge.

"Where are they?" I asked, still looking through my binocular.

"There," John pointed. "See those birds flitting above the *jesse*? The buff will be right beneath them."

The birds, which I assumed to be some sort of tickbird, were maybe a half mile from where we touched ashore. It was the only opening along the shoreline that afforded us a landing area.

It was as the bow of *The Queen* hissed to a stop in the sand on Namembere that the full realization hit me: I had fulfilled a lifelong dream, a dream I had had since first seeing the movie *King Solomon's Mines* at the age of thirteen. To a hopeless romantic like me, the sights, the sounds, the emotions that welled up inside of me that first evening in real Africa are simply beyond my ability to relate.

The trackers and skinners scurried ashore and immediately began preparing a fire for a dinner of steak and sausage. There was the smell of smoke and the sound of sizzling meat, the dull clang of utensils amid laughter, and the small talk about the events of the day and the anticipation of the next. There was a chill in the air, the kind that makes you inch closer to the fire and be glad you are wearing a down vest. I recall looking out over the lake at the biggest orange sun I had ever seen just as it was about to quench itself in the waters of the Kariba.

Around the fire Clem recounted tales of elephant hunting and his culling experiences of buffalo and lion and rhino; he electrified us with stories of charges stopped . . . and some that were not. He recalled what it was like in the old days, and he talked about guns and cartridges and places he'd seen and the animals he had hunted. It was all such wonderfully heady stuff.

I recall my last thoughts that evening as I nursed a snifter of KWV brandy and listened to the water lapping at *The Queen's* thighs. They were of buffalo and what it would be like having to go into the *jesse* after a wounded one. My last sip was kind of a toast to not having to find out.

The next morning Howard and I flipped a coin to see who would hunt buffalo first. I won—or lost, depending on your point of view. Howard and Clem would go to another part of the island to see if they could find sable or impala.

"Well, Jon, go pick yourself out a buffalo," said Clem. He said it like we were heading for the produce section of a market to grab a head of lettuce. "And take your gun with you," he grinned, knowing full well I had been clutching it in a death grip ever since breakfast.

Once John and I were into the *jesse*, it wasn't quite as thick as it looked from afar. There were stunted trees with singular trunks about the size of your forearm that grew to three or four feet high before myriad branches shot off to form a fairly dense bush that rose to a height of about seven or eight feet. If you got down on your knees, you could see for maybe fifty yards; standing, you couldn't see ten. A buffalo's hearing and sight are only so-so, but his sense of smell is extraordinary. There wasn't much of a wind as I recall, but what little there was we made every effort to put in our face before heading to where we had last seen the birds the night before.

The buff were still in the *jesse*, so we had no choice but to sneak on hands and knees into the vegetation. We were hoping to pick out a bull from the periphery of the herd. It was a little disappointing, then, that my first look at a real African Cape buffalo turned out to be one of legs, legs, and more legs. I was also amazed to see how tightly they crowded together; to where they were all virtually touching one another. I'll bet all eighty animals didn't occupy a half-acre.

The first time John and I got to within maybe twenty-five yards of the herd, close enough to see the sentry cows nervously eyeing us, trying to make out what it was they were seeing but not yet smelling. Suddenly, three hundred saucer-size hoofs thundered through the bushes in a cloud of choking dust. I could feel the ground shake and hear a loud swishing as huge bodies slid past, through, and over whatever brush was in their way.

That went on for nearly three hours. Whenever we'd get close enough to start seeing some of the upper halves of buffalo, they'd thunder off, usually away from us, but a couple times toward us to where they passed within ten yards on either side. They would then run a few hundred yards before stopping, regroup, and then close ranks again like canned sardines. Try as we did, we couldn't get them to leave the cover of the *jesse* for more open ground, which was never more than a few hundred yards away.

I now know how foolhardy what we were doing was, but having just that one day to collect my buffalo colored our judgment. In retrospect, maybe John figured the first time the herd stampeded our way would be enough for me to call a halt to the proceedings. I wasn't that smart, but then I wasn't dumb enough not to be scared, either. I was frightened all right, but it was that exhilarating kind of fright that has your stomach trying to float out of your body through your throat, the kind that has you swallowing hard because your mouth is completely dry.

Sensing that the game we were playing could end badly, John suggested we give it one more try. "They're getting more and more nervous each time we approach," he said. "I think we should push our luck only so far."

I, too, had the same feeling. "You're the boss, John. Whatever you decide is OK with me."

I had always thought being killed by a wounded, charging buffalo wasn't a bad way to check out, but being trampled by a herd of panicked animals that were just confused about which direction danger lay had all the romance of falling off a ladder.

John figured a change in tactics was in order for this last effort. "This time, if we get to where we start seeing horns, you get that gun of yours to your shoulder. Then try to follow through your scope what I'll be describing. It'll happen fast, so if I tell you it's a good bull, and you think you're looking at what I'm looking at, shoot!"

My Buffalo Baptismal

This certainly was not how I pictured buffalo hunting. It was, however, my only chance at one, and who knew if or when I'd ever get back to Africa.

"OK," I said, "let's give it a go."

So off we went one last time, walking when we could, crawling when we had to, until we were again looking at buffalo legs. This time the *jesse* was a little thinner, and we could see fairly well. As good luck would have it, we were able to put a huge, strategically located termite mound between us and the buffalo and thereby get closer without being seen.

Now I could see whole buffaloes. My attention riveted on sweeping horns that emanated from beneath a helmet that parted in the middle; on drooping ears and vindictive eyes, and on nostrils big enough to stick your fist into. Adrenaline time. I could no longer smell the acrid odor of fresh urine and dung that we had been crawling through for the past three hours. The unbearably ticklish meanderings of the mopane flies across my face no longer bothered me, nor did the heat or the scratches on my bare legs. Rivulets of sweat no longer stung my eyes.

"Ready?" John asked in an anxious voice.

I nodded as I eased the Ruger around the right side of the termite mound and peered through the scope. John was just behind and above me so anything he saw I should be able to see from the same perspective. He raised his binocular and a hushed litany began.

"Cow . . . cow . . . cow . . . calf . . . young bull . . . cow . . . bull! Nice one! See him? Right behind that bush with the limb broken and hanging to the ground! He's facing left."

I figured I'd take John's word for it as to whether it was a good bull or not, so I didn't even look at the horns. I just tried to find the outline of a buffalo aligned with the branch he was describing. When I did, I placed the reticle on the vague outline of what I visualized to be the body of a buffalo standing broadside and unleashed the then-new Sierra 300-grain spitzer bullet.

At the explosion the bush erupted in pounding hoofs and sliding bodies. When the billowing dust settled enough to see, I had long since dropped another round—this time a 300-grain Hornady solid—down the Ruger's gullet and levered the action shut. We eased forward to find nothing but a splotch of blood, the frothy pink that comes from a lung shot.

"Now I've done it," I said to John dejectedly, "wounded a Cape buffalo in this tangled labyrinth," as I gestured to the dense brush surrounding us.

"I don't think he'll go too far," said John. "You hit him pretty good."

We inched forward in small semicircles until John found another splotch of blood. This gave us direction. It took five full minutes to go ten yards. To say we advanced cautiously would be the quintessence of understatement. For the hundredth time I pushed forward with my thumb on the top-tang safety on the Ruger to be sure it was off. I then checked the elastic band I wore on my left wrist to make sure my two back-up rounds were still stuck there should I need a quick second shot—at least "quick" by single-shot standards.

Suddenly I caught movement in the bush about twenty yards in front of us. I cautiously raised my binocular to see an eye looking back at me. Then part of a boss materialized, then part of the neck and shoulders. I now could see what direction his body was facing. John, who was a couple yards in front of me, saw him too and motioned me up to his side.

"Hurry," he said, in the most urgent whisper I'd ever heard.

Only the upper half of the bull's neck wasn't obscured by gnarly limbs, but I figured that was enough for a spine shot. This time the Hornady solid did the job. The bull went down in a puff of dust. It was over. A flood of conflicting emotions engulfed me. I was happy, yet sad. I felt proud, yet humble. I was glad it was over, yet near tears knowing I might never have the chance to do it again.

A cursory autopsy revealed that my first shot had, indeed, gone into the chest, but a little high to have any immediate effect. It would have been a fatal shot, but "fatal" on a buffalo could mean a long time, time enough to exact revenge.

I often wonder what would have happened, what could have happened, had we not seen that the bull had circled back and was waiting for us to get a little closer. It could have turned out differently. I have since shot other buffaloes, bigger buffaloes, but none were as exciting as that first one.

Of all the things in the world I either covet or envy, it is one's first safari, for no matter how many times you return, a first one is all you get.

What If?

Chapter 31

I've often asked myself what if I hadn't sold that first article I wrote oh-so-long-ago? The one I slaved over for months, writing and rewriting until I couldn't ask Judith to type it yet again. Having submitted it to John Amber as an unsolicited manuscript, I was fully prepared that it would be rejected. I had even heard that some editors automatically toss this type of submission into the round file without even looking at them, but I found that hard to believe. I mean, even if 95 percent of the submissions that came in unsolicited were garbage, to not even look at a proposed article would be just plain stupid. After all, there could be a gem among the stones.

I was also well aware of stories, many apocryphal I'm sure, where successful writers/authors claimed they could have papered their walls with rejection slips when they first started out. Would I have had the determination and the optimism to keep writing, to keep accepting rejections time after time? I don't think so. If that first article hadn't been accepted, I surely would have sent it to another magazine, but how many pink slips I could have endured is something I've often asked myself. Would I have tried writing another piece and again gone through the submission process—sending it one at a time to each of the five or six national gun magazines that existed at the time? I was pretty sure that every editor that returned my first submission would probably recognize my name as having authored a piece they had previously rejected and would, thus, be even less inclined to give it a read. I'm not sure if that was ever true, but I definitely felt that way back then.

What if Judith hadn't volunteered to go to work to support me and the boys while I tried my hand at freelancing and babysitting? It was a momentous decision at the time for our young family. The more responsible thing to do after having lost my job at *Outdoor People of Pennsylvania* was to look for another one. After all, Judith's entry-level position at a Target-like store hardly paid enough to sustain a family of four, while I on the other hand, had a degree and some experience in the business world and as an editor. Though we really didn't discuss it as I recall, I made up my mind that if it didn't look promising after six months, I'd give up any thoughts of becoming a full-time writer for at least a few years until the boys were older.

The one thing I do know for sure is that I didn't get much encouragement from anyone. Well intentioned though they were, my mother's attempts at tempering my expectations may have had the opposite effect and strengthened my resolve. Just how important were those two pictures in my dad's "Garden of Memories" family photo album—the one of the mysterious lion hunter and his 1903 Springfield and the one of my dad with a row a dead mallards and his borrowed Winchester Model 97? Then there's the influence that the movie *King Solomon's Mines* had on me—a film that still brings me to tears whenever I hear those haunting drums as the credits roll by?

It could well be that, when all is said and done, it was that insignificant little man, Carl Hanley, who just might have been the greatest influence of all, simply because he said I couldn't do it. Remember, he was the one I worked with in my first job out of college, that man who lived his life in what Thoreau so eloquently described as "quiet desperation." Certainly, he set the bar for low expectations, a bar that I refused to accept.

Surely the "what ifs" in my life are no different from anyone else's in that we can all look back at how little incidents, whether planned or by happenstance, serendipitous or calamitous, either decided or ultimately changed the course of our lives. I was fortunate, nay, blessed, having a wife like Judith who so unselfishly gave of herself so that I could pursue my dreams. Never did I hear a word of discouragement during those merciful few months when we were just starting out and struggling to make it all work. But work it did, and so much better, so much faster, than I could have ever dreamed. How many men can look back on their lives and say they fulfilled every childhood dream . . . and then some? All I know is, I can.